The Prentice-Hall
Complete Secretarial
Letter Book

The Prentice-Hall Complete Secretarial Letter Book

Mary A. DeVries

Prentice-Hall, Inc.   Englewood Cliffs, New Jersey

Prentice-Hall International, Inc., *London*
Prentice-Hall of Australia, Pty, Ltd., *Sydney*
Prentice-Hall of Canada, Ltd., *Toronto*
Prentice-Hall of India Private, Ltd., *New Delhi*
Prentice-Hall of Japan, Inc., *Tokyo*
Prentice-Hall of Southeast Asia Pte. Ltd., *Singapore*
Whitehall Books, Ltd., Wellington, *New Zealand*

© 1978 *by*

Prentice-Hall, Inc.
Englewood Cliffs, N.J.

Library of Congress Cataloging in Publication Data

De Vries, Mary A.
   The Prentice-Hall complete secretarial letter book.

   Includes index.
   1. Commercial correspondence.   2. Form letters.
I. Prentice-Hall, inc. II. Title.
III. Title: Complete secretarial letter book.
HF5726.D48   651.7'5   78-8383
ISBN 0-13-695494-4

Printed in the United States of America

HOW TO USE THESE MODELS TO DO
YOUR BUSINESS CORRESPONDENCE
QUICKLY AND PROFESSIONALLY

It has been said that in the business world people talk more about the information explosion than the weather. No wonder—paper costs, postage costs, and processing costs are soaring, with no end in sight. As pressure for better and faster communication mounts, the secretary must rely more and more on good models to speed and improve her correspondence. The models in this book will help you cut time and costs in composing and processing letters, but that's only the beginning. Model forms and memos are also included to encompass the *whole* area of written communication.

Since secretarial practices change from time to time, it is logical to expect changes in the forms of business communication, too. Therefore, before preparing even one model for this book, I read and evaluated thousands of actual letters and models covering almost every area of business activity, as well as dozens of the latest books on business communication and letter writing. During this time I also interviewed numerous experts: communications consultants, instructors, and, of course, secretaries for whom these models are intended. The picture that emerged was quite different from what I had expected. It was obvious that a really good book of models must take a new approach, because the vast information overload in the business world has changed the old, familiar patterns of business communication. A modern, up-to-date book must fully reflect the *way* written communication has changed, not just in letter style (for example, a casual, friendlier tone today), but in *type* of correspondence.

Many letter-writing aids are simply not in step with the significant trend to replace the standard letter with the memo and the "speed message " in many instances. Nor does the literature adequately stress what tremendous time savers appropriate forms can be in many aspects of business communication. That's why this book has gone a step beyond the traditional book of model letters to include two additional parts on memos and forms.

Nearly 400 model letters, forms, and memos have been prepared, covering a broad range of subjects and situations. Each model can be quickly and easily adapted to your own needs simply by changing a word or phrase here and there. These models are grouped in three parts, followed by a discussion of aids to letter writing:

Part I   Letters
Part II   Memos

Part III   Forms
Part IV   Letter-Writing Aids

The table of contents and a special alphabetical guide offer you two options in locating models for use. The object is to help you choose the right model for your purposes and to find it quickly.

The contents page shows the model letters and memos arranged by major categories. Chapters 1 through 14 consist of both letters and memos the secretary writes and signs and those the secretary writes for the manager. Current information indicates that practices vary widely from office to office in regard to who signs a particular letter. However, the models shown here can be used in either case, so this need not present a problem in your choice of a model letter or memo to use. There are twelve categories of letters:

- Requests and Inquiries
- Reservations and Orders
- Acknowledgment Letters
- Reminders and Follow-ups
- Appointment Letters
- Introductions and Letters of Reference
- Employee Letters
- Letters of Appreciation and Goodwill
- Social Business Letters and Invitations
- Complaints and Adjustments
- Credit and Collection Letters
- Sales Promotion Letters

Memos are divided into the two most familiar types:

- Memos that Give Information
- Memos that Make a Request

Forms are organized in three groups, with the models listed alphabetically within each group:

- Forms for Effective Communication
- Record-Keeping Forms
- Forms and Travel Records for Meetings and Conferences

Within a chapter, models are divided into major sections. Chapter 10, for instance, is arranged according to letters about complaints and those related to adjustments. Under these two sections are listed specific *types* of complaints or adjustments. Finally, under the specific type of complaint or adjustment, you will see a clue to the model letter itself. All models are numbered, beginning with one in each chapter, for example, 10.1, 10.2, 10.3, to speed the process of locating them. Number 10.1 refers to the first model in chapter 10.

When you need a model letter complaining about a bill on which there has been an overcharge, you can (1) turn to the table of contents where chapter 10, Complaints and Adjustments, is listed; (2) check the section in that chapter on Making Complaints; (3) look for a model in that section concerning Billing Errors—Amount; (4) beneath the Billing Errors listing, read the model description: Overcharged for Purchase (10.8); (5) turn to chapter 10 in the book and look up model letter 10.8. This is the way the information would appear on the table of contents:

Chapter 10   COMPLAINTS AND ADJUSTMENTS
             Making Complaints
               Billing Errors—Amount
               10.8. Overcharged for Purchase

If instead it had said "Undercharged for Purchase," you could still have used the model simply by changing the emphasis from overcharge to undercharge.

This is a book of models and thus all possible space is devoted to actual letters, memos, and forms. However, you will also find a generous number of helpful hints on construction, tone, and emphasis in discussions that appear in each chapter. To complete the picture, part IV—Letter-Writing Aids—presents the technical aspects essential to good letter- and memo-writing practices:

- Basic Letter Styles and Forms of Address
- Principal Elements of Letters and Memos

The Model Selector Guide, located at the front of the book, offers a thorough, easy-to-use index for locating models quickly. There you can find almost any subject alphabetically and look up the model numbers beside it. For example:

Apologies
    to customers 2.14, 11.12
    for delay 2.14, 3.13, 13.17
    employees 7.7
    See also Adjustments

With hundreds of letters, memos, and forms at your fingertips—covering almost every conceivable business situation—you will be able to improve your business communication quickly and reduce the time you spend on it substantially. This book is guaranteed to unlock the door to easier, more productive letter writing and to bring you up-to-date on the latest trends and practices in using letters, forms, and memos.

I want to thank the hundreds of organizations, from all parts of the United States, that provided sample correspondence and other material for evaluation: businesses such as manufacturing, retail, and wholesale establishments; service organizations such as travel agencies, printers, advertising agencies, and consulting firms; nonprofit organizations such as colleges, professional societies, secretarial schools, research institutions, and churches; and publishing and communications firms such as magazine and book publishers and television stations. Letters and memos were collected from every conceivable source, touching upon activities as diverse as jewelry repair, the sale of insurance, long-distance moving, and computer programming. I especially appreciated the helpful advice and comments provided by secretaries, college and secretarial school instructors, business communicators, and particularly friends and business associates who helped me collect five thousand actual letters, memos, and forms for examination.

Mary A. DeVries

CONTENTS

Part I LETTERS

Part II M E M O S

14 MEMOS THAT MAKE A REQUEST

Part III   F O R M S

Part IV LETTER-WRITING AIDS

MODEL SELECTOR GUIDE

Part I

LETTERS

1

REQUESTS AND INQUIRIES

Requests and inquiries are two of the most common types of letters to come into and go out of an office. In fact, they sometimes make up the lion's share of a secretary's daily correspondence. It is obvious, then, why these letters must be handled quickly and efficiently. In a modern office a busy secretary has no time to waste needlessly on repetitive, routine tasks. The model letters in this chapter are intended to save you precious time each day as you process requests and inquiries. Simply tailor each sample letter to your own situation by substituting your own facts and figures. (The Selector Guide will direct you to sample letters of request and inquiry in other chapters; for example, chapter 5, Replies to Requests for Appointments.)

Depending on the practice in your office, you will probably write many of these letters for your own signature (e.g., 1.1, The General Inquiry); you may also write some of them for the manager's signature (e.g., 1.12, Granting a Request for a Future Date); and the manager may draft others and ask you to refine and polish them (e.g., 1.16, The Qualified Refusal). If you have any doubts about how to handle a particular letter, ask the manager what he or she prefers. The nice thing about requests and inquiries is that they usually fall into a pattern that soon becomes easy to recognize.

Inquiries may be general (e.g., asking for information about typewriters) or specific (e.g., asking about prices and availablity of typewriters with wide carriages and correcting keys). Note that many inquiries also include a request. Replies to inquiries fall into more categories (e.g., answering a specific question, offering more than the writer requests, or enclosing literature with the response). Letters 1.1 through 1.7 are examples of typical letters of inquiry and replies to inquiries. (See chapter 14 for examples of inquiries transmitted by memo.)

Some letters of request, although similar in many ways to a routine inquiry letter, often require more thought. For instance, a request for a raise (see model 1.10) necessitates great care in preparation; it must present a forceful, persuasive case for the writer. Similarly, responses to requests can be sensitive. Perhaps the response must be negative—saying no to someone without offending him. Letters

3

1.8 through 1.17 are examples of typical letters of request and responses to requests. (See also chapter 14 for requests made by memo.)

MAKING INQUIRIES

An inquiry must be straightforward and specific. (Of course, *all* letters should be courteous and considerate.) Keep the inquiry as brief as possible.

1. Explain why you are writing, if pertinent.
2. State specifically what information you want.
3. Indicate if you want the reader to take some action.

The following two models say just enough—but not too much—for the reader to be able to decide quickly what to do and how to reply.

THE GENERAL INQUIRY

1.1. About Services

Gentlemen:

We have heard about your new nationwide custom-processing service for photographers. Is this service available in Memphis? If not, please send us the address of the nearest lab. Thank you.

Sincerely,

Authorities disagree on the use of "thank you" to conclude a letter, particularly a routine inquiry like model 1.1. However, most writers and readers consider any brief statement of appreciation to be a mark of courtesy and any omission of one to be a mark of rudeness. Some offices follow the practice of concluding a letter addressed to a specific person with the friendlier, more casual phrase, "Thanks very much."

INQUIRY FOR SPECIFIC NEEDS

1.2. About Delivery Date

Dear Mr. Harmon:

Would it be possible to receive the fourteen 8 x 10 glossy prints I ordered on May 24 one week earlier than requested? Our photography workshop has been rescheduled for an earlier date and we'll need the prints by June 12 at the latest. Would it help if I picked them up at your studio to save mail time?

I'd appreciate anything you can do to meet this new deadline. Please telephone me at 616-7777 to confirm that the prints will be available by June 12; also, please let me know if I should plan to pick them up.

Thanks very much.

Sincerely,

Specific inquiries must provide specific information; if Mr. Harmon's photography studio had been larger or if the writer had worked in a larger office, the inquiry might also have included a purchase order number and other pertinent reference data.

REPLIES TO INQUIRIES

Since many inquiries come from potential customers, a prompt reply can contribute toward an eventual sale. At the very least a quick response can help build goodwill for your company.

1. Provide as much information as you can in your first response.
2. Give specific information.
3. If further communication or action is needed or is desirable, make a recommendation.
4. Thank the writer for his interest.

Models 1.3 to 1.7 provide typical replies to five common types of inquiries.

RESPONSE TO SPECIFIC QUESTIONS

1.3. On Procedures

Dear Mr. Sims:

It was good to hear you would like to display your cookware at our fair. Space is being reserved now for such exhibits, and I suggest you make your decision about taking a booth by August 20.

The enclosed literature will describe the physical attributes of the exhibit area and the entry form contains information on fees and hours during which exhibits will be open to the public. Basically, all you need to do to reserve a booth is complete the entry form and mail it with your check to this office. Details on setting up your exhibit will be sent promptly upon receipt of your reservation.

I hope the enclosed material will answer your questions, but do let me know if I can add anything. Thanks very much for telling us about your cookware. I'll look forward to seeing your exhibit at the fair.

Sincerely,

Even when you use an occasion such as this to do some selling on the side, your first objective must be to answer the writer's questions clearly and thoughtfully.

REPLIES THAT OFFER ADDITIONAL INFORMATION

1.4. About Orders

Dear Ms. Hendricks:

Yes, the discount on 35mm. cameras you inquired about is still available and does apply to the models you saw listed in our catalog. Through December 15 all brands will be sold at 25 percent off our regularly listed prices, and you may, indeed, order by mail.

The cameras are being offered at a discount in addition to our usual low prices. They are current models we are clearing out to make room for a supply of new models arriving in January. (The new models, of course, will not be available at these discount prices.) Just pick any camera shown in this year's catalog and deduct 25 percent from the listed price. As the catalog order form shows, we pay postage and handling on all mail orders over $10.

If we can provide more information to help you make a selection, please let us know. We appreciate your interest in our cameras.

Sincerely,

This letter does some "soft" selling, but it tries first to answer the writer's question—whether the discount is still available. Since Ms. Hendricks appeared to be interested in knowing as much as possible, the response also tells *why* the cameras are being discounted.

REPLIES WHEN THE INQUIRY IS VAGUE

1.5. About Statistical Information

Dear Mr. Collins:

We were pleased to learn your article on successful merchandising techniques for your school newspaper will use our company as an example. Two booklets that describe our company operations and products are enclosed.

I'll also be glad to send some statistical information as you requested. Please let me know what kind of statistical data you need: company figures, for example, number of employees, plants, and so on; or product figures, for example, products manufactured, shipped, and so on? Also, since our statistical information is so extensive, covering more than twenty years of operations, I'll need to know what years are of interest to you and whether you want various break-downs of statistics, such as products shipped nationally, or by region, state, or city. If you are uncertain about what you need at this early stage, perhaps you could describe your proposed article in detail, and I could then select figures I believe would be most useful to you.

Best of luck in your research. We're happy to be of help and appreciate your thinking of our company.

Cordially,

This letter depicts a typical situation. When inquiries are vague, the best thing to do is ask the writer to be more specific. However, take care not to let any sign of annoyance creep into your letter. As a representative of your company you must be courteous and helpful at all times.

REPLIES WHEN INFORMATION IS NOT AVAILABLE

1.6. About Products

Dear Ms. Jones:

We wholeheartedly agree that our vitamins and cosmetics should be made available over the counter in stores throughout the country—and we're working on that right now! Although it's a little too early as yet to specify exactly when this will occur or in which stores the products will be sold, we hope to have this information available by June.

The announcement of sales through retail outlets—large department stores, chain drug stores, and so on—will be made in our monthly catalog, probably in the May issue. Since you're on our mailing list, you'll be receiving the announcement in this way. Of course, we hope a store near you will carry our products; however, everything will continue to be available by mail, and you will receive a new catalog each month, just as before.

It's good to know you value our vitamins and cosmetics so highly. You may be certain we value your trust in us just as highly. Thanks for letting us know about your interest in the retail distribution of our products.

Sincerely,

Letter 1.6 shows another frequent situation—the need to say *something* that will satisfy the writer, even though the information specifically requested is not available. In these cases, avoid a negative reply such as "I don't know; write back later."

TRANSMITTAL LETTERS

1.7. About Prices, with Form to Be Completed

Dear Mr. Tryon:

Here is the current price list you requested. You'll notice that it covers our full line of automobile parts and accessories.

An order form appears at the bottom of the price list. To order the items you need, simply check them off in the spaces provided, complete the form, and return it to us.

Thanks for your interest. I hope we hear from you again.

Sincerely,

Transmittal letters are sometimes prepared as printed "Dear Customer" form letters, or printed with only the inside address and salutation typed in each time. However, if the items transmitted are few or if they continually differ (e.g., a report, a brochure, a price list, a sample of something, etc.), each transmittal letter may be typed individually. Model 1.7 could be used either as a printed form letter or as an individually typed letter.

MAKING REQUESTS

The inquiry often does no more than ask about something (what do your typewriter stands cost) but the request always asks to have something done (send us two typewriter stands). Like the inquiry, the request must be specific. It should:

1. Tell what you want (possibly why you want it).
2. Explain what action you want the reader to take.
3. Specify all pertinent facts, such as time, place, price, delivery.
4. Express appreciation if a favor or special effort is required.

Models 1.8 to 1.10 are examples of three common types of requests.

REQUESTS WITHOUT ALTERNATIVE

1.8. For Action

Dear Janice:

Would it be possible for you to have the display boards we ordered yesterday ready a few days before our Monday afternoon marketing meeting? I will be helping Mr. Dexter finish his presentation materials over the weekend; if the boards were already set up, we could test how well the display items work on the boards at the same time.

We're a little worried about one display and would feel much safer if we could check it out before Monday.

Please phone me at 666-1212 if you can have the boards here by Friday noon on June 5. Incidentally, I'll be glad to help you set them up. Thanks so much for your help, Janice.

Best wishes

Although model 1.10, below, is called "The Persuasive Request," all requests are persuasive to some degree, as you can see from letter 1.8. Often the "why" of the request is very important and should be mentioned early in the letter; however, all that is needed is just enough to persuade the reader to say yes—not pages and pages of facts that are of no use or interest to the reader. Notice in this model that the writer uses the recipient's name in concluding: "Thanks so much for your help, Janice." Experience shows this is an effective letter-writing technique and can be used frequently to good advantage.

REQUESTS WITH ALTERNATIVE

1.9. For a Decision

Dear Joe:

How would you feel about taking action to end the growing controversy over our proposed clubhouse? As treasurer of the Lakeville Country Club Association, you might be able to settle things once and for all.

The principal disagreement among members is over the size of the proposed clubhouse expenditure. Some people think the commitment of funds would be unrealistic for us. There's only one way to find out: get three bids from reputable contractors and have the bids and our financial status examined in depth. Specifically, you could propose to the membership that we retain a local accounting firm to undertake this examination and submit recommendations to us. The other alternative would be for you to make the study; however, I realize it would be extremely difficult for you to make a commitment to donate that much time and effort to such a project. Also, if the study came from the outside, no one could claim bias in the recommendations. Would you therefore want to get a quote from a local accounting firm?

Please let me know your decision as soon as possible, Joe. I would agree to either course of action, just so we do something to settle the debate before the controversy becomes even more heated.

Best regards,

When more than one alternative is given in a letter, the writer should ask certain questions before stating the alternatives: are they of equal merit; are all equally practical and desirable; would the choice of a particular alternative create special problems that should be mentioned; and so on. In model 1.9, the writer obviously prefers one of the two alternatives but is eager to do *something* and thus would agree to either of them.

THE PERSUASIVE REQUEST

1.10. For a Raise

Dear Dr. Carlton:

Today I'm starting my third year of employment at Raleigh Jr. College and my second year in your office. I've enjoyed every moment and hope the progress we've all shared has been satisfying to you, too. I'd appreciate it very much if you would review my accomplishments during the past two years and consider a salary increase for me effective the first of next month.

Since I've worked in your office, our secretarial and clerical staff has grown from one person to four, including part-time student assistants. As a result, my responsibilities have increased greatly, primarily in the area of training and supervising assistants. To handle the growing work load that made this staff expansion necessary, I've made a number of significant contributions: for example, I established a new filing system, streamlined the mail-processing function, developed a more effective follow-up system for our counseling activities, and prepared a work manual for all of us to use as a guide to office practices and procedures. In addition to these specific contributions, I feel my secretarial skills have improved substantially during the past two years, and that I am performing my duties more confidently and more effectively each day.

I hope the above examples of progress are evident in my record of performance at Raleigh, and that you'll agree they justify an increase in my salary.

Thank you very much, Dr. Carlton, for considering my request.

Sincerely,

A persuasive request is really a selling job, which means you have to state in your letter as many good reasons as you can think of to support your case. Such a letter requires careful planning. You should list and refine all the reasons you want to use before you even think about composing the letter. Once you begin writing, present your case in logical order. Guard against unreasonable requests and inaccurate statements.

RESPONDING TO REQUESTS

The request, like the routine inquiry, often comes from a prospective customer, and promptness and courtesy in replying are essential.

1. Be specific and clear in your response.
2. If you must say no or maybe, be considerate.
3. Recommend further action or communication, if necessary.

Models 1.11 to 1.17 are examples of seven typical situations requiring a variety of responses to requests.

REPLIES THAT OFFER MORE THAN REQUESTED

1.11. For Clarification

Dear Lynn:

We'd be glad to send you an address list of our society's membership on press-apply labels. However, the price of $35 a thousand I had quoted was for a standard printout; the charge for a printout on press-apply labels is $65 a thousand. Shall we go ahead on that basis? Please let me know—thanks, Lynn.

Best wishes,

When you suspect a person making a request has misunderstood something or lacks important information, *do not* proceed until you have sent a clarification.

GRANTING A REQUEST FOR A FUTURE DATE

1.12. For Interview

Dear Miss Pace:

Thank you for sending us your resume. We do have an opening in the file department and Mr. Johnson would be happy to discuss the position with you.

Could you come in on Thursday morning, November 5? Mr. Johnson will be free at 10:30 a.m. Please telephone me at 625-9999 if you are unable to come at that time. Otherwise, we'll look forward to seeing you then.

Cordially,

Although some letters, such as model 1.12, should be brief, they need not be abrupt. Notice how the last sentence of this letter adds a friendly, warm tone; in this case, it may also help to relax a nervous job applicant.

POSITIVE RESPONSES THAT SUGGEST ALTERNATIVES

1.13. To Assistance

Dear Ms. Marshall:

I was pleased to learn you would like to have someone from our office assist you in organizing a local chapter of our state's Human Resources Council. Naturally, I'm flattered you thought of me, and it's with regret that I must decline the opportunity to work with you on this project. My unpredictable schedule just wouldn't allow me to do justice to the effort.

Have you considered my assistant Hal Goldman? He's a "super-organizer" and seems to have boundless energy and enthusiasm once he gets involved in a project. Also, he's lived in this community most of his adult life and knows where to go and whom to see for support and cooperation in local activities. Since part of his job is to keep our office functioning smoothly while I'm travelling, he would be available most of the time. I know Hal enjoys this type of project work, and I'm certain you could count on a positive response from him.

Although I'm sorry I can't personally participate, it would be satisfying to me to know someone from our office was involved in this important venture. Many thanks for asking and please accept my good wishes for a successful Human Resources Chapter.

                                                        Cordially,

Model 1.13 illustrates a common situation—agreeing to a general idea but suggesting an alternative to the writer's specific request. A reply of this type should move rapidly into a persuasive case for the alternative suggestion, so the emphasis of the letter and its tone will be positive and will not discourage the person making the request.

TRANSMITTAL LETTERS

1.14. For Literature, with Documents Enclosed

Dear Mr. Cramer:

Here, with our compliments, are the three reports you requested: Wastewater Treatment; The Sloan Watershed Project; and Changing Rural Land-Use Patterns.

I hope this literature will be helpful to you. Thanks very much for writing to the Science Institute.

Sincerely,

Transmittal letters are usually brief, the intent being simply to say that certain items are enclosed (or are being sent separately). However, there is no reason why a transmittal letter has to be cold and unfriendly, as you can see from the last paragraph of model 1.14.

THE UNQUALIFIED REFUSAL

1.15. For Contributions

Dear Mr. Moore:

I regret very much that our company will be unable to contribute to your drive to secure recreational funds for underprivileged children in our community. As much as we would like to support all such worthwhile endeavors, our company is small, and we are forced to confine our donations to a single annual pledge to the Community Fund.

Please accept our good wishes for the success of your campaign for this important cause.

Sincerely,

A letter of refusal should include a reason for declining the request. Model 1.15 concerns a worthy cause and thus the letter closes with good wishes for the project's success.

THE QUALIFIED REFUSAL

1.16. Of Cooperation

Dear Paula:

Thanks for giving me a chance to review your proposal for a new system to handle registrations at our next seminar. You obviously spent a lot of time on this. Although I agree that the chaos we experienced at last year's seminar must be prevented in the future, I'm reluctant to recommend this new system to Mr. Parks.

The greatest difficulty I anticipate in the proposed system is the need to have the registration desk run by two persons from our secretarial staff instead of volunteers from the seminar. Although that might prevent chaos at the registration desk, I'm afraid it would introduce chaos in our office. We usually have a peak work load at the time of our seminars and really need additional, not less, help.

I know you would like to solve the problem—and so would I—but I feel we need to move in a different direction and find a solution that wouldn't affect our work capacity and capability at the office. If you can come up with an idea that avoids such pitfalls, let me know, and I'll be delighted to help you put it into effect.

Thanks for all your time and effort, Paula. I know everyone on the training committee will appreciate it.

Best wishes,

The qualified refusal is tricky to handle, as letter 1.16 suggests. Often the objective is to say "no, I won't, unless . . ." Like any kind of refusal, this one requires tact and consideration for the feelings of the recipient.

REFERRAL TO OTHER SOURCES

1.17. For Additional Information

Dear Mr. Inman:

Since our department no longer conducts market research, the information we have on machine tool orders and shipments is both limited and dated. Have you contacted Machine Control Magazine in Dayton? They have a very active research department and might be able to supply the figures you need. Also, you might write to the Department of Commerce's Metalworking Division for back issues of their quarterly industrial reports.

Good luck in finding the information you need, and thanks for thinking of us.

Sincerely,

It is always a matter of good public relations to be as helpful as possible to anyone who contacts you. This includes taking time to compose a pleasant, even if brief, letter pointing out a better source to the writer.

2

RESERVATIONS AND ORDERS

Accuracy is a principal consideration in handling reservations and orders, whether you are placing or acknowledging them. Thus, even when information is secured and conveyed by phone, it is usually confirmed by letter. The models in chapter 2 concern two important duties for most secretaries: assisting in travel preparations for the manager; and processing orders coming in and going out of the office.

In many offices the majority of these letters are written by the secretary for her own signature (e.g., 2.2, Making Reservations—Direct). However, in some offices the secretary may prepare certain letters for the manager's signature (e.g., 2.14, Apologies for Delay). Regardless of the practice in your office, the sample letters in this chapter can easily be adapted to your situation; just follow the general pattern of the letters using your own information in each case. (See chapter 13 for models of similar correspondence handled by memo and chapter 3 for additional models of orders acknowledged by letter. Consult the Selector Guide for specific model numbers.)

Letters pertaining to reservations are commonplace in most offices, depending, of course, on the number of out-of-town trips the manager must make. Examples of reservation letters are those requesting information (2.1), making and confirming reservations (2.2, 2.3, 2.7, and 2.8), and cancelling or changing reservations (2.4, 2.5, and 2.6).

Letters that process orders are especially common in some offices. Often, however, the order is placed or acknowledged by use of a special form (see 15.24 and 15.25), particularly in offices where there are too many orders going in and out each day for the secretary to be able to type individual letters for each. In other situations letters are prepared individually. In fact, in certain cases there is no other choice, and models 2.9 to 2.17 cover the principal categories of letters that process orders.

HANDLING RESERVATIONS

Reservation letters are usually brief but they must give all necessary facts to avoid mistakes that could create serious problems for the manager while he or she is travelling.

1. Be absolutely clear and specific in transmitting both requests and acknowledgments.
2. Give all pertinent facts, for example, times, places, dates, order numbers, check or credit card numbers, and so on.
3. Ask for (and give) written confirmations whenever possible.

Models 2.1 to 2.8 are typical letters a secretary will write when it is her duty to handle reservations for the manager.

REQUESTING INFORMATION ON AVAILABILITY, RATES

2.1. For Hotel Accommodations

Gentlemen:

Please send me rates for a single room with bath. Would you have something available from Monday afternoon, March 4, through the night of Wednesday, March 6?

I'd appreciate an immediate reply so I can make reservations right away. Thank you.

Sincerely,

Inquiries such as model 2.1 can be very brief, containing only the essential facts. It is not necessary at this point to give the name of the person for whom a reservation will eventually be made. (If time is short, of course, this type of inquiry would be made by telephone.)

MAKING RESERVATIONS—DIRECT

2.2. For Air Travel

Gentlemen:

Please reserve first-class space for Mr. David Lawson, assistant manager, Jones & Company. Mr. Lawson would like to leave Los Angeles on your flight number 523 to Chicago at 10:30 a.m., P.S.T., on March 4, and return from Chicago to Los Angeles on your flight number 716 at 3:45 p.m., C.S.T. on March 7. The ticket should be charged to Jones & Company's air travel card number 9511326. Mr. Lawson will pick up the ticket at the airport just before departure.

Please confirm this reservation immediately by wire. Thank you.

Sincerely,

Flight schedules change, and even if you recently received information from the airline, always list all facts (time, flight number, date, etc.) in your letter.

MAKING RESERVATIONS—
TRAVEL AGENT

2.3. For Foreign Travel

Dear Ms. Brock:

Please reserve a cabin-class stateroom for Mr. Louis Fortrell, director of promotion, Stone Millwork Company, on the Americana leaving New York for South Hampton on Tuesday, January 5, and returning on the Voyageur leaving South Hampton for New York on Friday, February 9.

Mr. Fortrell's itinerary is not yet complete. However, I would appreciate it if you could arrange first-class transportation and hotel accommodations for the following stopovers:

London: January 14–20
Brussels: January 22–February 1
Paris: February 3–7

Mr. Fortrell will make any late additions to or changes in this schedule after he arrives in Europe. He will be using his American Express card (number 37-115-3249-8776) for all arrangements.

We would like to have full details including rates on hotels and transportation as soon as possible. In the meantime, please let me know if you need further information. Thanks very much for your help.

Sincerely,

Foreign travel plans are almost always handled through a travel agent. Thus, as model 2.3 shows, if you give the agent places and dates, he or she will secure the information on rates and availability of transportation and hotel accommodations, and make all needed reservations for you.

CHANGING RESERVATIONS—
PAYMENT BY CHECK

2.4. For Train Travel

Dear Sir:

On September 9 I reserved a compartment on the Limited for Mr. Donald Glass, senior accountant at Boyle Accounting, leaving Richmond at 8:05 a.m., October 2, for Atlanta, and returning to Richmond at 7:45 p.m. on October 8 (ticket paid by company check).

Mr. Glass now plans to stop over in Atlanta a couple days and continue on to Miami before returning to Richmond. Therefore, I would like to reserve a compartment for Mr. Glass, leaving Atlanta on October 4 (preferably in the morning) for Miami and returning to Atlanta on October 8 in time to meet his 7:45 p.m. connection to Richmond.

Please let me know if this space will be available and the rate. Also, I would like to know if this ticket should be purchased additionally or whether there would be any cost saving if a new ticket for the entire trip were issued.

I'd appreciate an immediate reply so we can send you our check right away. Thank you.

Sincerely,

The rule in making reservations is the same, whether travel plans are new or revised: Give the transportation agent the necessary facts (day, time, method of payment, and so on) and request information or confirmation in writing.

CANCELLING RESERVATIONS—
NO ADVANCE PAYMENT

2.5. For Car Rental

Gentlemen:

On June 30 I reserved a car for one week, July 9 to 14, for Mr. Jack Moss, design engineer, Pitman Structures, Inc. As Mr. Moss will not be able to travel that week as planned, please cancel the reservation immediately. Thank you.

Sincerely,

Car rentals represent one exception to the rule regarding requests for written confirmation. In many offices arrangements for car rentals are made by phone (and cancelled by phone if time is short) and no advance payment or charge is made. However, follow the practice in your office.

CANCELLING RESERVATIONS—
PAYMENT BY CREDIT CARD

2.6. For Tour

Dear Miss Carson:

Last week Mr. Henry Stein, president of Watson Imports, picked up two tickets for himself and Mrs. Stein for a January 11-31 Mediterranean cruise on the Oceana. The tickets were charged to Mr. Stein's travel card account 775-6634-9110.

Because of an accident, Mrs. Stein will be unable to leave at that time; therefore, they would like to cancel the reservations (both tickets are enclosed). Please credit Mr. Stein's travel account for the full amount.

I'd appreciate having written confirmation of this cancellation. Thanks for your help, Miss Carson.

Cordially,

Most tours are arranged through travel agents who will make, change, or cancel reservations for you. However, they need the pertinent facts (date, charge account number, and so on) the same as any travel representative.

CONFIRMING RESERVATIONS

2.7. For Dinner

Dear Mr. Thomas:

This will confirm your reservation for a dinner table for twelve on Tuesday, March 4, at 7:30 p.m. in our Sunflower Room.

We will be happy to provide the full-course, roast beef menu you selected, with the services of a wine steward, at $12.90 per person.

If there is anything additional we can do to make the evening enjoyable for you and your guests, please do let me know. We appreciate the opportunity to help you plan this special occasion.

Sincerely,

Reservation confirmations can be brief, summarizing only the essential facts. But if you are providing a service and hope to have the customer return again, it is important to add a word of appreciation or a thoughtful offer of further assistance (e.g., the last paragraph of model 2.7).

PICKUP-DELIVERY ARRANGEMENTS

2.8 For Theatre Tickets

Gentlemen:

Please reserve two mezzanine seats for the November 14 evening performance of "The Window Dresser." Mr. Fred Beal, our company representative, will pick up the tickets at the box office on the afternoon of November 14.

A check for $13.65 is enclosed. Please let us know which seats are being reserved and confirm that the two tickets will be available at the box office for Mr. Beal on November 14. A stamped, self-addressed envelope is enclosed for your convenience in replying.

Thank you.

Sincerely,

Most tickets—theatre, travel, and so on—can be mailed, delivered by messenger, or held for pickup. Whichever method you choose, make clear in your letter the date desired for delivery or pickup.

PROCESSING ORDERS

When the need for personal handling precludes the use of a standard order form or acknowledgment form, orders must be processed by letter.

1. Specify clearly what you want to order. In an acknowledgment, confirm exactly what has been ordered.
2. Make certain all facts are correct and clearly understood regarding things such as price, quantity, and delivery date.
3. If any changes are necessary, carefully explain what is required.
4. Thank the customer for the order.

Models 2.9 to 2.17 are examples of the variety of orders that are processed by letter.

PLACING ORDER—PAYMENT BY CREDIT CARD

2.9 For Merchandise

Gentlemen:

Please send us the following item from your office furnishings department:

One (1), 6 x 9, Oatmeal, Fiber Blend Shag Area Rug by RugMakers, Ltd., $299.98 plus tax.

The purchase should be charged to the personal account of Mr. Martin West, senior vice-president, West Enterprises (account number 6621-0044-3967), and it should be delivered to West Enterprises, Suite 211, 1006 Highway North, Falls Church, Virginia 22042.

I'd appreciate written acknowledgment of this order, along with your estimated delivery date for the rug. Thank you.

Sincerely,

Although model 2.9 just gives the company address for place of delivery, some firms also specify the name of the individual to whom the item must be delivered.

PLACING ORDER—PAYMENT BY CHECK

2.10 For Service

Dear Miss Jennings:

Thanks very much for explaining the procedure to initiate business telephone service for Cole Records Company in our new Midwest office.

We would like to have a black desk phone with a fourteen-foot cord installed the week of October 7 at this location: Room 112, 23-14 Lafayette Avenue, Des Moines, Iowa 50336. One of our company representatives will be there from 9 to 5 o'clock each day to indicate the precise location for installation.

Our company check number 358 for $67.50 is enclosed, which includes a $25 deposit, $25 advance payment for one month's service, and $17.50 for installation plus tax. Monthly bills and correspondence should be sent to our eastern office: Cole Records Company, Inc., 511 West 42nd Street, New York, New York 10017.

Thanks for all your help, Miss Jennings. Please let me know if you need any further information. In the meantime I'd very much appreciate your confirmation of this order.

Cordially,

If advance payment is required for the service or product you are ordering, state the amount in your letter and what it covers, so the recipient will know instantly if anything is wrong.

CONFIRMATION OF TELEPHONE ORDER

2.11. For Office Equipment

Dear Mr. Ryan:

Thank you for your August 9 telephone order for one (1) model 320, camel-colored, high-back vinyl side chair, at our sale price of $149.98 plus $22 shipping and handling. The chair will be shipped from our factory in North Carolina in about four weeks; it will be sent to you C.O.D. as you requested.

We appreciate your order very much and hope we can be of service again.

Sincerely,

It is even more important to confirm a telephone order than a written order. The acknowledgment must restate all facts—full description, price and other charges, delivery date, and so on—to avoid any misunderstandings later. Details of phone conversations may soon be forgotten.

CANCELLING ORDER—PAYMENT BY CREDIT CARD

2.12. For Literature

Gentlemen:

On February 5 I placed an order for two correspondence courses: Basic Bookkeeping Course 343. The courses were charged to Mr. Ronald Page's First National Credit Card Number 1-606-2197-001.

Since the persons for whom this material was intended have been transferred to another division, we will be unable to use the courses. Please cancel the order and credit Mr. Page's account in full.

I'd appreciate having written confirmation of this cancellation. Thank you for your help.

Sincerely,

A cancellation of an order, like the original order, should state all pertinent data. If the order has already been received and can be returned, the letter should state that the unused material is enclosed for a full refund (if paid by check) or full credit (if charged to an account).

CHANGING ORDER—PAYMENT BY CHECK

2.13. For Maintenance

Dear Mr. Bloomington:

We would like to change our recent order for typewriter maintenance service at Benson Supplies, Inc. We had requested a maintenance contract for four of our electric office machines, and a check for $120 for one year's coverage was sent to you on July 15.

One of the typewriters included in this agreement has since been sold and we would like to change the contract to cover service for just the three remaining machines. In your June 4 letter to Mr. Barkley Briggs, associate director at Benson Supplies, you state that coverage for three machines would be $90. Please refund to Benson Supplies, Inc. the balance due as a result of this reduction in service.

I'm enclosing our present contract and will look forward to receiving a revised agreement as soon as possible. Thanks very much.

Sincerely,

Revised orders often involve refunds or additional charges. In the case of a refund, your letter must specify to whom a check should be sent or which account should be credited.

APOLOGIES FOR DELAY

2.14. Of Parts

Dear Mr. Creighton:

I'm very sorry for the unavoidable delay we've encountered in shipping the parts to you for your press. The recent truckers' strike created an unexpected backlog of orders at our factory, and all shipments had to be rescheduled. Now that the transportation problem has been solved, we will be able to ship your parts by October 5. I hope this date will be satisfactory.

Please accept our sincere apologies for any inconvenience the delay has caused. We appreciate your patience.

Cordially,

The tone of a letter of apology is particularly important since the letter must try to alleviate the customer's annoyance. An apology should be extended first and then a solution should be offered.

NEED ADDITIONAL INFORMATION TO
FILL ORDER

2.15. For Subscription

Dear Ms. Ritter:

Yes, we would be very happy to enter a subscription for you to Homebuilders' Newsletter and, as you requested, send an invoice for the full amount.

We'll need one further item of information to complete our records: would you prefer a one-year or two-year subscription (12 issues for $16 or 24 issues for $24)? As you can see, the two-year rate offers a substantial savings per copy.

As soon as we hear from you we'll complete your subscription records and your first issue will soon be on the way to you.

Thanks so much for your interest in Homebuilders' Newsletter. I hope you enjoy and profit from each fact-filled issue.

Cordially,

It's quite common for orders to come in with facts insufficient to fill them. If preprinted forms are not used for replying, a letter must be sent. Since you are dealing with a customer or prospective customer, your letter must not show any irritation that the writer forgot something obvious; rather, it should be pleasant and indicate your appreciation for the customer's order.

CONFIRMATION OF COST-DELIVERY TIME

2.16. For Supplies

Dear Mr. Jones:

This will confirm the offer regarding clipboards that I made to you by telephone yesterday. We can supply 400 gold-stamped, navy vinyl clipboards, 8 ½ x 11, with ruled tablet inserts, for $500 plus 5 percent sales tax, to be delivered to your offices on or before March 23. So we can meet your deadline, please let us know by February 15 whether you wish to have us proceed with the order.

If we can be of help in any other way, just let me know. Thanks very much for asking about our convention supplies.

Sincerely,

Confirmations of cost should clearly specify any extra charges such as shipping or sales tax. If you promise to deliver goods by a specific date, be certain to tell the prospective customer when he or she must place the order so you can meet that deadline.

TRANSMITTAL LETTER

2.17. For Shipment

Dear Carl:

Fourteen insured cartons of files and other materials are being sent to you today by Hiller Trucking Service. This will complete the transfer of records to our new office. As you know, I'll personally hand carry our bank books, books of account, and other vital records.

Hope everything arrives safely. I'll be joining you in a few weeks—in time to help you unpack!

Best regards,

Although we usually think of packing slips or special forms accompanying the shipment of most materials, there are other occasions when a separate, individually typed letter is needed, as model 2.17 shows. Often a copy of the transmittal letter is enclosed in each carton of material.

3

ACKNOWLEDGMENT LETTERS

An acknowledgment of correspondence received is common courtesy in a business office. Although many routine acknowledgments are handled with a standard form, others require more personal attention. The models in chapter 3 are grouped into two basic categories of acknowledgments: those that acknowledge a letter without answering it and those that acknowledge and also answer it.

Many acknowledgments are prepared and sent by the secretary in the manager's absence (e.g., 3.3, Personal Letters Received—Manager Is Away). Others are usually handled by the secretary routinely (e.g., 3.5, Orders Received), although some may be written by the secretary for the manager's signature (e.g., 3.9, Confirmation of Verbal Agreement). The format for most of these letters is simple and straightforward, which means the models shown here can be easily adapted to your own situation. (Chapter 13 gives examples of similar communications sent by memo. The Selector Guide will direct you to specific models of acknowledgment correspondence in other chapters.)

Simple acknowledgments, such as confirming the receipt of an order, are almost always brief and easy to process. Models 3.1 to 3.9 are examples of simple acknowledgments of correspondence or material received.

The second type of acknowledgment—one that also answers—is slightly more involved and sometimes requires more thought in preparation. The response, for example, could necessitate some research to provide a suitable answer. Letters 3.10 to 3.16 show some typical patterns for acknowledgments that also answer.

SIMPLE ACKNOWLEDGMENTS

A simple acknowledgment should not be considered unimportant just because it is basically straightforward and routine. Even the briefest, simplest acknowledgment conveys an impression of you and your company to the recipient.

1. Respond promptly.
2. Indicate what you received.
3. Express your appreciation for whatever you received.

The following nine models are examples of typical acknowledgments that respond without answering.

INFORMATION RECEIVED

3.1. With Documents

Dear Julie:

Thanks very much for sending the type catalog and price lists I requested. This will make it so much easier for me to typemark our quarterly reports.

I really appreciate your quick response—it all arrived just in time for our next report!

Best Wishes,

When someone makes a helpful gesture and rushes something to you, he or she deserves a sincere expression of thanks at the very least.

INFORMATION REQUESTED

3.2. You Send Documents

Dear Mr. Davis:

We were delighted to learn about your interest in our consumer reports. The index you requested is enclosed.

I hope this will be helpful to you in selecting specific reports to order. Do let us know if we can offer any further information.

Thanks so much for your interest.

Sincerely,

Model 3.2 illustrates a standard procedure in acknowledgments of requests for information: offer to supply additional information and thank the writer for his or her interest.

PERSONAL LETTERS RECEIVED—
MANAGER IS AWAY

3.3. Condolences

Dear Mr. Letterman:

Your letter announcing the untimely death of your associate James
Ringley arrived while Mrs. Baxter is away on business. I know she
will be deeply saddened by this unfortunate loss and will contact you
when she returns.

Sincerely,

This type of acknowledgment should be brief but have a sympathetic tone. It
should state that the manager will respond as soon as he or she returns. (If a close
friend of the manager has died, the secretary obviously would not wait until the
manager returns to relay the message.)

BUSINESS LETTER RECEIVED—
MANAGER IS AWAY

3.4. A Transmittal Letter

Dear Mr. Hefner:

Since Mr. Putnam will be away from the office until March 23, I'm
sending you the tapes you requested in his absence. As soon as he
returns I'll ask him if there is any additional information we could provide. In the meantime, I hope the enclosed tapes will be useful.

If there's anything further I can do to help until Mr. Putnam returns,
please let me know.

Sincerely,

Busy executives travel frequently and rely on their secretaries to acknowledge
correspondence in their absence. Model 3.4 is a simple acknowledgment in the
form of a transmittal letter sent while the manager is away. Typically, it promises
to alert the manager, Mr. Putnam, as soon as he returns.

ORDERS RECEIVED

3.5. For Books

Dear Mr. Franklin:

Thank you for your order for twelve (12) of our Second Annual Conference Proceedings. I've forwarded all information to our publications department, and I know they will give your order prompt attention.

Sincerely,

Although most orders can be simply and efficiently aknowledged by form, certain occasions warrant a personal acknowledgment. Model 3.5 concerns an order from an important member of an association; the opportunity is used to make personal contact with the member and strengthen the member-society relationship.

ORDERS CHANGED

3.6. For Merchandise

Dear Mrs. Blackstone:

We'll be happy to change your recent order for Sesame Stoneware service for eight to service for twelve. I've forwarded this change to our warehouse, and you should soon be receiving your new service for twelve.

We appreciate your interest in these lovely dishes and hope you will enjoy them for many years.

Sincerely,

Model 3.6 shows how to use a simple acknowledgment of a change in an order to build customer relations.

REMITTANCES RECEIVED

3.7. For Membership Renewal

Dear Mr. Phillips:

Thank you for sending along your annual fee for membership renewal. We appreciate your continuing participation in the society and hope you will enjoy and benefit from the many new programs and activities scheduled for the coming year.

Sincerely,

Even the simple acknowledgment of a remittance, if made by personal letter rather than form, can be used as an opportunity to build goodwill and solidify relations.

APPOINTMENT REQUESTED

3.8. For Job Interview

Dear Miss Harper:

Thank you very much for letting us know you would like to find a suitable position at Newton College. Ms. Rossberg will be happy to see you to discuss your qualifications and current job opportunities at Newton.

Please telephone me at 643-0100 to set a date for an appointment.

Sincerely,

Model 3.8 is a typical example of the simple acknowledgment. It does not offer any information about positions that are open nor does it comment on Miss Harper's qualifications and prospects for finding a job at the college. It does not even specify the time or place for an appointment but rather asks Miss Harper to phone the college to make these arrangements later.

CONFIRMATION OF VERBAL AGREEMENT

3.9. To Serve on Committee

Dear Hal:

Thanks again for asking me to serve on the Entertainment Committee at the club next year. As I mentioned by phone today, I don't foresee any complications in my schedule, so I'd be happy to serve on the committee.

I'll look forward to receiving details from you concerning the next meeting.

Best regards,

Although the manager would sign a letter such as this, the secretary may be expected to write it.

ACKNOWLEDGMENTS THAT ALSO ANSWER

Some acknowledgments must also supply additional information. Such letters may need extra attention and care in preparation. However, the same rules used for a simple acknowledgment apply here as well.

1. Respond promptly.
2. Indicate what you received.
3. Provide as much information as you can to answer the letter or request.
4. Express appreciation if something is received.

Models 3.10 to 3.16 are examples of the pattern used to acknowledge and answer a letter.

INFORMATION RECEIVED

3.10. With Missing Item

Dear Ms. Block:

Thanks for letting me know that a detailed description of my property has been sent directly to a number of prospects. The address list was enclosed with your November 5 letter, but the property description was missing.

Could you still send me a copy of the description? I'd like very much to see it. Since I'll be leaving on vacation in a couple weeks I'd appreciate it if you could put it in the mail to me this week.

Cordially,

Letters calling attention to the omission of enclosures should describe what was and was not received. If the missing information is needed by a specific date, be certain to make this clear.

PERSONAL LETTERS RECEIVED

3.11. With Congratulations

Dear Al:

I want to thank you for your thoughtful letter congratulating me on my recent interview in the Brentwood News. You're right—it was a welcome opportunity for me, as the interview gave me a chance to say some things I've long believed about our growing tax burden in Brentwood. I'm especially pleased to learn you agree with my remarks.

I appreciate your vote of confidence, Al. Let's hope it all does some good!

Regards,

Model 3.11 is an example of a response that not only acknowledges someone's letter but uses the opportunity to confirm the writer's stand on a tax issue.

BUSINESS LETTERS RECEIVED—
MANAGER IS AWAY

3.12. About Speaking Engagement

Dear Mr. Ellis:

Thank you for reminding Miss Webster about her promise to speak at your club luncheon on Wednesday, August 9. She's away on business now, but I know she's planning to return in time to address your group.

I'll bring your letter to her attention as soon as she returns and I'm certain she will contact you promptly to confirm these arrangements.

Sincerely,

Model 3.12 is an example of a letter that tries to satisfy the writer but assures him that the manager will soon be in contact.

ORDERS RECEIVED

3.13. Send Apology for Delay in Filling

Dear Mrs. Prentiss:

Thank you for your order for eleven (11) 8 x 10 executive reminder calendars. Our previous supplier discontinued this line last month, and I regret there will be a two- to three-week delay while we wait for a shipment from our new supplier.

The calendars should be here by October 12, and I'll phone you immediately as soon as they arrive.

Please accept my apologies for this unavoidable delay.

Sincerely,

There could be a number of variations of model 3.13: a recommendation for a substitute calendar that might be available sooner; a promise to look for another source if the order is urgent; and so on. In any case, though, the letter must thank the customer, explain the delay, and offer an apology.

REMITTANCES RECEIVED

3.14. With Error in Payment

Dear Mr. Addison:

Thank you for sending along your payment of our invoice number 1-03295J for the electrical wiring work completed in July, We note, however, an overpayment: the amount due is $140.20; your check total is $142.00. Therefore, our check refunding the overpayment of $1.80 is enclosed.

We appreciated the opportunity to handle your electrical wiring needs and hope you'll call on us again when we can be of further service.

Sincerely,

Ordinarily, a remittance such as that described by model 3.14 would not be acknowledged by letter. The error in payment, however, made it necessary to acknowledge the payment and explain why a refund was due.

ORDER SENT INCOMPLETE

3.15. You Suggest Substitute

Dear Mrs. Pollock:

We are sorry that two of the items listed in your January 14 order are temporarily out of stock. The two-foot brass planter and the set of our walnut-grained trays have been back ordered and will be available after March 1.

A copy of our winter sale catalog is enclosed, which shows a variety of other planters and trays—all available immediately should you care to select substitutes for the out-of-stock items. Just let us know and we'll change your order right away. In the meantime, the rest of the items you requested are being sent to you by parcel post this week.

We sincerely regret the delay in filling part of your order. Thank you
for your patience.

Cordially,

Letter 3.15, like model 3.14, concerns an acknowledgment that would not
likely be made by personal letter if if were not desirable to explain at the same time
that substitutes for the originally ordered items are available. Notice that the letter
also offers an apology.

INQUIRIES RECEIVED

3.16. You Recommend Appointment

Dear Ms. Sampson:

Although we expect our remote assembly control to be operational
within one month, we haven't yet collected and published the information you inquired about.

One of our chief researchers, Rudolph Kraeger, has been supervising most of the developmental activity on this project and could no
doubt answer many of your questions. If you would like to set up an
appointment with Mr. Keaeger, please phone me at 423-4000. I know
he would be happy to talk with you about the new control.

We appreciate your interest. Thanks very much for writing.

Sincerely,

An acknowledgment that only partially answers should advise the writer how
or where to find further information. Model 3.16 is an example of a situation
where there is no published information that can be sent by mail at present. The
only alternative source for immediate information then is the personal interview.

4

REMINDERS AND FOLLOW-UPS

How nice it would be if all business letters were promptly acknowledged by the recipients. Since many letters are not always acknowledged in time—or at all—reminders and follow-ups are an essential part of the secretary's daily correspondence. Usually, the secretary maintains a follow-up file to alert her on which date, for each letter, a follow-up or reminder must be sent.

A secretary will send many reminders and follow-ups under her own signature (e.g., 4.7, Unanswered Letters—Request for Prices). The manager would likely sign certain letters, however (e.g., 4.6, Invitation to Workshop Panelist), although the secretary might draft them. Most reminders and follow-ups have a standard pattern, and it should be easy to tailor the models in this chapter to your own needs. (The Selector Guide will lead you to other follow-up and reminder letters throughout the book: for example, chapter 12, Follow-up Sales Letters. See also chapter 13 for follow-ups and reminders prepared in the memo format.)

Reminders are frequently sent to confirm plans previously made and acknowledged. Thus, the reminder could cover almost any conceivable situation of this type, although the more common reminder letters concern appointments (4.1), meeting notices (4.2), invitations (4.6), expressions of interest (4.5), and requests for something (4.3 and 4.4). The reminder can also be considered a follow-up letter, for example, model 4.3, even though the stress is on "reminding."

The follow-up letter could pertain to as many or even more situations than the reminder—virtually anything. Models 4.7 to 4.15 concern typical situations requiring a follow-up: for example, an unreturned phone call (4.8), a letter received with something missing (4.12), an invitation for someone to return after an interview (4.14), and an order never received (4.15).

SENDING REMINDERS

Reminders are usually brief, although occasionally a situation requires the repetition of numerous facts. In either case the letter must be specific. To be of any value, of course, it must be sent in time for the recipient—who may have forgotten everything—to take whatever action was originally planned.

1. Specify the facts pertaining to the commitment (e.g., what is planned, when, etc.).
2. If pertinent, specify the date of the original commitment and whether it was made verbally or by letter.
3. If there is time, request a confirmation by letter (or phone).
4. Do *not* suggest that the recipient is thoughtless or forgetful.

The following six models are only a few of the possible circumstances requiring a reminder; however, as you will see, the tone and pattern of reminders is similar from letter to letter, even though the situation may change.

APPOINTMENTS

4.1. For Business Luncheon

Dear Steve:

This is just a note to let you know everything is set for our March 14 luncheon date at the Kingsley Inn. I have a table for five reserved in my name, and the others will meet us there at 12 o'clock.

I certainly hope nothing has come up to affect these plans for you, Steve, but do give me a call if you anticipate any problems in joining us. Otherwise, I'll look forward to seeing you then.

                                                    Best regards,

Letter 4.1 would be appropriate if the plans were made far in advance and it is conceivable that someone may have forgotten the date in the meantime. Often such reminders are handled by telephone; however, if a person is very busy it can be helpful to have something in writing. Dates and times are too easily confused and forgotten in phone conversations.

MEETINGS AND CONFERENCES

4.2. Meeting Notice

Dear Lisa:

I hope you're still planning to be at our August 30 meeting of the Berkshire Club. We expect to start the meeting at 2:00 p.m. in the conference room at club headquarters.

Since I'm trying to estimate attendance now that the meeting date is almost here, I'd appreciate it if you could telephone me at 669-4000 or drop me a note to confirm that you are still planning to attend.

Thanks very much, Lisa. Hope to see you then.

                                                    Cordially,

If you compare models 4.1 and 4.2 you can see how similar various types of reminders are even though the circumstances or events are different.

Many writers start all their reminder letters with the phrase "This is to remind you that..." As models 4.1 and 4.2 show, there are other introductions that can be used to vary this type of correspondence.

REQUEST NOT ACKNOWLEDGED

4.3. For Report Requested

Gentlemen:

Early last month I wrote to request twenty copies of your report, "How to Sell with Visual Aids," and your April 9 response stated that the copies would be sent shortly. As I indicated then, we wanted them to distribute at our June 1 sales meeting.

The reports have not yet arrived, but we are still interested in having them for use at our June 1 meeting. I'd appreciate it if you could let me know right away whether they will be delivered before that date.

Thank you.

Sincerely,

A reminder that involves a deadline should always ask for written acknowledgment by a certain date. Model 4.3, for instance, concerns a situation where the reports *must* arrive before June 1, and the writer needs to know if this is not going to be possible.

INQUIRY NOT ACKNOWLEDGED

4.4. For Information Requested

Dear Mrs. Blackstone:

I was wondering if you've had an opportunity to consider further my inquiry of August 5 about folding and inserting machines. You had replied that some literature would soon be on the way. The literature has not yet arrived, but we are still interested. In case my original letter has been mislaid, I'm enclosing a copy that lists the special features we need.

I'll look forward to hearing from you soon. Thanks very much.

Sincerely,

There are two occasions when you might want to enclose a copy of your original letter: (1) when you suspect the original was lost or (2) when the original con-

tained numerous essential details you do not want to repeat in your reminder
letter.

EXPRESSION OF INTEREST

4.5. In Equipment Demonstration

Dear Bill:

Last fall, after stopping at your plant to see the model 420 computer
in operation, I decided to wait until the 430 series was available before considering a purchase. You had suggested giving me a call later. Although I haven't heard from you, I was wondering if you now
have the new 430 on the floor. If so, I would still be interested in a
demonstration.

Please drop me a note or phone me at 224-9360 as soon as you can
arrange a private demonstration for me.

Thanks very much, Bill.

Regards,

Usually salesmen do not forget an interested customer or prospective customer. But, occasionally, when substantial time has passed, it is necessary to send
a reminder of your continuing interest. Model 4.5 closes by asking the recipient to
acknowledge the letter—something that all reminders should do.

INVITATION

4.6. To Workshop Panelist

Dear Mr. Shatner:

Have you had an opportunity to consider our invitation to you to participate in our training seminar as one of the workshop panelists on
Tuesday, March 14, at 2:00 p.m.? I wanted to remind you that our
deadline for the program is next Friday, February 5.

Because we haven't heard either way from you since extending the
invitation last month, I'm wondering if my letter of invitation went
astray. If so, please refer to the enclosed copy of my original letter,
which contains full details regarding the workshop.

I sincerely hope you'll be able to participate; your contribution would
add a great deal to the success of our seminar. Could you let me
know this week so we can finalize our program?

Thanks very much.

Cordially,

When you write to jog the memory of someone who should have responded to an invitation, it is necessary either (1) to enclose the original letter or (2) to restate all details—date, time, place, type of event, and so on. If the details are extensive, it is obviously easier to enclose a copy of the original.

THE FOLLOW-UP

All unanswered correspondence, phone calls, invitations, orders, and so forth must be followed up at predetermined intervals. Usually the secretary will check her follow-up file daily and send letters for everything still pending and due for follow-up on each day. The pattern of a follow-up letter is essentially the same as that for a reminder.

1. Specify all pertinent facts pertaining to the item or letter being traced.
2. Request a prompt reply to your letter.
3. Do *not* suggest the recipient is thoughtless or forgetful.

Models 4.7 to 4.15 are only a few examples of the virtually endless variety of follow-up letters. However, the basic patterns shown in these models can be adapted to almost any other type of situation requiring a follow-up.

UNANSWERED LETTERS

4.7. Of Request for Prices

Gentlemen:

Last month I requested prices on your two dial-a-matic color heads for standard black and white enlargers. The information has not yet arrived, and we would like to have it as soon as possible so we may place an order by the end of this month.

Could you send us the prices this week? Thank you.

Sincerely,

When you follow up this type of routine request for information, which is not directed to a particular person, it does not really matter whether you believe your original letter was lost or whether the company is just very slow in responding. Simply restate what you want as briefly as possibly and specify when you need the information.

UNRETURNED PHONE CALLS

4.8. Of Request for Appointment

Dear Marge:

I wonder if you received my telephone message last week concerning a possible appointment for you to see Timothy Beal, manager, Courtland Supplies, Inc. Mr. Beal wants to expand his plastic container line, and I thought you might be able to discuss our products with him.

If you could drop me a note or phone me right away, I'll set up an appointment at the earliest possible date.

Thanks, Marge.

Cordially,

An unreturned phone call can be irritating, but the tone of a follow-up letter in this situation must not show even a hint of annoyance. Simply restate what you wanted and ask for a quick reply.

GIFT NOT ACKNOWLEDGED

4.9. Holiday Expression

Dear Ned:

I can imagine how busy you've been recently directing the opening of a new store in your territory during the hectic holiday season, so I thought I should check something with you. Two months ago today Roger and I sent you a gift—a hand-crafted paperweight—to wish you a happy holiday and congratulate you on the grand opening; I'm wondering if it perhaps went astray in the unavoidable confusion of moving to the new store.

Could you let me know if it arrived safely? If not, it was insured, and we can contact the post office here right away.

Best of luck with the new store, Ned.

Cordially,

After two months a follow-up is in order when a gift has not been acknowledged. Model 4.9 suggests that the recipient has been extremely busy—something he can use as an excuse in case he has just been tardy in sending a thank you. The letter also describes the gift in case it accidentally ended up on someone else's desk. Finally, the letter explains what can be done if it never arrived.

INQUIRY FROM A PROSPECTIVE CUSTOMER

4.10. Interested in Merchandise

Dear Mr. Vinson:

Last month you inquired about our miniature player-recorder, and I wanted to let you know immediately that a new shipment of these machines has arrived. Would you like to come in and try one out?

The miniature version has most of the essential features of our standard size model but because of its compact size can easily be carried in one's coat pocket. It is ideal for anyone who travels a great deal, and even in the office, executives enjoy its small, light-weight characteristics for handy desk-top use.

I hope you can stop by soon to see for yourself how remarkable these little machines are. We're open from 9 to 5 o'clock Mondays through Saturdays. In the meantime, if you have any questions, just phone me at 430-3900 or 430-6888.

Cordially,

Inquiries from prospective customers should be followed up as soon as possible. In the situation described by letter 4.10, it was necessary to wait until a shipment of machines arrived. Note that the follow-up letter is relatively brief but does a little selling as well as relays the pertinent facts and responds to the original inquiry.

FOLLOWING AN APPOINTMENT

4.11. Company Hospitality

Dear Mr. Collins:

It was a thoroughly enjoyable experience to meet you and your associates last Friday and tour your plant facilities. I was very much impressed with your entire optical instruments manufacturing operation and thought the efficiency of your production crew was most remarkable.

Thank you also for the excellent lunch at your club. It gave me a chance to get better acquainted with your associates and learn more about our mutual interests.

I'll look forward to seeing you in Cincinnati next month at the precision optics conference.

Best regards,

Successful business relationships are maintained by appropriate responses to all contacts. Thus, a meeting where one executive enjoys the company hospitality extended by another must be followed up with a note of appreciation.

TRANSMITTAL LETTER RECEIVED

4.12. With Missing Enclosure

Dear Mr. Jackson:

As Mr. Ryan is away this week, I'm acknowledging your letter of January 30 to him.

You mentioned that you were including a tentative program for the Civic Center opening, but the program was not enclosed. If you could send along a copy right away, I'll see that Mr. Ryan receives it just as soon as he returns next week.

Thanks very much.

Sincerely,

Letters with missing enclosures should be followed up immediately. One should never assume the sender will later realize the omission and send the item along.

MEMBERSHIP APPLICATION RECEIVED

4.13. Dues Not Enclosed

Dear Ms. Fredericks:

Thanks very much for completing an application for membership in the Lewistown's Secretarial Society. If you'll send us your remittance of $14 for one year's dues, we'll be happy to process your request for membership immediately.

Cordially,

When a remittance is not enclosed with an application (or order) there is no way of knowing if the sender forgot to include it or did not realize that payment in advance is required. Therefore, simply follow up promptly with a request for the amount due and state that the application (or order) will be processed promptly upon receipt.

JOB INTERVIEW

4.14. You Ask Applicant to Return

Dear Mrs. Clark:

Mr. Baxter was very pleased with your recent interview and application for the position of office manager.

Would you be able to come in again to discuss the position with him further? He will be free on Thursday, August 11, at 9:30 in the morning.

I'd appreciate a call at 463-1000 if this time is not convenient. Otherwise, we'll look forward to seeing you then.

Cordially,

Follow-ups that concern an appointment must have the same ingredients as any letter regarding a specific date. Give the details regarding time, place, and so on, and ask the recipient to notify you if the time is convenient.

ORDER NEVER RECEIVED

4.15. Supplies Needed Urgently

Gentlemen:

On March 21 I placed a rush order for two cartons of your black cartridge film ribbons, number 2245781. As the ribbons have not yet arrived, I wonder if my original order went astray; if so, please consider this a duplicate.

Since we are urgently in need of replacements, I would appreciate having this order send immediately by United Parcel Service. The cartons should be delivered to our letterhead address, attention of Max Donnelley.

If these ribbons are out of stock or cannot be sent on a rush basis, please phone me right away at 782-3000. Thank you.

Sincerely,

When you are following up an order never received, take care in the wording of your letter. Notice that model 4.15 describes this as a *duplicate* order to avoid having it treated as a new, *additional* order for more ribbons.

5

APPOINTMENT LETTERS

Arranging appointments is an important part of the secretary's job. Although many plans for meetings and interviews are made by telephone, they are almost always confirmed by letter. Sometimes the appointment letter or your response to an appointment letter is the first thing a prospective visitor sees from your company. Since first impressions can be lasting impressions, it is essential that your letter be clear, accurate, and courteous.

In most offices the majority of appointment letters are written and signed by the secretary (e.g., 5.6, Confirming Appointment). Even appointment letters signed by someone else are frequently written by the secretary (e.g., 5.10, Cancelling Appointments with Company Official). Since appointment letters primarily concern details of time, place, date, and so on, they are generally brief and straightforward, which means it will be easy for you to change the basic facts and adapt the models in this chapter to your own situation. (Consult the Selector Guide for appointment letters in other chapters, for example, 3.8.)

Letters that make appointments can be grouped into two categories: (1) those that present all details without alternatives (5.1, 5.3, 5.5, and 5.6), the most common type of appointment letter, and (2) those that offer alternatives or leave certain details, such as the time, open (5.2 and 5.4).

Replies to requests for appointments vary somewhat more than letters making appointments. For instance, some responses grant the appointment (5.7 and 5.8); some change or cancel the appointment (5.9 and 5.10); and others refuse the appointment either temporarily or indefinitely (5.11, 5.12, and 5.13).

MAKING APPOINTMENTS

Since appointment letters deal with facts such as time and place, they have to be accurate. Also, because the letters do contain such specific information, they must be sent in time for the recipient to respond and comply with the suggested arrangements.

1. State the purpose of the appointment.
2. Suggest the time, place, and date.
3. Ask for a confirmation.

Just because letters making appointments must be factual and precise, they need not be abrupt and cold. Observe the pattern and tone of models 5.1 to 5.6, which represent the most common types of appointment letters.

APPOINTMENT FOR THE MANAGER—
TIME SET

5.1. To Make Presentation

Dear Mr. Boyd:

The enclosed walnut plaque is sent to you with our compliments. It's a sample from one of our recent shipments to Farnsworth Junior College. You'll notice it bears their seal in four colors.

Plaques such as this containing logos and seals are very popular with schools, clubs, and other groups. When produced in quantities of 100 or more they are inexpensive and can either be awarded or sold at a profit by the purchasing organization.

We would like to show you more samples and tell you what we could offer your college. Would it be possible to visit your office? I will be In Houston on Monday, April 9, and could stop to see you at 3:30 p.m. Please let me know if that time would be convenient for you.

Thanks very much.

Cordially,

Model 5.1 asks for a response, presumably by mail. If time had been short the letter could have asked for a telephone response or could have said someone would call the recipient on a certain date to confirm the arrangements.

APPOINTMENT FOR THE MANAGER—
TIME OPEN

5.2. For Plant Tour

Dear Mr. Winston:

Jeffrey Stevens, assistant production manager at Hill Market Services, Inc., will be in Detroit on Wednesday, August 13, and would like to arrange a tour of your plant while he is there.

Would it be possible for him to visit your facilities some time during the morning on Wednesday? Please let me know what time would be convenient.

Thank you very much.

Sincerely,

Some things such as a plant tour cannot be arranged at all imaginable times. Companies often conduct tours only on certain days at certain times. Model 5.2 therefore requests only a morning tour, but does not ask for a particular hour, leaving it up to the company to specify the time.

ASKING SOMEONE TO SEE THE MANAGER

5.3. About Budget Review

Dear Mrs. Kelly:

Mr. Brill would like to know if you could see him in his office on Tuesday, May 4, at 11 o'clock. He wants to review your recommendations for next year's budget.

I'd appreciate it if you would ask your secretary to telephone me at extension 511 to let me know if this time is convenient for you.

Thank you very much.

Sincerely,

Notice how the models of appointment letters shown here all deal in some way with the four basic facts—time, date, place, and purpose of the appointment—and close with some comment regarding confirmation of the proposed appointment.

REQUESTING APPOINTMENTS— WITH ALTERNATIVE

5.4. For Choice of Location-Time

Dear Helen:

Would it be possible to meet with you for about a half hour next week to discuss publicity plans for your upcoming warehouse sale? I have some ideas ready to present to you and we could move ahead with the media as soon as the concept is selected.

Since we have a few materials that can't be transported easily, perhaps you would prefer to stop by our offices, say, at 10:30 a.m. next Friday, November 9. Or, in case that isn't convenient, I could meet you in your office at 2:00 p.m. next Friday.

I'd appreciate a call from you as soon as you know which schedule would be most convenient for you. Thanks, Helen.

Cordially,

Sometimes there is a reason for offering an alternative for the appointment. In model 5.4 the writer wanted to mention that certain materials could not be easily transported; however, he also realized some clients do not like to be bothered with going out to their supplier's establishment for an appointment, so he offered a second alternative whereby he would call on the client in her office.

REQUESTING APPOINTMENTS—
WITHOUT ALTERNATIVE

5.5. In Manager's Office—Time Set

Dear Mrs. Lange:

Ms. Greenberg would like to know if you could come to her office at 3 o'clock on Tuesday, December 4, to discuss final arrangements for your children's trust fund.

Please let me know whether this time will be convenient for you. Thank you very much.

Sincerely,

Model 5.5 is a typical appointment letter. It specifies the time, date, and place without suggesting any alternatives. Of course, the letter nevertheless closes with a request to let the writer know if these arrangements are convenient. This letter assumes the recipient is familiar with the location of the office where the appointment will take place; if that were not the case the letter would have to give an address or further directions.

CONFIRMING APPOINTMENT

5.6. To New Employee

Dear Ms. Maxwell:

Last week Mr. Benson suggested you meet with him Monday morning, April 3, to discuss your new duties at Hillary Corporation. This is just to let you know he is looking forward to seeing you in his office at 8:30 a.m.

Best wishes

Model 5.6 is a confirmation of an appointment and thus does not ask the recipient to confirm the confirmation.

REPLIES TO REQUESTS FOR APPOINTMENTS

The situation may be reversed in a *reply* to the request for an appointment, but the letter must still concentrate on the same basic facts of time, date, place, and reason for the appointment.

1. Repeat the essential facts of the appointment.
2. If the proposed appointment is inconvenient, suggest an alternative and ask for a reply.
3. If you must say no, do it politely.

Models 5.7 to 5.13 illustrate patterns to use in granting, changing, and cancelling appointments.

GRANTING APPOINTMENTS AT TIME REQUESTED

5.7. To the Manager's Superior

Dear Mr. Bixby:

I'll be happy to meet you in your office Wednesday, January 20, at one o'clock, to discuss the Wilson report.

Regards,

There is no need for excessive detail or conversation in the simple confirmation letter. In this case the manager signed the letter since it was going to his superior.

GRANTING APPOINTMENTS AT TIME YOU SET

5.8. To Company Representative

Dear Phil:

I'll be glad to discuss the plans for our January inventory with you. How about meeting me in my office at 10:30 a.m., Tuesday, March 6?

Let me know if that time will be convenient for you. Thanks, Phil.

Best regards,

Even though model 5.8 is a confirmation, it suggests a time and therefore must conclude with a request for confirmation.

CHANGING APPOINTMENTS

5.9. With Business Associate

Dear Morgan:

An unexpected complication in my schedule at the plant is going to prevent me from meeting you for lunch on Thursday, April 4. However, I'm free on Monday, April 8. Would it be convenient for you to meet me then at the Palmer House about 12.30 p.m.?

I'm sorry I can't keep our original date, but I hope Monday will be just as satisfactory for you. Could you have your secretary phone my office to let me know?

Thanks very much, Morgan. I'm looking forward to seeing you soon.

Regards,

A letter changing appointments must briefly refer to the original appointment facts and specify the essential facts of the new appointment—time, date, place, and so on. The letter should also apologize for not keeping the original date and ask if the new arrangement is convenient.

CANCELLING APPOINTMENTS

5.10. With Company Official

Dear Mr. Harris:

I'm very sorry to let you know I'll be unable to keep our June 7 appointment to discuss the annual audit. Our West Coast office has been experiencing shipping problems and the president has asked me to fly out immediately to lend a hand. Since it isn't clear right now when I can return, I'll have my secretary set up a new appointment with you next week.

My apologies for any inconvenience this may cause you, Mr. Harris. I'll be looking forward to our meeting later this month.

Cordially,

The cancellation letter should give—briefly—a reason for not keeping the appointment and apologize for any inconvenience caused by the cancellation. If the meeting is to be rescheduled later, the letter should indicate that new arrangements will be made at a future date.

REFUSING APPOINTMENTS—
UNTIL LATER

5.11. To Supplier

Dear Mr. Proxmire:

Thanks for letting Ms. Adams know you have a new line of carbon-less sets available for applications, invoices, and other forms. As much as she would like to see them, I'm sorry to let you know that because of previous commitments she won't be free for several weeks.

Perhaps you could phone me at 920-0732 toward the end of this month to see how her schedule looks then.

Sincerely,

Model 5.11 is an example of a letter that says, no, not now, but perhaps later. However, a letter refusing an appointment should never suggest the possibility of a later meeting unless you or the manager truly intend to see the person then.

REFUSING APPOINTMENTS—
INDEFINITELY

5.12. To Overbearing Salesmen

Dear Mr. Billet:

Thank you for reminding us that you will be in town next Wednesday and would like to discuss your printing services with Ms. McCarthy.

As Ms. McCarthy has indicated on several occasions previously, we are very pleased with our present arrangements for printing and definitely will not be considering any other services in the foresee-able future. Therefore, Ms. McCarthy has asked me to tell you that a meeting would not be helpful at this time.

We appreciate your interest, however, and thank you for writing.

Sincerely,

Some people do not easily take no for an answer and it is necessary to become more firm with each refusal. Model 5.12 is an example of a refusal that is still reasonable friendly, although it clearly does say no. Business persons frequently try to leave the door open just a crack in case some day it will be necessary to do business with the person being turned away.

REFUSING APPOINTMENTS WITH A SUGGESTION

5.13. Referral to Another Department

Dear Miss Javorsky:

We enjoyed seeing the sample fabrics you sent last Thursday. However, this department is not in charge of fabric selection. You might write to Mrs. Lorin MacDonald, purchasing coordinator, Room 410, at this address. I'm certain she will be happy to hear from you and will contact you about an appointment if she is in need of materials. In the meantime, I'll send your fabric samples to her office.

Thank you for writing to Ned's Apparel.

Cordially,

It is common business practice to refer callers to another office whenever possible. This is helpful to everyone; in fact, it is a part of business life that people often need pointing in the right direction. Therefore, this type of appointment letter should always be friendly and informative, even though it says no to the immediate appointment request.

6

INTRODUCTIONS AND
LETTERS OF REFERENCE

References and introductions can be difficult to write, primarily because they involve an evaluation of someone's personal and professional characteristics. Such letters require diplomacy, tact, and honesty. What you say—and how you say it—may be critical both to the recipient and to the subject of the letter.

Because references and introductions can be so sensitive (e. g., 6.17, Refusing to Provide References), the manager may prefer to draft most of these letters, expecting the secretary to refine and polish them. However, in some offices the secretary will write many of them, although the manager will doubtless sign some (e.g., 6.8, Introducing a Successor). Others the secretary will send out under her own signature (e.g., 6.12, Requesting a Credit Reference). Practices differ substantially from office to office; if you have any doubts about which letters you should write and sign, ask the manager in your office.

Introductions, which you may give, request, or refuse, can involve individuals or organizations, friends or relative strangers. They may concern social or business situations, personal or professional characteristics. In short, introductions vary greatly. Fortunately, there are basic guidelines you can follow in all types of introductions, as shown in models 6.1 to 6.10. (Check the Selector Guide for examples of other correspondence pertaining to introductions, for example, 8.7.)

Letters of reference and recommendation, including those requested, given, and refused, are also varied and numerous. Often they concern financial and business matters (6.11 and 6.12), but one of the most familiar types of reference or recommendation letter, and the one that many secretaries will encounter most frequently, is the employment reference (6.13–6.19); thus chapter 6 offers a variety of models for these letters. Although references and recommendations obviously differ according to circumstances, most of them employ a basic pattern you can use for the letters you write in your own office.

HANDLING INTRODUCTIONS

A letter of introduction can be sent along with the subject of the letter or mailed in advance. If it is sent before the subject's arrival, it gives the recipient a chance to refuse the introduction. Since you are really asking a favor of the recipient, it is only common courtesy to give him or her an opportunity to say no.

1. Provide whatever basic information will be useful about the person being introduced.
2. Explain why the recipient might want to meet the subject.
3. Give the recipient an opportunity to decline.
4. If you are accepting an introduction, be appreciative; if you are refusing one, be tactful.
5. Thank the recipient.

Models 6.1 to 6.10 are examples of letters requesting, granting, and refusing introductions.

REQUESTING AN INTRODUCTION— BUSINESS

6.1. To Prospective Client

Dear Bob:

Last Friday my boss gave me a challenging new assignment—to approach the Midtown Dental Supply Company as a prospective client for our public relations services. I thought of you right away since Wilson's president, Carl Edson, was your college roommate.

I was wondering if you could write a brief letter of introduction for me. I'll be in Chicago on July 12 and in a couple weeks plan to request an appointment with Mr. Edson. But I thought it would be good if a letter of introduction reached him first.

If you can find time in your busy schedule to do this—and wouldn't feel you were imposing on your old college friend—I'd certainly appreciate it. Thanks a million, Bob.

Best regards,

When you ask someone to write an introduction letter, explain why and when you want to see the person. Conclude with an expression of appreciation.

REQUESTING AN INTRODUCTION—
SOCIAL

6.2. For Club Membership

Dear Jim:

For several months Annette and I have been thinking about joining the Belmont Country Club. Since you and Marge have been members for many years, we were wondering if you could introduce us by letter to the president, Donald Whipple.

It probably isn't essential to have a letter of introduction precede us, but we are new in town. It might be reassuring to Mr. Whipple to know that "someone out there" has heard of us and can vouch that we don't rob banks or burn books!

If you can find a moment to do this and wouldn't mind, Annette and I would be most grateful. Thanks ever so much, Jim.

Cordially,

Although model 6.2 concerns a social situation, notice how similar the pattern is to that of model 6.1, which involves a business matter.

INTRODUCING A PERSONAL FRIEND

6.3. To Business Associate

Dear Pamela:

One of my dearest friends, Adele Stahl, will be in Boulder the week of June 5. She's such an enjoyable person that I'd like very much for you to meet her, so I've suggested she phone you some time that week.

Adele is the head designer at Litman, Parnell, and Benjamin in New York. Since you oversee the design staff at Rocky Mountain Creations, I know you both would have a good time comparing notes.

I'd appreciate any courtesy you can extend to Adele, although we'll both understand if your prior commitments will make it impossible for the two of you to get together.

All good wishes.

Cordially,

In any introduction, keep in mind that you are asking a favor and the recipient may not want to comply—thus the "out" offered in the third paragraph of model 6.3.

INTRODUCING A BUSINESS OR PROFESSIONAL ASSOCIATE

6.4. To Prospective Employer

Dear Mrs. Nichols:

It's a pleasure to introduce Mike Ritter to you as a possible candidate for a position with your firm. I understand he will be contacting you soon to request an interview.

Mike is presently employed at Holt Chemical Laboratories as a supervisor. We previously worked together before I left Holt to move to the West Coast. During the five years of our association, he was the perfect employee—responsible, highly capable, and a thoroughly delightful person to know.

I'd appreciate any consideration you can extend to him. Thanks very much, Mrs. Nichols.

Sincerely,

The pattern for a letter introducing a business associate is similar to that for a friend; however, you can see the tone of model 6.4 is more reserved than that in model 6.3.

INTRODUCING A BUSINESS ORGANIZATION

6.5. To Colleague

Dear Bill:

Let me introduce to you the Medallion Uniform Service—an organization that could be of assistance to your company. We've been using Medallion services in Madison for seven years and have been completely satisfied with their continuing ability to provide low-cost, high-quality service. I've heard similar reports from other Medallion customers, for example, Madison Discount Mart and the Midwestern Bottle Capping Company.

A representative from Medallion will phone you next week to ask for an appointment to discuss what they can offer your company. In case you are interested in learning more about them, I'm enclosing one of the brochures they recently left with me. I'm certain you would be pleased with their service should you decide to give them a try.

Hope to see you soon, Bill.

Best regards,

A letter introducing a company should comment on the quality of its product or service and name a few of its customers. If it is not obvious, the letter should also indicate why the recipient might be interested in the company.

INTRODUCING JOB APPLICANTS

6.6. To Department Managers

Dear Mr. Olmsted:

I'd like to introduce Sandra Birney to you as a possible candidate for a secretarial position in your department. I understand you have two openings in the secretarial-administrative area.

Sandra has been working in our Scranton office for four years, but as you know we are terminating this facility on August 1. Considering her excellent training, solid secretarial and administrative experience, and pleasant personality, she would be a fine addition to your staff, and she is willing to relocate to Pittsburgh.

Since we are eager to find new positions for all employees left jobless by our branch closing, I'd appreciate any consideration you can extend to Sandra. I've asked her to phone you next week to inquire about a possible interview.

Thanks very much, Mr. Olmsted.

Sincerely,

As model 6.6 shows, a letter introducing a job applicant should refer to the candidate's previous experience and personal character. Although the letter can be sent along with the candidate, it is often desirable to send it in advance.

INTRODUCING SALES REPRESENTATIVES

6.7. To New Customers

Dear Mr. Solomon:

Nichols Wax Company is pleased to introduce Charles Wagner, our new representative in the Washington-Baltimore region. Charles has a thorough understanding of the problems and requirements in floor cleaning, maintenance, and refinishing for businesses. He is well qualified to discuss with you your needs in this area, and I know you'll enjoy his friendly, helpful attitude.

Charles will phone you soon for an appointment to stop by and meet you personally. I hope you'll be able to see him then. If you need anything in the meantime, however, you can reach him at 202-661-7000.

Cordially,

The tone of the letter is important in correspondence that introduces a sales representative. The letter must convincingly suggest the customer would enjoy and benefit from talking to the salesperson. If the letter pushes too much, the customer might react adversely and refuse to see the representative.

INTRODUCING A SUCCESSOR

6.8. For Retiring Executive

Dear Ethel:

It's a pleasure to introduce to you our new manager of quality control, Tom Walters. He is succeeding Earl Steiner who retired last week.

Tom will soon be visiting our Phoenix branch, and I know he'll want to meet you and learn about your cutting and stamping work. You'll enjoy his enthusiastic approach to everything he does. Tom is an intelligent and dedicated organizer and somehow everything and everyone functions better when he is around.

You can be expecting a call or letter from his secretary very soon to let you know when he'll arrive. I'd appreciate it if you would welcome Tom and brief him on your operation.

Thanks very much, Ethel.

Cordially,

There are two types of letters to introduce a successor in business: a general introduction to all employees, and an individual letter to specific employees, such as model 6.8. The general letter would be similar except instead of asking a specific person to assist the successor, it would ask everyone to welcome and assist the new person.

COMPANY POLICY PROHIBITS

6.9. For Former Employee

Dear Ms. Russell:

As much as I would like to provide the letter of introduction you requested, I'm very sorry to let you know that company policy prohibits this practice.

Because we use so many part-time and temporary employees, it is difficult for us to get to know everyone as fully as we should. We thus limit our comments to standard replies to requests from companies for references. As an alternative to the letter of introduction, I would suggest you have your prospective employers submit routine queries to my office, and I'll be happy to respond to them.

Please accept our good wishes for much success in finding a suitable position.

Sincerely,

Model 6.9 is an example of a letter that says no politely. Following the typical pattern for this type of letter, it offers a reason for the refusal, suggests an alternative, and closes by wishing the recipient good luck.

CANNOT JUSTIFY INTRODUCTION

6.10. For Troublesome Candidate

Dear Mr. Attleboro:

I'm sorry I cannot provide the letter of introduction you requested. Since your employment with our company was terminated because of the serious consequences of your behavior on the job, it would not be appropriate for me to write a letter on your behalf that ignored this problem.

Nevertheless, I sincerely hope you will benefit from past experience and overcome your difficulties. With determination, I'm sure you can achieve success in a suitable new position.

Sincerely yours,

Model 6.10 concerns a situation where the person requesting a letter of introduction was fired because of serious trouble he caused. The writer, therefore, has refused to give him a letter of introduction, because he believes it would be unethical to comment without mentioning the incident. This is a highly sensitive type of letter. Although it firmly says no, a final paragraph is added to temper the harshness of the refusal and, it is hoped, to encourage the recipient not to give up but to do better in his next position. However, any statement along this line must avoid a pious, preachy tone, which would only antagonize the recipient.

LETTERS OF REFERENCE AND RECOMMENDATION

Letters of reference and recommendation, like letters of introduction, require diplomacy, tact, and honesty. Since they comment on the character and ability of a person (or organization), they can be sensitive and must be skillfully composed.

1. Provide information that will be helpful to the person receiving the letter of reference or recommendation.
2. Be as objective and honest as possible in your comments, but also be considerate in the way you say something.
3. If you are requesting a reference or recommendation, express your appreciation.

Although letters of reference and recommendation often need careful thought and planning, a basic pattern can be followed in the majority of cases, as shown in models 6.11 to 6.19.

REQUESTING A BANK REFERENCE

6.11. For Business Loan

Dear Ms. Brunatelli:

Michael Dudley has applied for a business loan with us and has given the First National Bank as a reference. His application states that he has both a regular checking account and a NOW account at your bank.

I'd appreciate knowing how long he has had these accounts and what the balances usually average in each account.

Thanks very much for your help.

Cordially,

A request for a bank reference usually mentions the type of account(s) and asks for (1) the length of time the applicant has had the account(s) and (2) the average balance in the account(s). (Often forms are used to request or give such information.)

REQUESTING A CREDIT REFERENCE

6.12. For New Customer

Dear Mr. Forgione:

Wendall Smith and Associates has requested that we extend credit terms to them on future purchases of supplies from us. Donald Travis, general manager of the firm, has given the name of your company as a credit reference.

I'd appreciate it if you would comment on their performance in honoring such commitments. Your comments and recommendations will be held in the strictest confidence.

Thanks very much for your assistance.

Sincerely,

As models 6.11 and 6.12 show, requests for references concerning finances are similar. The first paragraph indicates who the applicant is and what his financial relationship is to the·person or firm receiving the request. The second paragraph indicates what type of information is desired, and the final paragraph concludes with a brief word of appreciation.

REQUESTING A REFERENCE FROM FORMER EMPLOYER

6.13. For Job Applicant

Dear Mrs. Whiteside:

Miss Carol Brogan, one of your former employees, has applied for a secretarial position in our Training Division and has given your name as a reference.

I'd appreciate it if you could tell us something about her experience and ability. Your comments will be held in the strictest confidence.

Thanks very much for your help.

Cordially,

Sometimes firms enclose a form that makes it easier for the recipient to reply. Paragraph 2 might then read: "I'd appreciate it if you would use the enclosed form to comment on her ability and experience," or a sentence might simply be added: "A form for your convenience in replying is enclosed."

GIVING AN EMPLOYMENT REFERENCE—BUSINESS

6.14. About Former Employee

Dear Mr. Wyatt:

Mrs. Mary Kennedy was employed as our office manager for nine months in 1976 before she left to join another organization. Although her stay with us was brief, we were pleased with her performance. Her secretarial and administrative skills were excellent, and her capabilities in working with and supervising other employees were outstanding. She acted responsibly and conscientiously at all times, and we were sorry to have her leave so soon.

It's a pleasure to recommend Mrs. Kennedy as a valuable addition to the appropriate organization.

Sincerely,

A recommendation must always be honest. Model 6.14 acknowledges that the candidate did not stay very long with the writer's firm, although in every other respect she was an ideal employee.

GIVING AN EMPLOYMENT REFERENCE—PERSONAL

6.15. About Former Student

Dear Mr. Wilcox:

Robert Andretti entered Morgantown University in 1970 and received the bachelor of arts degree in economics in 1974. During that time he was a student in three of my social science classes.

I would heartily recommend Robert for the position you described. Although I'm not familiar with his employment record, I can assure you he was a model student: creative, intelligent, well organized, and cooperative. With his friendly manner and congenial personality, it was always a pleasure to have him in my classes.

Let me know if there's anything further I can offer.

Cordially,

The personal reference is similar to the employment reference in format. The principal difference is that the stress is on the candidate's personal characteristics with little or no indication of his business background.

OPEN LETTER OF RECOMMENDATION

6.16. About Colleague

To Whom It May Concern:

I'm pleased to have this opportunity to comment on the important contribution Matthew Miida made to the success of Royal Advertising Associates. For five years he was responsible for all of our art production, including each stage of preparation from concept to mechanical.

In spite of the great variety of literature we handled—magazines, newsletters, books, catalogs, posters, brochures, ads—he was able to apply his extraordinary talent and broad experience in each instance, enabling us to serve many different types of clients. Mr. Miida is a truly gifted artist, and I have great respect for his high-quality work and his responsible and trustworthy character.

Matthew Miida would be an asset to any firm concerned with the preparation of artwork. I believe the appropriate organization would benefit immensely from his contribution.

Sincerely yours,

The open letter of recommendation follows a pattern similar to that of any other recommendation, and like any other reference letter it should be honest and informative. Headings vary; some firms object to the general "To Whom It May Concern" head and use something more specific such as "To All Prospective Employers."

REFUSING TO PROVIDE REFERENCES

6.17. For Difficult Former Employee

Dear Mr. Bronx:

I'm sorry to let you know I cannot provide the letter of reference you requested. Your employment record with us was unsatisfactory, and it is our policy in these situations not to furnish such letters. However, I personally wish you luck in finding more satisfying and successful employment elsewhere.

Sincerely,

The refusal to provide a reference is similar to the refusal to provide a letter of introduction (model 6.10). Although you must say no firmly if circumstances require it such as they do in model 6.17, your letter should not anger the former employee or discourage him from trying to be successful in a new position.

THANK YOU FOR EMPLOYMENT REFERENCE— POSITION ACCEPTED

6.18. By Job Applicant

Dear Ms. Eddington:

Your letter of recommendation to Mr. Colter was so effective that I have been offered the position of administrative assistant. It's a wonderful opportunity and I intend to accept the offer immediately.

Thanks for all your help. I really appreciate it.

Sincerely,

Thank yous for references can be brief. Model 6.18 typically acknowledges how important the letter of recommendation was and expresses genuine appreciation for it.

THANK YOU FOR EMPLOYMENT REFERENCE—
POSITION DECLINED

6.19. By Job Applicant

Dear Mr. Trilling:

I want you to know how much I appreciated your recent letter of recommendation to the Boston Wentworth Corporation. Although they did offer me a position, it was not quite what I was looking for. I have therefore decided to decline it and continue looking for something more suitable.

I hope I may continue to use your name as a reference. Thanks so much for all your help, Mr. Trilling.

Sincerely,

Even though positions are not found or are not accepted, it is only common courtesy to thank someone who has written a letter on your behalf. Model 6.19 expresses appreciation, explains that the job offer was not accepted, and mentions that further letters of reference may be needed.

7

EMPLOYEE LETTERS

Internal business communication is just as important as external correspondence. Although a substantial portion of internal communication is handled verbally or by memorandum and speed message (see Part II: MEMOS, chapters 13 and 14), a surprising number of employee situations are best handled in the traditional letter format. Sometimes the writer wants to personalize the correspondence as much as possible or perhaps give it a more thoughtful, formal appearance than the memo would provide. At these times the memo would appear too general, too informal, and too much of a hasty form of communication. However, regardless of whether the communication is prepared in memo or letter format, most companies will mail it by means of interoffice mail and thus avoid the cost of applying postage to individual letters if there are large numbers involved.

Some letters in this chapter you would write specifically for the manager's signature (e.g., 7.13, Refusing to Give Raise); others, however, would be appropriate for your own use as well (e.g., 7.11, Giving Advice—Without Being Asked). When you prepare employee letters for someone else's signature, the extent to which you write or rewrite depends on the practice in your office. Perhaps the manager relies on you to draft most of these letters, merely supplying the facts to you; or, if the letter concerns a highly sensitive situation, perhaps the manager prefers to give you a rough draft, which you refine and polish.

Motivational letters are common in many companies, particularly in those that have more than just a few employees. Although individually these letters serve a specific purpose (e.g., to thank an employee for something), generally they serve to motivate employees—to increase their job satisfaction and encourage them to work harder and perform better. Examples of motivational letters to employees are welcome letters (7.1), thank you letters (7.2, 7.3, and 7.9), letters promoting support and unity (7.4, 7.5, and 7.6), apologies (7.7), and letters of advice (7.8, 7.10, and 7.11).

Unfortunately, some situations necessitate criticism, not commendation; and sometimes it is necessary to say no—tactfully, but firmly. Letters of rejection require special attention because they must accomplish a specific purpose without antagonizing or discouraging the employee and thus adversely affecting his or her future performance. Examples of such letters are refusals to give something (7.13), rejections of something offered (7.12 and 7.16), criticisms (7.14 and 7.15), and refusals to accept responsibility for something (7.17).

Consult the Selector Guide for similar nonemployee models found in other chapters throughout the book.

MOTIVATIONAL LETTERS

Perhaps the most important thing to remember in writing a motivational letter is what NOT to do:

1. Avoid any appearance of beating a drum or lecturing from a soapbox.
2. Do not get so carried away with lavish compliments that you sound insincere.

If you make a point honestly and thoughtfully, your letter stands a much better chance of inspiring and motivating the employee.

The eleven models that follow are examples of the wide variety of motivational employee letters commonly written in the modern business office. Although you will be substituting your own facts and figures in each situation, try to retain the simple, straightforward style and the smooth, conversational tone the models project.

LETTERS TO NEW EMPLOYEES

7.1. Welcome

Dear Bob:

It's a pleasure to welcome you to the new training center at A.G. Harvey Chemical Corporation. With your extensive background in industrial training, I'm certain you will find numerous opportunities to use your many talents and capabilities.

You will soon meet the rest of our "family" at the center, and I know you won't be disappointed. They all share your enthusiasm for thorough and constructive training procedures, and their dedication is matched by their enjoyment of the special sense of fellowship we share at the center.

Remember, my office is just down the hall from yours. Stop by any time, and do let me know if I can answer any questions about your duties or help you become better acquainted with the training center.

Best regards,

The welcome letter is the most common type of letter to new employees. It is usually intended as a friendly gesture, with one employee saying hello and welcome to another and offering to be of assistance to the newcomer. This type of welcome letter, shown above, is brief and does not go into detail about job duties or company rules and regulations.

THANK YOU LETTERS—GROUP

7.2. For Special Efforts

Dear Staff Members:

It comes as no surprise to me that Samuels & Davis Company just completed its spring shipments on time—in spite of our recent equipment problems. With all of you devoting 200 percent of your time and energies to emergency adjustments and rescheduling difficulties, how could we fail?

I'm truly impressed by your unhesitating efforts on behalf of the company and want to extend my gratitude to each of you. I know this past month has been a difficult time—long hours, late hours, and weekends away from your families. But without this united effort, we would never have been able to satisfy all our customers, and as you know, the loss of even one customer would have had an adverse impact. However, thanks to you, our customers received their merchandise on schedule and operations are back to normal.

The loyalty and devotion you displayed over an extended period merit the highest commendation, and I have made arrangements for each of you to receive a special citation at our annual awards banquet. Samuels & Davis Company can truly be proud of its employees. My sincere thanks for your selfless and generous contributions.

Cordially,

This type of thank you letter stresses the employee's unselfish devotion to the company. The sincere praise gives the employee a desire to continue to make contributions.

THANK YOU LETTERS—INDIVIDUAL

7.3. For Suggestion

Dear Jeanne:

Your suggestion to cut rising printing costs by estimating and combining our orders for stock with other departments is precisely what we need. I think you've found a realistic way to trim our somewhat strained budget this quarter, and the potential savings should appeal to other departments as well.

If ever you have any further thoughts on ways to improve our operating procedures, please send them along. New ideas are always welcome in this department; in fact, constructive suggestions are of benefit to the entire company.

For all of us—thank you!

                                        Sincerely,

In letter 7.3 the writer specifically asks for further contributions.

ENCOURAGING EMPLOYEE SUPPORT

7.4. For New Policies

Dear Jerry:

Now that registration has nearly ended for our four-week, in-house training program, it is clear that participation may fall short of our expectations. We believe the small turnout is in part the result of our failure to communicate fully to each employee the important benefits of this new evening program. As production supervisor, perhaps you would have an opportunity to discuss the program personally with many of the production personnel.

As you know, Reynolds Data-Processing Company has decided to offer a brief training session twice this year on a voluntary-participation basis, free of charge, to all employees. It's an excellent opportunity for an employee to increase his knowledge in this growing field and prepare himself for advancement—all without cost and with a minimum of effort. It will undoubtedly bring some employees a step closer to promotion and a salary increase. As a side benefit the program will provide a chance for employees to get to know each other better—to make new friends—as they share a very pleasant and highly interesting hour together twice a week next month. Certainly those who finish the program will have a better understanding of the service that Reynolds supplies and their functions in the company in relation to others.

If the program succeeds, it will be Reynold's policy to offer in-house training sessions similar to this each year. Of course, we'll need your help and the help of many others to make this possible. Please talk to your production staff today. Let them know abut the exciting possibilities of this program and how the investment of just a few hours of their time now can produce substantial dividends for them later.

                                        Sincerely,

Letters encouraging employee support sometimes require more detail than others. The employee should never be asked to support something blindly; the reasons should be summarized in the body of the letter clearly and logically, followed by the request for support.

LETTERS THAT UNIFY

7.5. Stimulating Company Pride

Dear Staff Members:

I just received some exciting news for all of us at House of Fashion—for the third successive year we have been asked to present a one-hour fashion show at the State Merchandising Association's annual convention!

You are all aware that competition in our industry is fierce; it is a distinct honor to be chosen again and again by one of the state's most prestigious associations. Since House of Fashion's success is really your success, I know you must be as thrilled as I am that the results of our mutual efforts throughout the year continue to be recognized and rewarded.

I for one am delighted to be part of a winning team. Let's continue to work together to keep House of Fashion at the forefront.

Cordially,

The object of this letter is to stir up enthusiasm for the company. One sure way to arouse enthusiasm in others is to be enthusiastic yourself.

NEW YEAR'S RESOLUTIONS

7.6. About Performance

Dear Staff Member:

Have you ever thought that New Year's resolutions are rather silly because no one keeps them anyway? I have, but the truth is that not all resolutions are silly and not all of them are broken. Quite the contrary. A realistic and worthwhile resolution can and should be kept at any time of the year.

I've decided to take the plunge again this year—how about you? To be certain I won't make my resolutions on January 1 and break them on January 2, I've made my list both simple and sensible. For instance, I haven't vowed to work a ten-hour day instead of an eight-hour day, because it's not important whether I sit in my office eight or ten hours. How much I accomplish when I am there is important, however. If I can perform better, I might be able to do more in eight hours than I would otherwise do in ten.

I'd like to invite you to join me in this effort to improve performance. Somehow I think it will be easier for each of us to keep our resolutions if our co-workers have the same objectives. And when it's time to share in the rewards, we will all feel we have truly earned them.

I'm genuinely looking forward to working with you this coming year. Please accept my thanks for your good work in days past and my good wishes for success and prosperity in days to come.

Happy New Year!

New Year's letters are usually of two types: a brief, simple greeting or a greeting combined with a call to greater and better things. Letter 7.6 uses the occasion to motivate the employee to perform better in the future. To avoid having the letter end up in the wastebasket, the writer uses the second paragraph to add a realistic, down-to-earth tone before asking the employee to make a resolution in the third paragraph.

LETTERS OF APOLOGY

7.7. About Misunderstandings

Dear Helen:

You're absolutely right—my project report is due this Friday, the 14th, and I'm embarrassed to say I haven't yet finished it. In haste, I had erroneously noted on my calendar that it would be due next Friday, the 21st. Although I've been pursuing a frantic appointment schedule for nearly a month, I don't know how I could have confused the dates. I'm very sorry.

I'll start working on the rest of the report today and guarantee it will be on your desk by next Tuesday. In the meantime, is there something else I could do to alleviate any problems my tardiness may have caused? Please let me know.

I appreciate your patience, Helen—thanks so much.

Cordially,

This letter follows a sound rule in business: if you're wrong, admit it, apologize, and make amends. An apology must try to lessen the frustration you may have caused the other person.

ADVICE TO EMPLOYEES

7.8. About Company Benefits

Dear Employee:

I'm proud to report that each year Marc Davis, Incorporated, has increased the number of benefits available to its employees. Last month a brochure describing current employee services was circulated in all departments, and by now you have had a chance to read about our programs and raise questions about your personal participation in them.

I urge you to review our company programs again and think about each one in terms of its applicability to you. Ask yourself if you are really receiving all the benefits to which you are entitled and, if you are not, why not. Perhaps you have not completed the necessary forms, or perhaps the extent of services available to you is not clear. For example, are you taking advantage of our matching-funds tuition plan? Are you using our free, volunteer medical services—x-rays, eye examinations, and so on?

If you have any questions about whether you are receiving all benefits available to you, write to our director of personnel services, Jerome Hanley, immediately. If your questions cannot be answered by mail, Mr. Hanley will be glad to see you to discuss our employee services in detail. Simply phone his secretary, Ms. Jackson, at extension 396 for an appointment.

I sincerely hope you will continue to enjoy and profit from the ever-expanding roster of company benefits at Marc Davis.

With warmest regards,

It is often necessary to give advice to employees; such letters must make it clear to the employee why he will benefit from taking the advice. If the letter proposes specific action, instructions must also be stated clearly, as, for example, in the third paragraph of letter 7.8.

INCREASE IN SALARY

7.9. As Reward for Productivity

Dear Frank:

It's always a pleasure to extend some tangible evidence of our appreciation for a job well done. Yes, your increase in salary from

$15,800 to $17,000 a year has been approved! It will become effective January 1.

I can't think of anyone who deserves a raise more than you. I know you have an excellent team, but it's largely through your innovative efforts and good judgment that productivity in your department broke all records this year. You may be certain your accomplishments have been duly noted, and we're all grateful for your contribution to the company.

Congratulations on the raise, Frank. Keep up the good work.

Best regards,

See chapter 8 for other letters that use expressions of congratulations goodwill to motivate employees.

GIVING ADVICE—EMPLOYEE REQUESTED

7.10. About Difficult Assignment

Dear Jan:

I hope you were exaggerating when you said you were having second thoughts about your latest assignment. It's going to be a tough job to reorganize administrative services, but I really believe you can handle it.

I'm flattered that you asked for my opinion, especially as the assignment sounds so familiar. My own department was having similar problems a few years ago—an increasing staff and decreasing productivity. We needed not more people but more efficient people. After streamlining operations, certain positions simply were not justified, and a staff reduction seemed mandatory. Of course, I'm not qualified to make a judgment about your department, but if you've concluded that a staff reduction is essential, I think you should make the recommendation without hesitation. It's not easy to suggest letting someone go, but it's just not fair to the others to have someone on the payroll who isn't making a contribution. In time your staff would resent that even more than they would object to some staff dismissals.

If you'd like to discuss this further, Jan, why don't we have lunch some time this week? You know I'd be happy to help any way I can. Give me a call, and we'll set a date.

Cordially,

There is one thing to guard against in letters giving advice—being held responsible later if something goes wrong. Notice the safety valve in the letter above: "Of course, I'm not qualified to make a judgment about your department," meaning, "It's your decision: please don't blame me if it doesn't turn out right."

GIVING ADVICE—WITHOUT BEING ASKED

7.11 To Assistant

Dear Polly:

It's good to see the progress you've made in setting up our office library. we're all eagerly waiting for the rest of the publications to arrive.

Have you had an opportunity yet to devise a checkout system? I noticed someone from the sales office removing a book this morning without signing it out. This could become a problem as borrowing increases and books disappear from the shelves without any indication where they've gone. I know you're pressed for time now, so how about working up a temporary checkout system to tide us over until something more official can be established?

Let me know if you have any questions, Polly. And thanks for doing such a fine job with our long-awaited library.

Best wishes,

Letter 7.11 has a mild criticism in the advice, softened with a compliment and rendered gently so the assistant will not be hurt or discouraged.

LETTERS OF REJECTION

Letters to employees that say no must be written with special care. No one likes to receive a refusal and feelings can be hurt if the rejection is not presented with tact and consideration for the recipient. However, it does not help to beat around the bush or try to soften the blow with insincere compliments.

1. If something is offered, such as a suggestion, thank the employee.
2. Tell him or her why—gently but firmly—it cannot be accepted.
3. If possible, give the employee some encouragement for future efforts.

It is extremely important to avoid discouraging the employee. A discontented and possibly humiliated person would not likely perform well in the future and possible would not even stay with the company.

The next six letters are examples of employee letters that reject something. Since they cover the most familiar situations of this type, you can easily use your own facts and adapt each one to your specific situation.

REJECTING A PROPOSAL

7.12. Of Business Associate

Dear Tom:

I read with great interest your proposal to expand our field operations. Thanks for taking time to present this idea. Although it sounds like an excellent plan, I'm sorry we can't take advantage of it now.

As you know, we're making preparations to introduce several new household products, and recent figures indicate this operation is going to draw on all our available resources for the next eight months. We just wouldn't have the capital, manpower, or training capability to broaden our territory now. But, who knows, if the new products are successful, this could open doors, and your plan might then be ideal. You may be certain I'll remember your suggestion if the right time comes.

I wish I would receive more good ideas like yours. It would make my job a lot easier. Thanks, Tom.

Best regards,

If the proposal in letter 7.12 were totally unrealistic for now and for the future as well, the slant of the letter would have to be changed to avoid any suggestion of future use. The compliment and thank you would remain in any case.

REFUSING TO GIVE RAISE

7.13. Because of Budget Restraints

Dear Mr. Steiner:

I have carefully reviewed your request for a raise and am sorry to let you know the company cannot grant the increase.

Although your record at Letterman, Inc., is satisfactory, and the company appreciates your interest in making further contributions, current budget restraints prevent us from making any salary increases. However, all salaries in your division are scheduled for review in six months, and you will be notified if there is any change in conditions then.

In the meantime, I hope you will continue to enjoy your work at Letterman.

Sincerely,

If Mr. Steiner's record had been more distinguished, the tone of this letter would have been raised to indicate a raise in the future was very likely. However, even though Mr. Steiner has not won any medals for outstanding performance, the company does not want to discourage him so he performs poorly or even quits.

CRITICISMS OF EMPLOYEES—INDIVIDUAL

7.14. About Performance

Dear Mr. Rydell:

The board has completed its review of your activities and expenditures during the past six months. Generally, we believe you have met most of our expectations satisfactorily. There is one matter, however, we would like to discuss with you.

Although you did not exceed the allotted budget for the past quarter, we notice you used surplus funds to make two business trips to San Francisco and Montreal. Your stated objective was to solicit memberships in the association and sell copies of our manual. We strongly believe this is a poor investment of time and funds. It simply is not economical to spend over $1,000 on a week of travel in an effort to sell some $3 manuals; nor is it wise to spend $100 an evening taking interested persons out on the town in hopes of receiving one or two $15 memberships in return.

I'd appreciate it if you would make arrangements for an Executive Committee meeting within the next few weeks. Specifically, we would like to discuss (1) more efficient and economical ways to promote membership and sell publications, and (2) the more advantageous use of surplus funds. I'll look forward to hearing your suggestions at the meeting.

Regards,

This type of letter concerns a sensitive situation, which means the manager might prefer to draft it—or most of it. The object here is to reprimand Mr. Rydell but give him a second chance and avoid hard feelings in the process. Thus, the last paragraph states that at the meeting they will discuss future procedures, *not* argue about Mr. Rydell's past mistakes.

CRITICISMS OF EMPLOYEES—GROUP

7.15. About Conduct

Dear Employees:

Yesterday afternoon, in the scramble to leave work at 5 o'clock, an employee's car struck the car of a customer in our parking lot. Although damage was minor and no one was injured, this customer was astounded at the wild and rude behavior of our employees, who were dangerously and carelessly speeding away.

It is entirely possible we will lose an important customer as a result of this objectionable behavior, but there is something that concerns me even more: the threat to the safety of all persons, whether customers, employees, or innocent bystanders. This reckless behavior must cease immediately, and I am requesting that each employee in this company observe all rules of common courtesy in the presence of others and—at all times—act with full regard for the safety and well-being of others. If voluntary cooperation is not sufficient to provide a safe atmosphere for everyone, I will have no choice but to impose a strong regulatory measure.

I hope the next report I receive will be quite different. Although not all employees were guilty in this instance, all can benefit from a greater awareness of the serious consequences that confront us when we forget the basic rules of common courtesy and consideration.

Yours sincerely,

The writer in letter 7.15 decided to issue a stern reprimand but give everyone a chance to improve his or her own conduct before imposing harsh restrictions.

DECLINING OFFER OF HELP

7.16. On Committee Assignment

Dear George:

I appreciated your offer to help me with the committee's resource survey. It's good to know someone out there wouldn't mind giving up golf for a few Saturdays!

Everything is off to a good start, however, and if I don't hit any snags, I'll be able to manage without extra manpower. But if there's any change in the situation, you'll be the first to know! Thanks for the offer, George.

Best personal regards,

Sometimes when offers of help are declined, it is best not to close the door completely, as shown in letter 7.16.

REFUSAL TO ACCEPT RESPONSIBILITY FOR PROBLEM

7.17. In Letter to Superior

Dear Mr. Johnson:

I was distressed to learn our city services proposal was denied because it was based upon an advocacy position. When I prepared it, I was under the impression this was the position held at headquarters in New York.

The instructions I received (photocopy enclosed) say nothing about funding being contingent on a pro and con approach. As you can see, these instructions came from our New York office. No doubt the original instructions from the Endowment Fund, which probably contained the pro-con clause, were retained at headquarters.

If you would agree to it, I would be glad to write a new proposal for a study of both sides of the city services issue. This time, however, I think it would be a good idea if I received a copy of the Endowment Fund's instructions, along with the guidelines from headquarters.

Please let me know if I should proceed with a new proposal.

Sincerely,

Any refusal to accept responsibility for something must clearly state why—and the reason(s) must be adequate. If possible, the letter should close with some gesture to help correct the situation anyway. If the letter blames someone else, great care must be taken. Harsh, perhaps inaccurate, accusations can lead to trouble and even lawsuits. Letter 7.17 avoids blaming any individual and merely makes an explanation without specifically criticizing someone else.

8

LETTERS OF APPRECIATION
AND GOODWILL

Communication in the business world goes far beyond activities that affect the exchange of goods and services. Whatever the ultimate business purpose may be, people must deal with people. Thus letters that influence the feelings and attitudes of others are of critical importance. Successful public relations is greatly dependent on the effectiveness of letters of appreciation and goodwill; although these letters are usually brief and easy to compose, their importance should not be underestimated.

The secretary can easily write the majority of these letters (e.g., 8.6, Favorable Mention), although the manager may sign many of them. Occasionally the manager may feel more qualified to draft the basic letter but will leave it up to the secretary to polish it. (e.g., 8.16, Thank You with Rejection). In either case, these letters are rarely complex and you should find it relatively simple to use the models in this chapter as your guide. (Refer to the Selector Guide for similar models throughout the book, for example: chapter 6, Thank You for Employment Reference.)

It is not likely one could ever send too many letters of appreciation. Few letters are so warmly received and so effective in promoting good human relations. Models 8.1 to 8.16 are examples of the numerous occasions that warrant an appreciative response.

Successful public relations is a highly desirable goal of any organization, and letters of goodwill are vital in building public confidence and encouraging favorable attitudes toward your company. Many situations can be used for this purpose, from sending holiday wishes (8.17 and 8.18) to offering praise for a worthy suggestion (8.20 and 8.21).

The letter of congratulation is a very distinct type of goodwill letter. Although it is often very personal and thus effective in cementing business friendships, it is also highly effective as a tool in building good public relations for the company. Models 8.24 to 8.32 reveal how letters of congratulations can create feelings of goodwill among individuals and organizations.

LETTERS OF APPRECIATION

Some persons have difficulty expressing themselves warmly in a letter; others fall into the opposite trap of becoming too flowery and gushy. Letters of appreciation will sound insincere if they are too restrained or too overflowing.

1. Be natural and sincere in your expression of appreciation.
2. Explain why you appreciate what was done.
3. If appropriate, offer to reciprocate.
4. Also, if appropriate, encourage the recipient to contribute further.

Letters of appreciation can be sent in any instance where someone does something thoughtful or commendable. The following sixteen models are examples of the many situations that would warrant letters of appreciation.

PROMPT PAYMENT

8.1. By New Customer

Dear Mr. Willis:

I want to thank you for your letter and remittance for our recent land-scaping work. It was a pleasure to be of service to you and I sincerely appreciate your prompt payment.

If we can be of further help in planning and finishing your lovely resort grounds, please do let me know. I'll look forward to hearing from you again.

Cordially,

Naturally, one does not write a personal letter to thank everyone who pays a bill. Some businesses, however, use this occasion to build good relations with a promising new customer. The letter should express appreciation for the prompt payment and indicate it was a pleasure to be of service.

PERSONAL FAVOR

8.2. By Business Associate

Dear Brad:

I sincerely appreciated your help in completing our proposal for a new wing at the recreation center. Without your assistance I would certainly have missed the deadline. But thanks to you, we made it, and I'm very confident the proposal is a good one and will be adopted.

If ever I can reciprocate, Brad, just let me know.

Best regards,

Like most letters of appreciation, a letter commenting on a favor can be brief. It should sincerely express gratitude and offer to reciprocate.

OFFER OF ASSISTANCE TO FIRM

8.3. By Colleague

Dear Roy:

It was very thoughtful of you to offer to take over my three evening classes so I can attend the machine tool show in Chicago next month. I had planned to cancel them as a last resort, but if you can fill in, it would be so much better.

I'll phone you next week so we can arrange to go over the lesson plans together. Thanks a million, Roy.

Best regards,

The letter of appreciation for an offer of assistance (1) expresses gratitude, (2) accepts or rejects the offer, and (3) suggests the next step if the offer is accepted.

MESSAGE OF CONGRATULATIONS

8.4. Upon Election

Dear Mr. Johnson:

Thank you so much, Mr. Johnson, for your kind letter of congratulations and warm wishes. It was good to hear you supported the environmental protectionist stand that led to my election to the Barkley Society's board of directors. With your help and that of all the others who believe in our cause, my job will be much easier.

Cordially,

Responses to letters of congratulation will vary slightly depending upon whether the situation involves a new job, an award or honor, or something else. In all cases, though, a *brief* expression of appreciation is usually preferable, unless the writer is seeking additional support or for some other reason needs to comment further on his achievement.

MESSAGE OF SYMPATHY

8.5. Upon Death of Spouse

Dear Edna:

Thank you for your thoughtful expression of sympathy and offer of assistance. Marie considered you one of her dearest friends. Your kind words were very comforting, and I appreciate knowing I can call on you if the need should arise.

Sincerely,

Letters of appreciation should always be sent in response to expressions of sympathy. Replies usually are very brief—no more than one to three sentences.

FAVORABLE MENTION

8.6. In Article

Dear Mr. Fenton:

I was surprised and pleased to read the flattering remarks about my recent Community College address in your article, "The Last of the Pioneers." Your books and articles always—and justifiably—have an extensive readership, so I'm especially happy to know you approve of my universalist philosophy.

My sincere thanks, Mr. Fenton.

Cordially,

A letter of appreciation for complimentary remarks should indicate where you read or heard the remarks and what they referred to and offer thanks for the favorable mention.

INTRODUCTION

8.7. To Prospective Client

Dear Fred:

I just talked to the purchasing manager at Crystal Distributors and he would like to see me next week! Since he mentioned your name it's obvious your letter of introduction opened the door for me.

Thanks ever so much, Fred. I truly appreciate your effort and hope I can be of help to you some day.

Best regards,

Model 8.7 is a typical appreciation letter. It refers to the recipient's effort, tells why the act was appreciated, gives thanks for it, and offers to reciprocate.

RECEIVING ADVICE

8.8. From Subordinate

Dear Angela:

I think you should be the first to know our loose-leaf service is a huge success; after all, you were one of the first to recommend publishing our market studies in this format. Fortunately, we all had sense enough to realize your advice was right on target.

I'm making a point to let others around the office know about your important contribution. For now, Angela, please accept my sincerest thanks.

                                                        Best wishes,

Sometimes writers include a sentence in letters such as model 8.8 encouraging the recipient to contribute further, for example, "Keep up the good work," or "Any further ideas you have will be most welcome."

HOSPITALITY—OVERNIGHT GUEST

8.9. Of Business Associate

Dear John:

Thanks for a delightful weekend with you and Janet. I so much enjoyed visiting with both of you in your home, and those wonderful meals were a very special treat for me. You must give me a chance to reciprocate the next time you're in Buffalo.

My best to Janet.

                                                        Cordially,

Acknowledgments of hospitality, like all appreciation letters, are brief. Since they often concern thanks for personal attention, the letters frequently have an especially warm and personal tone.

HOSPITALITY—DINNER GUEST

8.10. Of Business Associate

Dear Ken:

Thank you so much for that splendid dinner at the Carriage Inn last Thursday. The meal was outstanding and the conversation stimulating—an unbeatable combination.

It was good to see you again, and I'll be looking forward to our next meeting.

Best regards,

Notice how the same general pattern can be used from letter to letter. Model 8.10, for instance, takes the same approach as model 8.9, extending a warm—but brief—expression of thanks.

CONFERENCE SPEAKER

8.11. An Invited Guest

Dear Mrs. Kline:

Thank you for your generous comments about my speech at the Eastern Merchants' conference. It was a pleasure to appear before this distinguished group, and I'm pleased to know my remarks were meaningful in some way.

Sincerely,

This type of appreciation letter would vary depending upon the recipient. If the letter were directed to the person who had originally invited the speaker, for example, it would also have to express thanks for that invitation, even though presumably a thank you letter for that purpose was sent earlier.

INVITATION TO OPEN HOUSE

8.12. Of Supplier

Dear Mr. Ripley:

Thank you for the invitation to your open house and reception on Wednesday, March 11. It will be a pleasure to help you celebrate the opening of your new offices in Kansas City, and I'll look forward to seeing you on the 11th at three o'clock.

Cordially,

This type of thank you for an invitation assumes the invitation was informal. Had it been formal, the reply also would have to adopt the formal style (see chapter 15, model 15.12).

BONUS RECEIVED

8.13. A Special Reward

Dear Mr. Severin:

I was delighted to receive your letter telling me a bonus would be forthcoming for my work on the Benson project. Thanks ever so much.

The project was challenging and I'm glad I had the opportunity to tackle it. Although I never dreamed a bonus was in store, you may be certain it is most welcome. Mrs. Franklin and I truly appreciate the company's generosity.

Many thanks, Mr. Severin.

Cordially,

A letter of appreciation for a bonus or salary increase must obviously express sincere thanks. Sometimes the writer refers to his or her spouse's gratitude as well. If the bonus is a reward for doing something special, it also should briefly acknowledge the activity and indicate that it was a pleasure to make the contribution.

AFTER A COMPANY TOUR

8.14. With Client

Dear Mr. Hollister:

Thank you again for arranging such an informative tour of your company. I'm confident I have a much better understanding of your activities in Louisville and that this will enable us to improve our service to you.

I sincerely appreciated your time and thoughtful attention, Mr. Hollister, and now will look forward to having you visit our facilities in Deerfield.

Best regards,

Model 8.14 concerns a tour of a client's establishment; thus, it includes a statement of how the knowledge gained will help the writer's company provide better service. The general thank you for a tour would be almost the same, except it should omit this statement and might also omit the concluding suggestion that the tour host visit the writer's facilities.

THANK YOU WITH REQUEST

8.15. For Favor

Dear Ms. Godine:

Your layouts for our spring catalog just arrived and they look absolutely marvelous! Thanks for working so hard to keep our tight production schedule.

Although I'm completely satisfied with the layouts, I wonder if you could do one more thing: design a tear-out card insert to be placed just inside the back cover (copy enclosed). This is something that came up at our staff meeting yesterday afternoon, and I just received the copy this morning. Fortunately, it will be a separate piece that won't disturb the other pages. I'd really appreciate it if you could get the design for this insert to me by the end of this week.

Many thanks for your usual good work, Ms. Godine. We're all very pleased.

Cordially,

When you must include a request for something in your letter of appreciation, be certain the request does not totally overwhelm the expression of gratitude. Preferably, begin and conclude the letter with words of appreciation, keeping the request in a middle paragraph.

THANK YOU WITH REJECTION

8.16. Of Work Unacceptable

Dear Mr. Lewis:

As much as I appreciate your promptness in filling our June 17 order for 4,000 invoices and matching window envelopes, I regret we cannot accept the finished product.

If you'll compare the ink on the enclosed new invoice with that of the letterhead on which this letter is written, you'll notice a distinct difference in color. Although we might have been willing to live with a slight variation, this extreme change would cause problems since all of our materials—invoices, brochures, and so on—are color matched. I don't know what caused this problem—possibly in the rush the ink was not mixed correctly.

I'm sorry to bring you this news. Perhaps the paper itself can be retained and portions of it cut for later use as small memo or note paper. We will be placing an order for these items in August. In the meantime, I'd appreciate a call from you as soon as possible to discuss replacing the stationery order.

Thanks very much, Mr. Lewis.

Sincerely,

A thank you letter that includes a rejection will either reject something with no request for a replacement or it will say no but ask for a corrected version. Although model 8.16 rejects an order, the writer has no desire to end his relationship with the supplier. The letter expresses appreciation for the supplier's promptness, and the mild tone of it indicates the supplier is thought to be a fair and cooperative person. If this were not the case, the letter would probably place more stress on the error and build a case that the supplier could not avoid. Either way, however, a letter such as this should never display anger or frustration, but should be civil and businesslike.

GOODWILL LETTERS

Individually, goodwill letters serve many purposes, but in general they are used to build good public relations. The essence of a goodwill letter is its attitude, and the writer should keep this guideline foremost in his or her mind.

1. Use an appropriate occasion to say something thoughtful or flattering.
2. When you offer something, do not ask for or expect an immediate favor or reward in return.
3. Be natural; write warmly and sincerely, but without excess.

Models 8.17 to 8.23 illustrate but a few of the countless occasions that can be used to send a letter of goodwill.

HOLIDAY-SEASONAL GREETINGS— CUSTOMER

8.17. To Long-Time Customer

Dear Frank:

During the holiday season I'm always reminded of the many things for which we at Porter Industries can be grateful. At the top of our list every year is the fine relationship we enjoy with good customers like you.

This is the eleventh year we've been doing business with you—can you believe it? I know I've enjoyed every year and look forward to many more. In particular, it's always a pleasure to work with you, Frank.

All of us at Porter send you and your associates our very best wishes for a beautiful and bountiful holiday season.

Cordially,

Holidays are perfect occasions for a letter of goodwill. A letter to a customer should comment on the good business relationship and close with holiday greetings. Except for a friendly remark about looking forward to many more years of friendship or good business relations, such a letter should *not* become commercial and try to do some selling on the side.

HOLIDAY SEASONAL GREETINGS— EMPLOYEES

8.18. To All Employees

Dear Employee:

This has been a busy and exciting year for all of us at Browning and Beale. Thanks to your loyal and dedicated efforts, we have much to look forward to in the coming year.

Although we're not a large company, we have gained solidarity and strength through our many friendships and our cooperative spirit. I feel very proud and happy to have you on our team, and I hope we will be able to make your position at Browning and Beale more satisfying and rewarding each year.

Warmest regards to you and yours over this holiday season, and my sincerest wishes for a peaceful and plentiful New Year.

Cordially,

Holiday greetings to employees vary from brief letters of good wishes to more involved commentaries on the employee's participation in the company's progress. Some (e.g., model 7.6) focus on the subject of New Year's Resolutions.

TRIBUTE TO EMPLOYEES

8.19. A Retiring Worker

Dear Staff Member:

It's both my sad and pleasant duty to let you know our maintenance manager, Gerald Fitzpatrick, has reached that enviable position of independence: retirement.

Although we will miss having Gerald just around the corner ready to solve all our problems, we know he has earned the right to "do his own thing." I can't think of anyone who has been more essential to our daily operations. Gerald has been our link between go and no-go for nearly thirty years. It's astounding to recall how many times his superb maintenance skills and know-how have kept us from disaster.

Let's hope he doesn't go too far away to hear a sudden cry for help! But in the meantime, why don't you join me in sending him your warm wishes as he embarks on his new life of freedom and leisure.

Cordially,

The tribute to an employee is a general letter of praise sent to other employees or business associates. If this were an individual letter to the retiring employee, it would follow the same general pattern and tone, except the remarks of praise and good wishes would be personally directed to the employee.

COMMEND SUGGESTION, WITH REJECTION

8.20. Of Assistant

Dear Louise:

I was fascinated with your suggestion for a departmental newsletter. Thanks so much for your thoughtful plan. I'd like to consider the idea again a little farther down the road. At present our staff time and resources are too limited for us to add an extracurricular activity, but we all hope that situation will eventually improve.

For now, I just wanted you to know how much I appreciate your suggestion. In fact, creative and imaginative ideas like yours are always welcome. Many thanks, Louise.

Best wishes,

A rejection will not build goodwill unless the tone is clearly one of appreciation and encouragement in spite of the refusal. Model 8.20 downplays the fact it is saying no by beginning and ending the letter with a warm expression of thanks and particularly flattering remarks. Whenever possible *all* situations should be used to encourage and improve human relations.

COMMEND SUGGESTION, WITH ACCEPTANCE

8.21. Of Assistant

Dear Dick:

That was a great idea of yours to use medium-weight manila second sheets for our rough drafts. I placed an order this morning and you were right—the savings over the bond paper we were using will amount to $3.50 a ream, which will be very significant over a year's time.

Your excellent suggestion is going to be of real benefit to the company, Dick. Many thanks for your help.

Best regards,

Model 8.21 adopts the same general approach as most other goodwill letters. It uses a newly accepted idea as an opportunity to build good human relations by complimenting the assistant who suggested it.

LETTERS WITH GIFT

8.22. To Customer

Dear Ms. Anderson:

Now that we've completed photographic coverage of your fifth annual conference, I just wanted you to know how grateful we are for the opportunity to provide this service to you each year. Please accept the enclosed personalized photo album as a small token of our appreciation.

Sincerest thanks for your confidence in us, Ms. Anderson. It's always a pleasure to work with you.

Cordially,

A letter to a customer with a genuine gift—not a sales gimmick or product sample—should offer the gift with a sincere expression of appreciation of warm wishes. This type of letter, however, should *not* try to sell anything. Whether gifts may be given or accepted depends on company policy, of course.

FREE OFFER WITH NO STRINGS

8.23. To Prospective Customer

Dear Mr. Kirby:

Since we're practically neighbors now, I want to welcome you to Sunset Hills on behalf of all of us at Neil's Dry Cleaning Service Center.

We know the first few weeks after moving into a new community can be a difficult time. There are always a million things to do and lots of unexpected expenses. Clothes and dry goods sometimes arrive wrinkled, dusty, and soiled. Because we know this so well, we'd like to make your move a little easier for you. Here, with our compliments, are five coupons that will permit you to have up to fourteen garments or other items dry cleaned free of charge within the next three weeks.

If there's anything else we can do to make your introduction to Sunset Hills more enjoyable, all you have to do is call. We're delighted to have you as our neighbor and look forward to meeting you soon.

Cordially,

Notice that model 8.23 does not qualify the offer. It is completely free with no strings attached. Of course, the writer hopes the recipient will patronize his or her establishment, but the immediate objective is to build goodwill.

LETTERS OF CONGRATULATIONS

People respond positively to praise and recognition. Because of this, letters of congratulations can be a valuable tool in a business person's efforts to win goodwill.
1. Write sincerely and enthusiastically, without evidence of envy.
2. Devote your comments to the recipient's accomplishments and do not make other remarks that would overshadow it.

Situations that warrant letters of congratulations are innumerable, both in business and socially. Models 8.24 to 8.32 are examples of some of these occasions.

AWARD GIVEN

8.24. To Employee

Dear Jim:

Congratulations! I was so pleased to read in the paper this morning that you had received the Lovett Award for Outstanding Community

Service. I've followed your relentless efforts to beautify our downtown shopping area for two years and it's clear you've been our champion from the very start. We at Gibson Tool Company are happy and proud to know one of our employees has received such a coveted award.

You truly deserve this recognition of your generous and invaluable contribution, Jim. I don't know what we—or Lovett—would do without you!

Regards,

The length and content of a congratulatory letter will obviously differ with the occasion. However, model 8.24 illustrates one thing that should be repeated in all such letters: the spirit of unselfish, enthusiastic praise for the recipient.

PROMOTION

8.25. Of Business Associate

Dear Ted:

I was delighted to learn about your promotion—congratulations! You've certainly earned it, and I know you'll find your new responsibilities exciting and challenging.

Best wishes for success in the new position, Ted.

Cordially,

Most letters congratulating someone upon promotion are brief, the purpose being simply to offer congratulations, say that he or she deserves the promotion, and wish the person well in the new position.

BANQUET ADDRESS

8.26. Of Guest Speaker

Dear Mr. Hollingsworth:

Let me congratulate you on making one of the finest speeches that members of our organization have ever had the privilege of hearing. The audience was practically spellbound by your astute analysis of small business failure in America. I thought the applause would go on all night when you presented your five-point plan for progress.

Your ideas are ingenious, and I want to thank you sincerely for sharing them with us. We hope you'll join us soon again as our guest at a future luncheon.

Cordially,

Whether a letter to a guest speaker is sent as a congratulatory note or a straight thank you letter depends on the circumstances. Model 8.26 concerns a situation where the speaker deserved a word of congratulations for developing and presenting a particularly ingenious plan.

OUTSTANDING CONTRIBUTION

8.27. For Community Service

Dear Leonard:

You must be very proud of your recent success in prodding community leaders to take a tougher stand on law and order. Without your courageous citizen's campaign to control vandalism and street crime, I believe we would be even worse off today than we were a year ago. But thanks to you, the proper authorities are acting to reverse the alarming trend we've experienced.

There may not be a specific medal available for your contribution, but you have unquestionably won the gratitude of those of us who live in Ridgeway. Because of your persistent efforts we all feel much safer on the streets today.

Sincerest congratulations, Leonard, for a job well done.

Regards,

Model 8.27 illustrates a key point to remember in deciding when congratulatory letters can be sent. Expressions of commendation and praise are appropriate whenever someone makes a contribution, whether or not the effort is publicly acknowledged and whether or not any award has been bestowed.

BUSINESS ANNIVERSARY

8.28. Of Customer

Dear Mr. Jarvis:

It's a pleasure to send you our sincerest congratulations on the silver anniversary of Ramsey Builders. We at Logan Lumber Company consider it our good fortune to have had you as a customer for the last ten of those twenty-five years.

It's common knowledge that Ramsey Builders is one of the most respected firms in this part of the country. You truly have something to celebrate on this occasion; from its birth, your firm has made steady progress and growth, winning countless friends in every sphere of the business world along the way.

We look forward to Ramsey Builders' next twenty-five years and wish all of you the great success and satisfaction you so richly deserve.

Cordially,

In a congratulatory letter to a customer it would be easy to stray from the purpose of the letter and stress your relationship with and your service to that customer. But this must be strictly avoided. As model 8.28 shows, the remarks should focus on the customer's time of glory.

BUSINESS ACHIEVEMENT

8.29. A New Development

Dear Ms. Arnold:

During a visit to the lab yesterday I had an opportunity to see your new test gauge in use. It's a magnificient instrument! You must be proud, indeed, to know this highly useful tool is your own creation. Its accuracy is amazing and it is surprisingly easy to use. How exciting to think of the many potential applications for it outside as well as inside the classroom.

Sincerest congratulations on this remarkable achievement, Ms. Arnold. Your work is an inspiration to all of us.

Best wishes,

A congratulatory letter concerning a new development (or new product, new service) should be enthusiastic and comment intelligently, even if briefly, on it. In model 8.29 the writer took time to learn a few basic facts about the new gauge, for example, it is accurate, easy to use, and has a number of potential applications. Such remarks make it seem as if the writer is truly interested in the new development.

NEW BUSINESS

8.30. Of Former Employee

Dear Stan:

How wonderful it was to learn your new agency is open and ready for business—congratulations! With your experience and proven capability in advertising, I know your organization will be a huge success.

My very best to you, Stan. I'm so pleased all your good work has paid off.

Cordially,

One thing always to guard against in writing letters acknowledging the good fortune of others: letting a hint of envy creep into the letter. This can happen unintentionally. For example, a remark such as "some people have all the luck" could be made in good humor, but the recipient might mistake it for sour grapes.

ON MARRIAGE

8.31. Manager's Assistant

Dear Joe:

Edna and I send you our sincerest congratulations on your coming marriage. Our very best wishes to both of you now and in the years to come.

Cordially,

Although marriage congratulations can be as brief as model 8.31, they will vary depending on how well one knows the recipient, whether one is invited to the wedding, and so on. Model 8.31 would be suitable in most instances, however.

COMMEND PERFORMANCE

8.32 Employee Recognition

Dear Jane:

Congratulations on doing such a beautiful job redecorating our offices. I knew you were talented and creative, but this time I think you even broke your own record! I can hardly wait for more people to visit, so we can show off the results of your hard work.

Thanks a million, Jane. I love all of it.

Best wishes,

As you can see from model 8.32, many letters are really a combination of appreciation and congratulations. This model focuses on congratulations for outstanding work but closes with a word of thanks.

9

SOCIAL-BUSINESS LETTERS
AND INVITATIONS

Business and social activities inevitably overlap at times, and circumstances often require a social-business letter or invitation. Sometimes this letter is sent on special social-business letterhead that is usually smaller than standard business stationery (consult printers and stationery stores for samples). Although social-business correspondence is more personal than other types of business communication, and is thus effective in building business friendships, it is also an excellent means to build favorable public relations for your company. The secretary plays a key role in helping the manager maintain good social-business relations by recognizing and alerting him or her to occasions when a social-business letter or invitation would be appropriate.

The majority of social-business letters are prepared for the manager's signature. It is likely the manager will also ask you to prepare and order *formal* business invitations. Chapter 15 includes several examples of formal invitations and replies (see 15.12–15.15). In many offices the secretary drafts most of the social-business letters (e.g., 9.1, Luncheon Invitation) according to instructions from the manager. Of course, there are always situations when the secretary might send a social-business letter under her own signature (e.g., 9.11, Refusing Invitations to Party). The models in this chapter follow a standard pattern that can be used in composing your own letters; however, as you substitute your own facts, take care to retain the warm, personal tone that characterizes most of these letters. (Consult the Selector Guide for models of social-business correspondence in other chapters.)

Most invitations are issued by letter, as models 9.1 to 9.6 illustrate. This informal style of communication is typically used for invitations to lunch, dinner, a party, an open house, and so on. It is also common in soliciting memberships in professional societies, requesting donations, and asking someone to speak at a special event.

Replies to informal invitations are also sent by letter. Models 9.7 to 9.12 are examples of the style and tone to follow in accepting or declining invitations. Most replies will be either an acceptance or a refusal. Occasionally, however, the manager may decide to accept after first refusing or vice versa (see 9.12).

In addition to preparing the specific invitation or reply to an invitation, the secretary regularly handles miscellaneous letters for social occasions. Although a list of potential situations would be endless, models 9.13 to 9.21 concern many of the common social occasions: expressions regarding birthdays, holidays, thank yous, condolences, gifts—generally, any special event.

ISSUING INVITATIONS

Once you have determined that an informal (letter) invitation is appropriate for the occasion in question, the next step is to decide exactly how informal the tone of the letter should be. Obviously, the tone of a letter asking a friend to have lunch would be more casual and personal than that of a letter to a prominent person asking him or her to address a conference.

1. Specify what the occasion is, e.g., a dinner.
2. Indicate the reason for the invitation, e.g., to celebrate an anniversary.
3. Specify all details about the event, such as time, place, and who will be there.
4. Request a reply by a certain date.

Letters of invitation are appropriate for many occasions; models 9.1 to 9.6 show the pattern and tone to use in composing these letters.

LUNCHEON INVITATION

9.1. To Business Associate

Dear Henry:

Would you be able to have lunch with me on Monday, June 9? If you're free, I'd like to have you be my guest at the Harcourt Inn.

My associate Jim Kimberly will also be there, and we plan to meet about 12:30 p.m. in the cocktail lounge. Jim, you may recall, is the engineer you met at our offices last month. He's still fascinated with your new building designs!

Let me know if you can join us, Henry. I hope you can. Jim and I are both eager to see you again.

Cordially,

Model 9.1 is a typical letter of invitation to someone the writer knows well—thus, the casual tone.

PARTY INVITATION

9.2. To Employees

Dear Employee:

The officers of Kenworthy Corporation cordially invite you to a summer festival party at the South Pacific Clubhouse on Wednesday evening, July 21. This will be an informal get-together for all employees to show our appreciation for your hard work during this long, hot summer!

Cocktails will be served at 7 o'clock followed by a South Pacific smorgasbord at 8 o'clock. There will also be entertainment, fun, and relaxation for everyone until midnight.

We sincerely hope you can attend. Please send your reply to Jeannette Carson in the Business Office by July 15.

Cordially,

Although this is a general invitation to all employees, notice that it contains the same elements as a letter directed to a specific individual; it specifies the nature of the event, who is coming, where and when it is to be held, how long it will last, and the date when a reply is needed. Model 9.2 is an invitation for employees only; sometimes spouses are also invited, and the first sentence of the letter would then be revised to indicate this.

SPEAKING INVITATION

9.3. At Seminar

Dear Dr. Reisterhoff:

Members of the Society for the Evaluation of Human Issues have long admired your behavioral research activities and would enjoy learning more about your work. We would like to invite you to speak at the opening general session of our seminar on human issues to be held at the Bayside Motel, Atlantic City, New Jersey, on November 11, at 9 a.m. Since this session runs forty minutes, a twenty-five-minute address followed by a ten- to fifteen-minute question and answer period would be ideal.

About fifty persons are expected to attend, most of them instructors, researchers, and other persons with backgrounds in the social and behavioral sciences and all of them concerned with the investigation of human issues. We are particularly interested in your findings pertaining to the effect of local opium production on the social-cultural populace of Burma. I know you recently filmed a documentary on this subject and could offer some valuable insights to our members.

In case you are able to be with us, I'm enclosing a data form for you to complete, which will provide us with appropriate information to use in publicizing your appearance. Details concerning transportation and accommodations for speakers are included on the enclosed summary information sheet.

We do hope you can join us on November 11. I'd appreciate having your reply by September 15 so we can finalize our program.

Sincerely,

The extent of information that should go into a speaking invitation letter depends on what type of accessory information sheets can be enclosed. If miscellaneous details can be sent by way of such enclosures, the letter can be kept relatively brief. Nevertheless, it should give basic facts—time, place, and so on—and request a reply by a specific date.

MEMBERSHIP INVITATION

9.4. In Professional Society

Dear Ms. Jackson:

The board of directors of the Batemen Cultural Society cordially invite you to join the membership of this prestigious organization. As a Spanish instructor you would especially enjoy the many benefits available to participants, such as monthly meetings concerning international cultural and historical events and the exchange of ideas with colleagues who share your interests.

As the enclosed brochure explains, the Bateman Cultural Society is dedicated to the preservation and understanding of traditional cultural relationships throughout the world. The society's explorations through special projects and regular meetings are highly interesting and extremely valuable to all mankind.

We would welcome your membership and hope you will take advantage of the enclosed application form so your participation can begin immediately.

Cordially,

Clubs and associations often solicit memberships by letter of invitation. Usually these letters are limited to general features of the organization and provide more detailed information by enclosing brochures and other material. Although the letter *invites* the prospect to join the organization, the membership usually has a price tag. Sometimes, in an effort to sound less like a sales letter, and when enclosed material clearly explains related charges, the invitation itself avoids mentioning fees.

INVITATION TO SUPPORT
CHARITABLE ORGANIZATION

9.5. To Business Associate

Dear Paul:

As you know, I was recently appointed treasurer of the Winthrop Foundation. One of my new duties is to tell you and other interested persons something about this very worthwhile organization and invite your support during the coming year.

The Winthrop Foundation serves the greater Detroit area by providing emergency funds and manpower during times of health-related crises. This aid might be anything from offering medical attention, supplies, and shelter to desperate flood, fire, or accident victims to setting up temporary hospital facilities when epidemics or other disease crises overload regular health-care establishments.

Time and again during the past twelve years of the foundation's existence it has demonstrated how much our metropolitan area needs this type of organization. But, to survive, any charitable organization needs many contributions from people like you and me who one day may benefit from its life-saving assistance.

I hope you can see your way clear to support the foundation this year with a generous contribution. Anything you can give will be greatly appreciated and put to good use. Many thanks, Paul

Best regards,

An *invitation* to support something is really a request to give something. Usually the pattern is to begin with an invitation to support the cause or organization, followed by a synopsis of its features, and concluding with a request for a contribution.

INVITATION TO SPECIAL EVENT

9.6. An Open House

Dear Mrs. Hollingsworth:

The board of trustees of Marden Technological Institute cordially invite you to an open house on Thursday, April 9, to mark the opening of the Center for Advanced Studies. Since you have freely given so many hours of your time to fund-raising efforts for the new center, we sincerely hope you can join us on this happy occasion.

The center will be open from 10:00 a.m. until 5:00 p.m. on Thursday for visitors to view these magnificient facilities. Cocktails will be served in the Faculty Lounge from 5:00 until 7:00 p.m. for you and other special friends of the Institute.

We're all looking forward to seeing you again, Mrs. Hollingsworth. Please do let me know if you can join us for cocktails at the conclusion of visiting hours.

Cordially,

Facts given in an invitation such as model 9.6 might vary slightly depending on the recipient. For example, no address for the center is given since the recipient obviously is very familiar with its location. Nevertheless, this letter, like all invitations, must otherwise be specific in details of time, place, nature of the event, who is coming, and so on.

REPLIES TO INVITATIONS

Courtesy demands that one respond promptly to an invitation. When time permits, the reply should always be in writing.

1. Repeat the essential details of time, date, and place.
2. Express pleasure when accepting an invitation.
3. Express regret and give a reason when declining an invitation.

Models 9.7 to 9.12 show examples of several types of acceptences and several types of refusals of invitations by letter.

ACCEPTING INVITATION TO SPEAK

9.7. At Club Dinner Meeting

Dear Mr. Santos:

It will be a pleasure to speak at the Retailers Club dinner meeting at the Holiday Inn on Friday, May 19, at 8:00 p.m.

I'll be glad to focus on the subject of the effect of large chain stores on small business development in the Southeast. As you suggested, I'll limit my address to thirty minutes.

Your invitation is most welcome, and I'm looking forward to meeting you and your colleagues in the Retailers Club.

Cordially,

Acceptances of speaking engagements should repeat the essential details—time, place, topic, and so on. When the invitation requests biographical data and a photograph, state in your acceptance letter that these items are enclosed or will be sent later. When an acceptance must be qualified, for example, based upon a change in the suggested topic, give an explanation and, if appropriate, recommend an alternative.

ACCEPTING INVITATION TO LUNCH

9.8. With Colleague

Dear Natalie:

Yes, I certainly am free on the 14th to meet you for lunch at the Red Lantern. Many thanks for asking. I'll look forward to seeing you at 12:00 noon in the Jungle Lounge.

Regards,

As you can see from model 9.8, an acceptance of an invitation to lunch can be brief. However, it should (1) display enthusiasm and appreciation for the invitation and (2) repeat the essential details.

ACCEPTING INVITATION TO
MEMBERSHIP

9.9. On Special Committee

Dear Mr. Barker:

Thanks very much for the invitation to serve on the Harvest Club's Education Committee. I appreciate the opportunity to participate and will be glad to accept a position on the committee.

I'll look forward to receiving further information about my duties and details about the next meeting.

Cordially,

The invitation being accepted in model 9.9 was really a request to work on a volunteer basis. Nevertheless, as you can see, when something is presented as an invitation, the reply of acceptance or declination must show appreciation.

REFUSING INVITATION TO SPEAK

9.10. At Conference

Dear Mr. Kittering:

I'm so sorry I can't accept your thoughtful invitation to speak at the Annual Crafts Conference in Seattle on August 8. My schedule calls for me to lecture in Houston most of that week.

Perhaps you would like to consider Professor George Parks from Rowland Art Institute. He is well qualified to address your prospective crafts audience and, if he will be free then, would no doubt be delighted to participate.

I very much regret that I can't join you in Seattle but do appreciate your thinking of me. Thanks very much.

Sincerely,

The refusal to an invitation to speak should express pleasure at being asked and regret at having to decline, giving a reason for the declination. If possible, the letter of refusal should suggest another speaker.

REFUSING INVITATION TO PARTY

9.11. For Employees

Dear Mr. Hartley:

Much to my regret, a previous engagement on March 24 will prevent me from attending the Business Department's party for members of the staff and their friends.

Thank you anyway. I very much appreciated the invitation.

Sincerely,

The declination of an invitation to a party (or other social-business event) can either specify exactly why the invitation is being refused (e.g., you will be visiting someone out of town) or merely indicate that you have a previous engagement without saying what it is.

REFUSING INVITATION AFTER
INITIAL ACCEPTANCE

9.12. For Lunch

Dear Margaret:

I'm very sorry to let you know that an unexpected complication in my schedule has arisen and I'll be unable to join you for lunch on September 5 as I had planned. Some important customers suddenly decided to pay us a visit and I've been assigned the task of ushering them around on September 5 and 6.

I did so appreciate your invitation, Margaret, and am very disappointed that we won't have a chance to visit on the 5th. Let's hope we can get together after my schedule clears up a little.

Best wishes,

The refusal of an invitation after first accepting it is similar to the initial declination: express pleasure at being asked, regret at having to decline, and give a reason for the refusal. A sentence can also be added, as shown in model 9.12, expressing hope to see the friend or associate later. However, the remark should not obligate the person sending the invitation to extend another one later.

LETTERS FOR SPECIAL OCCASIONS

In addition to invitations, social-business correspondence involves many letters for special occasions: birthdays, anniversaries, holidays, illness, death, and many other social-business events. Like all social-business letters, the letters for special occasions help build effective human relations among individuals and good public relations for your company.

1. Write naturally and sincerely.
2. Indicate the reason for your letter.
3. Focus your remarks on the recipient and the occasion and do not detract from it with other discussion.

Models 9.13 to 9.21 are examples of the many occasions that are acknowledged in social-business writing.

SENDING BIRTHDAY WISHES

9.13. To Business Associate

Dear Steve:

According to my calendar November 16 is a red-letter day—yours! This is to wish you the happiest birthday celebration ever.

All the best, Steve, on November 16 and on every day that follows for many years to come.

Regards,

Birthday wishes vary greatly depending on how well you know the person, how old the person is, whether or not age can be mentioned, and so on. Model 9.13 is appropriate for many instances since the tone is warm and friendly; yet it avoids remarking on the person's age and does not make overly familiar comments that some people might feel were too personal.

SENDING EXPRESSIONS OF SYMPATHY—INDIVIDUAL

9.14. On Loss of Spouse

Dear Jonathan:

Mrs. Wilson and I were deeply saddened by the death of your wife, Janet. We both enjoyed and respected her friendship and will miss her very much.

Our heartfelt sympathy goes out to you and your family. Do let me know if there's any way I can be of assistance in the weeks ahead.

Sincerely,

Sympathy letters will vary slightly, depending on your relationship with the recipient and his or her spouse. If you did not know the deceased very well, you might change the second sentence to "We know that everyone enjoyed and re-spected her and will miss her very much." In either case, the letter should avoid a macabre or flowery tone.

SENDING EXPRESSIONS OF SYMPATHY—COMPANY

9.15. On Loss of Official

Dear Lou:

I was shocked to learn of Marshall McKay's untimely death yester-day. I know this will be a serious loss for you and many others at the Berkshire Corporation from both a personal and business standpoint.

My sincerest sympathy to you and your associates.

Regards,

Like the letter of sympathy on an individual basis, the letter concerning the death of a company executive must be brief and avoid excessive sentimentality. Unlike the letter to an individual upon loss of spouse or close friend, the company letter may omit the offer of assistance.

LETTERS TO ACCOMPANY GIFTS

9.16. For Associate's Anniversary

Dear Madge:

Here's a little gift for you to help you celebrate your tenth anniversary at Norton Finance Company. Considering your solid record of prog-ress and achievement and the many friends you've made during these ten years, I know this is a significant and happy occasion for you.

Very best wishes, Madge, for continued success and satisfaction in your career.

Cordially,

Letters to accompany gifts must briefly indicate that a gift is enclosed and ex-plain the reason for the present. Any further comments should focus on the recip-ient and the cause for celebration—not on the gift.

LETTERS OF GOOD WISHES,
WITH REQUEST FOR FAVOR

9.17. To Department Head

Dear Carl:

I just saw some of your new textured papers and I think they're superb. Somehow you always manage to find the latest thing on the market and your selections are always a huge success.

This new textured series is the most exciting yet, and I was wondering if you could make up a small swatch book for us to keep in the public relations office. It would help us greatly to have the samples right at hand as we're talking with customers. If this isn't too much trouble I'd certainly appreciate it.

Keep us posted on your amazing discoveries, Carl, and best of luck with the new series.

Cordially,

Sometimes it is possible to combine expressions of good luck with requests for something, such as model 9.17 shows. However, the practice should be limited to situations where the request will not overshadow the expression of good wishes. Preferably, begin and close the letter with flattering remarks and keep the request in a middle paragraph.

THANK YOU FOR GOOD WISHES,
WITH FAVOR GRANTED

9.18. To Assistant

Dear Abe:

I really appreciated your complimentary remarks and good wishes on my promotion. Thanks so much.

Of course, I'll be glad to consider you for the Sherman account now that my new duties permit me to make such assignments. I'll be in touch with you about this just as soon as I've had a chance to review the status of this account.

Best regards,

When you receive a letter combining both a request for a favor and congratulations or good wishes, the only thing to do is respond with a combination thank you and acknowledgment of the request. Your reply might (1) grant the favor, (2), refuse it (see 9.19), or (3) agree to think about it and decide later.

THANK YOU FOR GOOD WISHES, REFUSING FAVOR

9.19. To Assistant

Dear Mary:

Thanks ever so much for your thoughtful letter. I'll certainly take your good wishes with me when I join our midwestern field staff next month.

It was very flattering to learn you would like to transfer with me. Knowing your fine capabilities so well, I wish this were possible. Unfortunately, there just aren't any administrative assistant openings in the Midwest at present. However, you might alert our personnel office here that you would like to transfer should a suitable opening arise later.

When the time comes, if you're still interested in moving I'll be most happy to recommend you for a transfer. Just let me know, Mary.

Best wishes,

Like any letter of refusal, the combination thank you and refusal letter should be considerate. To the extent possible it should have a positive tone even though it says no. It should give a reason for the refusal and, when practical, suggest other action to the recipient.

THANK YOU FOR GOOD WISHES, NO STRINGS

9.20. Birthday Greetings Received

Dear Carroll:

How nice of you to remember my birthday. Your warm wishes will make my day much more enjoyable; in fact, I think I'll take your advice and celebrate in style!

Many thanks, Carroll.

Regards,

The simple thank you letter can be very brief. The important thing is to indicate genuine appreciation for the good wishes received.

THANK YOU FOR SPECIAL KINDNESS

9.21. During Family Illness

Dear Bob:

I want to thank you for all your help during Ellen's recent illness. Although she's getting along fine now there were times when it was touch and go, and it was essential that I be at the hospital and assume extra responsibilities in caring for the children.

Without your assistance at the office I could never have managed to be away from work that much. I don't know how you did it. I'm sure it put an added strain on your own work load. Both Ellen and I are grateful for your unfailing support and kindness during this difficult time. I just hope some day I can be of help to you.

Sincerest thanks, Bob

                              Cordially,

Any response to a special act of kindness must show sincere gratitude. Although the letter can be relatively brief, it should comment enough about the act of kindness to let the recipient know his or her efforts were truly appreciated and worthwhile.

10

COMPLAINTS AND ADJUSTMENTS

Human errors, misunderstandings, and miscellaneous business problems breed complaints and the need to make adjustments. Eventually you will probably find yourself on different sides of this unavoidable facet of business correspondence, both making and receiving complaints and subsequent adjustments. If there is a bright side to this area of communication, it is that complaints and adjustments can be used to your advantage to discover and correct problems. Fortunately, most situations can be resolved to everyone's satisfaction if the entire process is approached positively, without anger or resentment.

Routine complaints and adjustments (e.g., 10.1, Incomplete Shipment) are written and signed by the secretary in most offices. Even letters the manager may want to sign (e.g., 10.2, Unsatisfactory Performance—Individual) can often be drafted by the secretary. Occasionally a particularly sensitive or unusual complaint or adjustment can best be written by the manager (e.g., 10.5, Criticism of New System), although you may be asked to polish and refine it. (See the Selector Guide for other models of complaints and adjustments throughout the book, e.g., 7.15. Some complaints and adjustments are also handled by memo. For such samples, see chapter 13.)

If a failure in business operations, production, or personnel performance affects you adversely and unfairly, a complaint is usually justified. Letters of complaint often deal with matters such as shipments (10.1 and 10.6), employee performance (10.2), company service (10.3), and company products (10.4). An especially common source of complaint is the billing error (10.7 to 10.10). All of these complaints will differ depending on the focus of each criticism (e.g., complaining about a late shipment is quite different from complaining about someone's performance) and the seriousness of the complaint. Nevertheless, there is a general pattern you can follow in most letters of complaint, as shown in models 10.1 to 10.10.

Handling adjustments requires tact and understanding. If someone is unhappy it is important to correct the situation or you might lose a customer or friend of the company and the company's image could be damaged. Like letters of complaint, adjustment letters might involve almost anything from a claim for damage (10.12) to an explanation of unsatisfactory work (10.18), and the composition of adjustment letters will vary according to the type of adjustment being made and the seriousness of the problem. However, models 10.11 to 10.20 show a general pattern and tone to follow in writing your own adjustment letters.

MAKING COMPLAINTS

Some persons complain at the slightest inconvenience; others never speak up even under the worst conditions. The best position to take is probably somewhere between those two extremes. The only way to be certain you are not moving too far in either direction is to avoid writing a hasty letter in anger and to take time to evaluate your justification in making a complaint.

1. State all details relative to the complaint.
2. Specify what type of adjustment you desire.
3. Be firm but do not display anger or an unreasonable attitude.
4. Be fair in your criticism and request for resolution.

The following ten models are examples of the wide variety of complaints you may have to write in your office.

INCOMPLETE SHIPMENT

10.1 Of Stationery

Gentlemen:

Our May 5 order for 10,000 company letterheads and matching envelopes has arrived incomplete. The correct number of letterheads was included with the shipment we received yesterday, but only 5,000 of the matching envelopes were delivered.

If the additional 5,000 envelopes are en route separately, please disregard this notice. If they are not, I'd appreciate your letting me know the anticipated delivery date right away. It's very important that we receive the rest of our order as soon as possible.

Thank you very much.

Sincerely,

Notification of a problem with a shipment should specify details such as delivery date, product in question, quantities ordered, and so on. If it is important to have the problem corrected quickly, this should be made clear. However, never ask someone to rush something to you when you really have no urgent need for it. This model illustrates the mildest form of complaint—little more than routine notification of an error or problem and a request for rectification.

UNSATISFACTORY PERFORMANCE— INDIVIDUAL

10.2. Of Employee

Dear Ms. Jackson:

I would like to request a replacement for Miss Lynda Belknap, the part-time clerk-typist sent to us last week from your agency. I'm sorry to let you know her performance has been unsatisfactory.

We had indicated to you our need for someone with good typing skills, but Miss Belknap apparently has minimal typing experience. Her speed is too slow, and the quality of her work is insufficient for our needs. Although in every other respect we were satisfied with her work, it is imperative that our clerical assistants be fast and accurate typists. We would therefore like to have a replacement ready to begin next Monday, the 14th.

I'd appreciate a phone call from you in advance to discuss the qualifications of the new assistant so we can avoid further problems. Thanks very much.

Sincerely,

It is likely that the writer of this complaint was more annoyed than the letter indicates. However, she restrained herself (1) because she wanted further help from the agency and (2) she did not want to condemn the employee's performance excessively or unfairly. Nevertheless, the letter makes it clear the situation is unacceptable and must be corrected. If the problem had been more serious, the writer might have insisted on some credit adjustment as well.

UNSATISFACTORY SERVICE— COMPANY

10.3. Late Deliveries

Dear Mr. MacAllen:

For several months we have been experiencing late deliveries from your company on parts for our hand-operated power tools. This unfortunate situation is causing many of our customers to question the prompt service and maintenance guarantee that is part of our sales policy.

Naturally, we are concerned about the growing dissatisfaction among our customers and believe we must find a solution without delay. Therefore, I'd appreciate it if you would let me know immediately what can be done to correct this situation. I'm sure you will understand that if you are unable to provide deliveries on a reliable schedule, we will have no alternative but to seek another source for our power tool supplies and parts.

I'll look forward to hearing from you within the week, and I do hope you'll have a solution for this persistent problem of late deliveries. Thanks very much. I appreciate your cooperation.

Sincerely,

Model 10.3 is an example of a letter that basically "lays it on the line": correct the problem and do it now or we will go elsewhere for our parts. However, notice that the letter makes the point clearly without unrestrained anger, name calling, or excessive criticism. The writer wants results but does not want to insult or anger the recipient so much that he will be disinclined to make an effort to correct the problem. This is not the only alternative, of course. Under other circumstances the writer might have stated he wants to end relations with the supplier and have all deliveries cease immediately.

UNSATISFACTORY PRODUCT

10.4. Defective Addressing Machine

Dear Mr. Baker:

I'm sorry to let you know the model 1920 addressing machine installed last month is malfunctioning. We have followed all instructions very carefully, and your serviceman has called twice to investigate the problem. But the equipment is apparently defective.

Please let us know when we can expect a replacement from you. Our next mailing is scheduled for August 9 and we will need properly functioning equipment installed by the first of the month to meet this deadline.

Thanks for your help and cooperation. I'll look forward to hearing from you shortly.

Sincerely,

There are several alternatives when a product is unsatisfactory: (1) ask for a replacement, (2) ask for further repairs, or (3) ask to return the equipment and receive a refund. Model 10.4 concerns a common response—the writer believes it is at least worth trying a replacement since there is nothing to lose by doing so.

CRITICISM OF NEW SYSTEM

10.5 To Department Head

Dear Mrs. Vinson:

Your efforts to simplify and reorganize our billing procedures have been a welcome sign of long-overdue reforms in this area. I've followed with interest the new system established by your department last month and would like to offer some comments for your consideration.

The new system allows for billing of all society members on a single anniversary date, once each year, with the usual second, third, and delinquent notices. Apparently this confines the task of invoice preparation to a single month during which additional typing assistance can be easily acquired and supervised. No doubt this exclusive focus on the total billing function at one time encourages many efficiencies and an extra lever of control.

Unfortunately, the single billing date also discourages seasonal and periodic monetary returns. We now must hope all members are best able to pay in April or soon thereafter. If they are not, since there is no dispersion of collections, they will simply become delinquent members. It is no longer possible to increase renewals through use of regular monthly and seasonal payment periods. Moreover, our receivables are now heavy in the spring and weak at other times, even though our expenditures do not follow a similar pattern. In short, by solving a few problems such as the ease of hiring temporary help only once a year, we may have introduced more serious problems pertaining to cash flow and year-round payment potential.

Possibly we should have another look at the new system, and I'd like to have your thoughts on this matter. Why don't you drop me a line and perhaps we can get together later for lunch to discuss it further. I'll look forward to hearing from you soon, Mrs. Vinson. Thanks very much.

Cordially

Criticism is most effective when it is constructive. If it alienates or offends the recipient it will probably be ineffective. Therefore, model 10.5 opens with a word of praise. Next, the criticism that follows is supported with specific detailed facts and suggestions. Finally, the letter closes courteously and in a friendly tone recommends lunch and more discussion.

OMISSION OF ENCLOSURES

10.6. Vital Data Missing

Dear Mr. Kirby:

As I explained by telephone this morning, your shipment of forty data-processing manuals (DATA PROCESSING TODAY, Ramon, 0073621, $8.98 ea.) arrived just in time for the opening class at our Central Training Center. However, we were disappointed to discover the supplementary instructor's guide and answer key was missing.

Since classes have already started we are urgently in need of this supplementary instructor's material. The course lasts only four weeks, so you can see the material will be of little use unless it reaches us without further delay. Therefore, I'd appreciate it if you would investigate whether this material is being sent immediately by priority mail.

Thanks very much for your help.

Sincerely,

The writer in model 10.6 obviously has a problem. Class has started and he is already using the textbooks that arrived. Since it is too late to cancel the entire order and look elsewhere for suitable material, he has little alternative but to pressure the supplier to get the missing supplementary aids to him as soon as possible. Thus, an urgent phone call to the supplier is followed with a letter repeating the details of the problem.

BILLING ERRORS—MERCHANDISE

10.7. Goods Not Ordered

Gentlemen:

We have just received your June 30 invoice no. 06400 for $120.88 for one dozen no. 221, carbon typewriter ribbons. Our records show that one dozen ribbons were ordered from you and received in April. However, they were paid by our check no. 713 for $120.88 on May 15.

Therefore, invoice no. 06400 was apparently sent in error and I'm returning it with this letter.

Sincerely,

Unfortunately, it is not completely unusual to be billed twice for the same purchase or to be billed for someone else's purchase, or just to be billed for something neither you nor anyone else ordered. Unless this error is repeated, though, a harsh or stern complaint is not justified. Therefore, simply return the invoice and explain carefully why you should not have been billed.

BILLING ERRORS—AMOUNT

10.8. Overcharged for Purchase

Gentlemen:

We have just received your August 17 invoice no. B1-2992 for $170.69 for one black, three-drawer, Masterlock file cabinet. According to the sales slip presented to us at the time of purchase, the total price should be $159.70.

Therefore, we are returning your invoice no. B1-2992. If you will issue a corrected invoice, we will be happy to send you our payment promptly upon receipt of it.

Sincerely,

Model 10.8, representing another type of billing error, is similar to model 10.7. Notice that in each case the incorrect invoice should be returned to the sender.

BILLING ERRORS—CREDIT CARD

10.9. Returned Ticket Not Credited

Gentlemen:

Account 12-343-001, Regina M. Edwards, Brock Department Stores

Your April 1 statement to Ms. Edwards shows a charge of $37 for a flight from Washington, D.C. to New York City. However, the reservation for this flight was cancelled by telephone and the ticket returned to you on March 4.

I'd appreciate it if you would send me a corrected statement showing that Ms. Edwards' account has been credited for the full amount of the returned ticket.

Thank you.

Sincerely,

Billing errors pertaining to charge accounts are handled much the same as errors related to other types of purchases. However, it is helpful to begin the letter with a subject line that states the account number, the account holder, and his or her company's name.

BILLING ERRORS—COMPUTER

10.10. Persistent Error

Dear Mr. Parsons:

On July 1 we received our fifth bill from your company for $124 for a model 86 electronic calculator. The other four invoices (March 1, April 1, May 1, and June 1) were promptly returned to your credit department with a letter repeating each time that we have never leased, purchased, or even seen a model 86 calculator. Although we once maintained an account with you, it was cancelled a year ago when our company offices were moved to another location. Since then we have made no purchases of any sort from you either on account or by cash. However, your latest invoice was accompanied by a letter stating that the machine, which we do not have, will be reclaimed if we do not make immediate payment.

Since our previous letters were apparently ignored and since your computer seems determined to perpetuate this situation, I'd appreciate it if you would personally locate the error and have it corrected immediately.

Thank you for your help.

Sincerely,

When a billing error becomes persistent, it is time to bypass the computer and get in touch with someone who is likely to be in a position to help you. This means you should address your letter to a specific individual or, if you cannot find a name, use a title such as manager, customer relations, or manager, billing department, or manager, credit department. Although you may be furious if the problem has been persistent, keep the tone of your letter firm but cool and calm enough to get some positive results. Angry threats and wild statements might cause someone to classify your letter as that of a crank, and it could then end up in a wastebasket.

HANDLING ADJUSTMENTS

It is always advisable to handle matters of adjustments promptly, whether your letter grants an adjustment, refuses to make one, or just offers an explanation for something.

1. Be considerate and understanding in your letter.
2. If you are at fault, apologize and try to rectify the situation.

3. Do not allow your explanations to sound like justifications for a fault.

Like complaints, adjustments can vary greatly. Models 10.11 to 10.20 are examples of the major types of adjustment letters: requests for adjustment, letters of explanation, and letters granting or refusing an adjustment request.

REQUESTING A REFUND

10.11. Merchandise Returned

Gentlemen:

I am returning for a refund one six-ounce jar of Magic Miracle Lotion, which I purchased on July 6 by check for $6.75. Your catalog description states that if a customer is not fully satisfied, the unused portion of the lotion may be returned and a full refund will be sent promptly. After one week's use, I am convinced the lotion is ineffective and wish to take advantage of your money-back guarantee.

Please make the refund check payable to Lois J. Harrington and send it to 903 Mockingbird Lane, Princeton, New Jersey 08540.

Thank you very much.

Sincerely,

A request for a refund should describe the object enclosed, list its price, indicate how it was paid for, and specify where the refund should be sent. If a special return policy is involved, the letter should also make reference to this.

CLAIM FOR DAMAGE

10.12 Merchandise Broken

Gentlemen:

Upon unpacking the framed print delivered to me on November 4 by Allied Truck Delivery Service, I found the glass over the picture had been cracked in transit, with one sharp edge piercing the print beneath.

Since the package was insured by the mailer, Novis Art Gallery, Concord, Massachusetts, I would appreciate having your claims adjuster call as soon as possible to inspect the damaged merchandise. If you have a claims form I should complete in the meantime, please send it to me at the address shown on this letterhead.

Thank you very much.

Sincerely,

Model 10.12 concerns a claim to be filed with the transporting company. Other claims might be registered with the sender, with the U.S. Postal Service, or with some other agency. In most cases a form must be filled out; sometimes an adjuster must call to inspect the damage or you must take the merchandise to the adjuster's office. In all cases, act promptly and notify the appropriate person immediately upon discovering the damage.

REQUEST FOR DISCOUNT

10.13. On Delayed Shipment

Dear Mr. Bradley:

Your representative informed me today that the sales brochures we ordered on May 7 are almost ready but will not reach us by the deadline we had agreed upon. These brochures were intended in part for distribution at our annual conference and in part for a mail campaign to sell the books and journals advertised in them.

Because we will not have the material to distribute at our conference, we will experience a substantial loss in book sales; usually we sell about 500 copies at these events when appropriate sales literature is available. In view of this problem, and since you failed to meet the deadline specified with our order, I trust you will provide a satisfactory discount on the order as partial compensation for the loss this delay will cause. A reduction of 40 percent of your charges would seem appropriate since that is the percentage of brochures we had intended to use at the conference.

I'd appreciate receiving your confirmation of this proposed settlement as soon as possible. Thank you.

Sincerely,

To justify a request for a discount based on a delayed shipment, you must (1) indicate that an earlier delivery date was guaranteed and (2) show how you will definitely suffer a loss because of the supplier's failure to meet the agreed-upon deadline. You can also specify a desired discount, although the eventual settlement may well be less than the amount requested. As long as your facts are accurate, the type of complaint illustrated in model 10.13 is completely justified.

GRANTING ADJUSTMENT—BILLING

10.14. Error Corrected

Dear Mrs. Swanson:

We are enclosing a corrected invoice for the linens sent to you on December 2. The price of $64.50 has been changed to $46.50.

Please accept our sincere apologies for this clerical error and any inconvenience it has caused you. We very much appreciate your interest in our merchandise and hope we will have an opportunity to serve you again.

Cordially,

When granting an adjustment for an error made by your company, state the correction details—item purchased, erroneous charge, corrected charge, and so on—and extend a sincere apology for the error and any inconvenience it has caused the customer. If further sales might be possible, you might close with some indication that you hope to be of service again.

GRANTING ADJUSTMENT— DAMAGE CLAIM

10.15. Merchandise Replaced

Dear Mr. Willis:

We were very sorry to learn the portable vacuum you recently ordered arrived with a cracked hull. Thank you for returning the damaged product so promptly.

A replacement model of the same style, size, color, and price is enclosed. It has been carefully inspected before packing to insure that you will not be troubled again with a similar problem.

We sincerely regret the delay and the inconvenience this has caused you but hope you will now be pleased with your new vacuum.

Thank you for your patience.

Cordially,

The response to a damage claim is determined by the customer's request and the company's policy. Many companies ask the customer to return the product and then offer him or her a choice of a replacement, a refund, or credit on a later purchase. With model 10.15 the customer had returned the product and had requested a replacement product. Similar to all adjustments responding to a justifiable complaint, this model offers an apology for the problem and any inconvenience it has caused.

EXPLANATION FOR DELAYED SHIPMENT

10. 16. Supplies Overdue

Dear Miss Cramer:

We are very sorry our shipment of frame kits to you has been delayed. The factory that manufactures the unfinished frames sent to us for finishing had experienced some problems in filling our orders last month. However, we received a new supply of frames on Tuesday and expect to finish them immediately and ship your kits on May 24.

We sincerely regret any inconvenience this has caused you and hope your order will soon be filled to your satisfaction.

Thank you so much for your patience.

Cordially,

Customers are entitled to an explanation of overdue orders. One thing to guard against in such letters is a tendency to make weak excuses sound like a justification for the delay. Before you compose the letter decide what the facts are and state them briefly and accurately. If there is no good reason for the delay, do not invent one or try to dress up a poor one, but simply apologize and indicate when the order will be filled.

EXPLANATION OF OVERSIGHT

10. 17. A Missing Part

Dear Mr. Shaw:

We're very sorry your humidifier was delivered with the roto-belt missing. A new belt is enclosed for you now.

Roto-belts are shipped to us separately and they are supposed to be fitted on the humidifiers as soon as they are unpacked. Apparently someone accidentally overlooked the unit that by chance was delivered to you.

Please accept our sincere apologies for this oversight and any inconvenience it may have caused you. We appreciate your interest in our humidifiers and hope yours will contribute to many years of your comfort and good health.

Cordially,

The letter explaining an oversight is patterned similarly to other adjustment letters such as models 10.15 and 10.16. Letters are not always sent in these cases, but a thoughtful explanation is a good way to improve customer relations.

EXPLANATION OF UNSATISFACTORY WORK

10.18. Poor Printing Quality

Dear Mrs. Clark:

You are absolutely right—the quality of printing on your November issue of Executive Newsletter is below our usual standards. Although I believe it meets the minimum standards of the trade, I agree completely that the printing can and should be improved on future issues.

My pressman tells me the press used for 11- by 17-inch work was performing poorly the week your newsletter was run. Since then we've had the serviceman look at the machine and the problem has been corrected. You may be certain our production supervisor will monitor the press runs more closely hereafter so this problem will never occur again.

We appreciate your concern and are very sorry you were unhappy with the job. Please accept our sincere apologies. We value your business and are going to do our utmost to provide high-quality work for you at all times.

Sincerely,

Follow a basic rule when you have to explain unsatisfactory work: when you are wrong, admit it and apologize. The customer is likely to be irritated in such a situation and will not tolerate feeble excuses or a rationale for low-quality work. In addition to giving an explanation, you should stress your intent to avoid such problems in the future and your sincere desire to satisfy the customer.

REFUSING ADJUSTMENT ON LATE DELIVERY

10. 19. Of Merchandise

Dear Mrs. Pendleton:

We were very sorry to learn your order for one dozen crystal goblets arrived after your reception for Senator Juliet. Unfortunately, our store has no policy providing for a reduction in cost of merchandise under these circumstances.

However, if the crystal has not been used, it can be returned for a full refund or for credit toward another purchase. Should you decide upon one of these alternatives, simply return the unused crystal to the customer service desk at our Madison Avenue Store where it was purchased and specify your choice of credit or refund.

We sincerely regret any inconvenience you have experienced and hope we'll have an opportunity to serve you again.

Cordially,

A letter refusing to make an adjustment should be especially tactful and considerate. Avoid a blunt, abrupt no. Model 10. 19 offers two alternatives to the customer's request for a discount: a full refund or credit toward another purchase. Any refusal letter will seem less harsh if other alternatives or suggestions are offered so the customer does not feel it is all a total loss.

REFUSING TO GRANT A REFUND

10. 20. On Sale Merchandise

Dear Mr. Rhoades:

We were very sorry to learn you were not satisfied with the cassettes purchased during our spring sale last month.Unfortunately, our store does not allow for returns or refunds on sale merchandise.

Although we cannot offer a refund on the sale cassettes, we do have a full line of other tapes and cassettes at regular price; any of these could be returned unused and unopened if you later decided against them.

We very much regret that you are unhappy with your purchase and
hope your next selections will be much more satisfactory.

Cordially,

Model 10.20 is similar to model 10.19 in that the tone is sympathetic even
though the letter is saying no. Also, this model makes a suggestion so the customer will know a sincere effort is being made to help him in spite of the policy
that prevents him from receiving the refund he wants.

11

CREDIT AND COLLECTION
LETTERS

Business writers often stress that we live in a credit society or an age of credit. Certainly, it is true that matters of credit and collection affect nearly every type of organization, large or small. Thus, it is important in the modern business office to be familiar with the types of correspondence generated in credit and collection activities, whether your own office handles these matters or whether your company has a credit department for this purpose.

Although financial matters are often sensitive, many of the letters pertaining to credit and collection are routine requests and responses. The task often falls to the secretary to write such letters, frequently mailing them under her own signature (e.g., 11.4, Providing Credit Information). In many offices the secretary will compose the letters for the manager's signature (e.g., 11.5, Inviting New Accounts—Business). When communications reach a serious level (e.g., 11.11, Cancelling Credit of Company), it is possible that the manager will want to draft the basic letter, although the secretary may be expected to refine and polish it. No matter who signs the letter, most credit and collection correspondence follows a very definite pattern you can use in composing you own letters; many credit and collection situations, in fact, are so routine they are handled by forms and form letters (see 15.8 and 15.9). (The Selector Guide will lead you to other credit and collection models throughout the book, for example: chapter 6, Requesting a Credit Reference.)

Credit letters deal with the financial status of a person or company—someone's ability to pay or someone's history of meeting his or her obligations. Both individuals and businesses are constantly concerned about their financial reputations and this concern must be carefully considered and respected when composing credit letters. Credit correspondence typically involves requests for credit or credit information (11.1–11.3 and 11.5–11.7) and responses to those requests (11.4 and 11.8–11.12).

The way you handle your collection correspondence depends on the size of your company and the number of situations you must handle. The most familiar approach to the problem of overdue accounts is the collection-letter series (11.13–11.18). This series provides examples of each step in collection proceedings, from the casual reminder to the final, last-resort prelude to legal action.

WRITING CREDIT LETTERS

In one respect credit letters are goodwill letters because they concern the relationship—past, present, or future—between two parties. This immediately suggests that the credit letter must try to preserve or establish a satisfactory relationship while still accomplishing its financial purpose.

1. When requesting credit, assuming the request is realistic, provide all information the recipient will need to process the request.
2. When responding to credit requests, be completely honest and accurate but also be considerate of the writer's feelings and needs.

Models 11.1 to 11.12 provide examples of the major types of credit letters: requesting credit or credit information; supplying credit information; and responding to requests for credit.

REQUEST FOR CREDIT—INDIVIDUAL

11.1. To Department Store

Gentlemen:

I would like to open a charge account at Baker's Department Store. Please send a credit application to me at 1440 Newbury Street, Charlotte, Vermont 05445.

Thank you.

                                          Sincerely,

This model shows the simplest form of credit request. Most stores have their own credit applications that must be completed. So the letter of request for credit does not provide any facts but merely asks for the application, which is then completed and returned to the store.

REQUEST FOR CREDIT—BUSINESS

11.2 To Supplier

Dear Mr. Adams:

The Wahlgreen Construction Company is continually in need of quality paint and home building supplies at attractive prices. We are familiar with your fine products and would like to place some orders with you in the coming months.

Would you be able to provide your usual credit terms to us for quantity purchases? I'm enclosing the name of our bank and three suppliers with whom we have done business in the past. Please let me know if you need further information for us to open an account with you.

Thanks very much for your consideration, Mr. Adams. We look forward to an opportunity to use your supplies in many of our future construction jobs.

Sincerely,

There are a number of ways for a business to seek credit on purchases. You might get letters of referral and recommendation from other credit sources before asking a new supplier for terms. Or you might simply ask for an application, using much the same approach as in model 11.1. The example shown here illustrates a third and common procedure—writing to ask for credit, indicating that purchases will be forthcoming, and enclosing the names of credit references instead of the actual letters. Model 11.2 also indicates that further information will be provided if needed.

REQUEST FOR CREDIT INFORMATION

11.3. About New Business

Dear Mr. Brewster:

Middle River Sporting Goods has just sent us a large order with a request to make this and future purchases on account. The manager, William Wright, gave your company's name as a credit reference.

Since Middle River is a new store, your experience with them may be limited. However, I'd appreciate having your evaluation of their potential and your recommendations regarding an extension of credit. Your comments, of course, will be kept strictly confidential.

Thanks very much, Mr. Brewster. I appreciate your help and cooperation.

Cordially,

Requests for credit information about businesses are similar, whether the business is new or well established. Assuming a form is not sent for the recipient to fill out, the letter usually asks the reference source to comment on his or her experience concerning the applicant's performance in previous credit situations. The reference source should be assured that all remarks will be held in the strictest confidence. Naturally, any letter of request must conclude with an expression of appreciation.

PROVIDING CREDIT INFORMATION

11.4. About Customer

Dear Mr. Gibbs:

Our experience with Whitcomb Industries has been excellent. According to our credit department, they have faithfully paid our invoices within thirty days throughout the nearly three years of our association. Most of their purchases have ranged between $2,000 and $4,000 a month.

Based on our own satisfaction with this account, I believe you could justifiably consider extending a similar amount of credit to Whitcomb Industries.

Let me know if there's anything else I can do to help. Best regards.

Cordially,

One of the most important requirements in providing credit information is accuracy. You should not make decisions for others, of course, but your facts should be clear and reliable, whether they are complimentary or negative. Model 11.4 comments on a good customer. Notice, however, even this letter carefully states that the recipient *might* (not should) consider extending a *similar* (not unlimited) amount of credit.

INVITING NEW ACCOUNTS—BUSINESS

11.5. For Office Supply Store

Dear Ms. Ringley:

We would like to make it easier for you to keep your office well supplied with the myriad of materials you need every day, from paper clips to sophisticated business forms. Therefore, we have opened an account for you in the name of your company; your credit is good at Carson's Office Supply and no application is necessary.

Our accounts for preferred customers such as your company are based on a thirty-day billing cycle (terms 2%, 10 days). Throughout each month you may make as many purchases of any size as you wish, with no minimum number required at any time. Whether you phone, write, or call at our store, all you need to do is give us your order and your name. Incidentally, we provide free, same-day delivery service for local customers.

We hope you'll enjoy the convenience of having an account at Carson's. I know we'll enjoy having you as a customer and look forward to hearing from you soon.

Cordially,

It is common practice for some establishments to add new customers by offering credit before they even ask for it. The letter inviting such business must provide details concerning the terms, billing cycle, whether an application must be completed later, and so on. It is important to avoid alarming the prospective customer with any suggestion of obligation on the customer's part. If there are benefits that accompany the account, such as free delivery service, they should be mentioned as well.

INVITING NEW ACCOUNTS—INDIVIDUAL

11.6. For Clothing Store

Dear Mrs. Lewis:

Did you know that Porter's Department Store has just expanded its line of household products to include lawn and garden tools and outdoor furniture? Actually, we have increased the number of products in all our departments during the past few months to make Porter's the most complete clothing and home service center in your area.

I thought you might like to know that in just another month, on August 20, our fall clothing sales will begin. So you can take advantage of the great savings that will be offered on men's, women's, and children's wear, I'm enclosing one of our charge-card applications. As you can see, it's very brief and will take only a minute to complete. If you mail it to us or leave it at our credit office within the next few days, we will be able to process it and, upon approval, send you your new charge plate in time for use during our big August sale days. Just check on the application whether you prefer our thirty-day, full-payment plan or a revolving account that offers low monthly payments on all purchases up to $300.

Why not take a minute right now to complete your application. A charge account at Porter's will make your shopping so much easier and enjoyable. We hope to hear from you soon.

Sincerely,

Model 11.6 represents another example of seeking new customers by offering credit before the prospective customer asks for it. In this case, however, the prospect is asked to complete an application, so credit is *not* guaranteed in the initial letter.

ACTIVATING OLD ACCOUNTS

11.7. At Service Establishment

Dear Mr. Greenberg:

We haven't seen you since last October and are wondering if our service was not completely satisfactory. If anything displeased you, I'd appreciate knowing about it so we can make amends without delay. Just call me at 224-3000 and I'll take care of the matter at once.

It was always a pleasure to see you at Mike's Foreign Car Service, and if your car is due for servicing soon, I'd like to offer you a 15 percent discount for this work as a special welcome-back gift. Incidentally, we have a new supply of foreign car accessories on hand now, and throughout this month are selling all discontinued items at a 10 to 30 percent reduction. We'll be glad to put whatever you select on your account: even though we haven't seen you recently, your credit is still good at Mike's.

Come in soon, and I personally guarantee we will do our best to see you are completely satisfied from this day on.

                                        Cordially,

Letters reactivating old accounts will vary, depending on how long the customer has been gone, why he probably left, and so on. Model 11.7 is typical in that (1) it adopts a thoughtful tone and (2) it offers an enticement, in this case discounts.

REFUSING CREDIT—WITH ALTERNATIVE

11.8. To Company

Dear Mr. Brooks:

We appreciated your interest in our new plastic storage containers and want to thank you for inquiring about credit.

As much as we would like to extend credit to your firm, an investigation of the references you supplied indicates there were occasional problems in making periodic payments on schedule. It is our policy in such cases to ship merchandise only C.O.D. or after advance cash payment. Perhaps you would like to place orders now on this basis and apply for credit privileges again in another six months.

Thanks very much for thinking of us. I hope we'll have an opportunity to provide the storage containers you need.

                                        Sincerely,

A letter of refusal should always be as thoughtful as possible. In model 11.8, the writer does not want to lose a prospective customer and thus recommends cash orders now and a reapplication for credit later.

REFUSING CREDIT—WITHOUT ALTERNATIVE

11.9. To Individual

Dear Mrs. Samuels:

Thank you for your recent application for a charge account at The Gift Shoppe. It was a pleasure to learn of your interest in our gifts.

As much as we would like to open an account for you, the credit information we received indicates you have experienced serious difficulties in making payments on your other accounts. Unfortunately, our policy prevents us from opening accounts under these circumstances.

Meanwhile, we hope you will take advantage of the many exciting gift selections in our store available on a cash basis.

Sincerely,

When credit information points to a consistently poor credit risk, there is no point in suggesting the applicant reapply soon again. In this model, the writer does not even mention sending merchandise C.O.D. However, he does close with a routine suggestion that the customer shop on a cash basis. Notice the letter adopts a relatively gentle tone, however, even though the writer doubtless is quite unimpressed with the applicant's record.

REFUSING SPECIAL CREDIT TERMS

11.10. Quantity Discounts

Dear Mrs. McDaniel:

We were happy to learn you are considering our detachable countertops for your lakeside cottages. They are, indeed, popular in motels, cottages, and other resort accommodations that have a combined living-kitchen area. However, I'm sorry we have no provision for quantity discounts on orders in the range of 25 to 30 units. It would be necessary for us to order above 100 units from the factory to receive a markdown we could pass along to our customers.

I do hope this won't discourage you from selecting our countertops for your cottages. We can guarantee they are not only attractive but highly durable and thus well suited for heavy tourist usage. We also believe the price of $39.50 per unit, including installation, is very reasonable in itself and that it would be hard to find a better value anywhere.

Let us know if we can take your order now so we can make certain the countertops will be ready for installation before the June rush begins. I know you'll be delighted with them.

Sincerely,

When credit is refused for some reason unrelated to the applicant's record, every effort should be made to retain the customer's business. Model 11.10 illustrates a case where there is nothing wrong with the customer's credit; the writer simply cannot offer a discount. Therefore, the letter says no, but does a selling job in hopes of getting the order anyway.

CANCELLING CREDIT

11.11. Of Company

Dear Mr. Parks:

Much to my regret, I must inform you we will have to stop extending credit to your company, effective immediately. As the enclosed statement of your account shows, your balance of $5,670.80 is long past due, and no payments have been made in the past ninety days.

We hope a check for the overdue amount will be forthcoming in the next few days. In the meantime, though, I'm sure you will understand we are unable to continue this outstanding indebtedness any further.

Sincerely,

Letter 11.11 should not be confused with a collection letter. The main purpose of this communication is simply to cancel the credit arrangement, even though the letter also asks the debtor to make payment. The assumption is that other correspondence has been and will be generated to collect the past-due account. In other cases, though, the writer might prefer to combine the letters, with cancellation and collection a joint objective in a single letter.

SETTLING MISUNDERSTANDINGS

11.12. Of Payment Plan

Dear Ms. Jacobs:

Thank you for returning our September 1 invoice No. 26170 for $212.98. You are absolutely right that you should be billed in installments for this charge.

Apparently our billing department misunderstood my instructions. I have informed them you are to billed monthly at the rate of $20 plus a service charge of 1.5 percent on the unpaid balance. A corrected invoice will be sent to you shortly.

Please accept our apologies for this misunderstanding. We appreciate your calling it to our attention.

Sincerely,

When someone—buyer or seller—misunderstands payment matters, the problem should be straightened out immediately. If the customer has misunderstood, the situation should be explained carefully, but he or she should never be criticized for failing to understand the terms of a sale. If the seller has made a mistake, as is the case in model 11.12, it should be rectified promptly and an apology issued immediately.

THE COLLECTION-LETTER SERIES

A single letter does not always result in collection of an overdue account. Knowing this, collection writers plan their correspondence with the assumption that they may have to write several letters, each one becoming more forceful than the one before. This program of collection correspondence is often called the collection-letter series.

1. Create a campaign of four to six letters, from a casual reminder to a prelude to legal action.
2. Gauge the tone of the letters from the beginning, with a friendly reminder, to the conclusion, with a final, strong plea preceding legal action.
3. Know the facts of the situation thoroughly before developing the content of any of the letters.
4. Always give the customer an opportunity to meet his obligation, no matter how late.

Models 11.13 to 11.18 represent a typical series of six collection letters. If fewer letters are desired, models 11.15, 11.6, and 11.17 (series #3, #4, and #5) could be combined into one or possibly two letters. Although many writers employ humor in their letters, most collection letters are more straighforward, as this series illustrates.

COLLECTION LETTER #1

11.13. A Casual Reminder

Dear Mr. Lawrence:

Just a friendly reminder that your payment of $70.98 will be very much appreciated.

If your check is already in the mail, please disregard this notice and accept our thanks. If it is not, won't you take a moment to mail it today?

Cordially,

The first letter sent when an account becomes overdue is usually short and friendly. The letter often suggests the check may already be in the mail, and the customer is told how much the payment will be appreciated.

COLLECTION LETTER #2

11.14. A Strong Reminder

Dear Mr. Lawrence:

Another thirty days have passed and your payment of $70.98 has not yet arrived.

Since we have not heard from you we assume the balance is correct and that your records agree with ours. Won't you therefore send us your check today or let us hear from you right away before this unpaid balance affects your credit standing?

Your cooperation will be very much appreciated, Mr. Lawrence. Thank you.

Sincerely,

Letter #2, often sent thirty days after #1, becomes more serious and uses stronger language. The customer is told (1) the payment due must be correct since he has not questioned it, and (2) he may lose his credit standing if he does not pay promptly or at least explain why he is not sending payment.

COLLECTION LETTER #3

11.15. The Discussion Letter

Dear Mr. Lawrence:

We were disappointed that we did not hear from you in response to our last letter concerning your overdue account of $70.98.

Since we have mailed several statements and letters to you, Mr. Lawrence, without any word in return, I'm growing somewhat concerned. Perhaps you are experiencing problems that make it difficult for you to pay this amount all at once. If you are having difficulty making the full payment, and you'll tell me about it, in confidence, of course, I'm sure we can set up an easy payment plan for you.

Please let me hear from you right away, Mr. Lawrence. We'll both be much happier when this matter is resolved to our mutual satisfaction.

Sincerely,

Letter #3 opens a discussion channel. It indicates to the customer that everyone has problems and if he will just explain what his are, perhaps an easier payment plan can be worked out. This letter gives the customer a good chance to discuss things before the seller starts getting tough. Letter #3 might be sent thirty days after the previous one. Some companies at this point begin speeding up the correspondence with shorter intervals between letters.

COLLECTION LETTER #4

11.16. An Urgent Message

Dear Mr. Lawrence:

Although we have sent you numerous statements and letters regarding your past-due account of $70.98, we have heard nothing from you.

I'm sure you will understand we are unable to continue waiting patiently in silence. Therefore, it is essential that this account be settled at once and we urge you to make the necessary arrangements without delay. If there are circumstances beyond your control, we urge you to tell us about them immediately.

Please put your check in the mail or contact us right away. We must hear from you at once to avoid further action.

Sincerely,

The tone of letter #4 becomes strong and urgent. The essence of the message is that time is running out and the customer must act quickly or other measures will have to be taken.

COLLECTION LETTER #5

11.17. The Special Appeal

Dear Mr. Lawrence:

For several months we have been writing to you about your long past-due account of $70.98. We must know your intentions immediately.

We realize, of course, that many overdue accounts are the result of unexpected financial difficulties. In these cases we make every effort to help our customers find a better arrangement for making payment. However, we have not heard from you and cannot offer such help until we know your situation.

Please send us something today. Our company is no longer in a position to continue to maintain your account under the present conditions. If we do not hear from you at once, we will have no choice but to pursue other collection procedures.

Sincerely,

Letter #5 makes an appeal to fear. It says in effect that the time has arrived when the seller can no longer carry the account and must take other collection measures, which usually suggests a collection agency or legal action.

COLLECTION LETTER #6

11.18. Prelude to Legal Action

Dear Mr. Lawrence:

Since you did not reply to my letter of January 1, I regret we must take other action to collect the balance of your past-due account. $70.98.

If we do not receive your check by February 1, you will next hear from the Harris-Blackwell Collection Agency. We hope you will take this final opportunity to avoid further damage to your credit standing, not to mention the additional costs you may incur if legal action is also necessary.

Just send us your check by February 1, and the matter will be resolved before we take this action.

Sincerely,

Letter #6 is the final collection attempt before the account is turned over to the collection agency or lawyer. Usually the customer is given ten days to two weeks to make payment. To leave no doubt in the customer's mind that the seller means business, the lawyer or collection agency is usually named in this final letter of the series.

12

SALES PROMOTION LETTERS

In one respect most letters are sales letters in that they sell something—a service, an idea, goodwill, and so on. But the letter specifically intended to promote sales is in a class by itself. Its success, directly or indirectly, can pave the way for company profits; its failure can cause a loss. Sales promotion letters, thus, are often judged by the monetary return they produce; in all cases they are judged by their effectiveness in stimulating a response. Ideally, these letters are addressed and sent to specific individuals. However, in large mail campaigns it is common to send letters using "Dear Customer" or "Dear Friend" or a similar salutation. Length of the letter depends partially on how much printing and postage you can afford. Many writers try to stay within one page to keep costs down and also because they believe their prospects will not read more than a brief message.

Sales promotion letters are frequently prepared by specialists, although even then essential information must be given to the writer. Therefore, the secretary must at the very least be familiar with the content and construction of these letters. In many offices, though, it will be part of the secretary's duties to assist in writing the letters; some may even go out under his or her own signature (e.g., 12.4, Transmittal Letter to Prospect). In the majority of cases, the manager and the secretary will probably share in the preparation of sales correspondence, and most of these letters will go out under the manager's signature (e.g., 12.6, Paving the Way for a Salesman's Call). Since most sales promotion letters are designed first to get attention, second to arouse interest and desire, and third to encourage action, they must follow a particular pattern. This means the models in this chapter can easily be used as guides in composing your own letters. (Refer to the Selector Guide for other letters throughout the book that include promotional messages e.g., 11.6.)

A principal type of sales promotion letter is the introduction of a service or a product. Sometimes this letter includes a sample product or some literature (12.3 and 12.4); frequently the letter just introduces the service, product, or something related to these things such as a payment plan or the representative servicing a particular area (12.1, 12.2, 12.5, and 12.6).

Once the contact has been made with a customer, a good sales program must plan a variety of follow-ups. These letters vary greatly with circumstances. Sometimes more information must be provided (12.9 and 12.11). Often special tactics must be employed to entice prospective and former customers to purchase something (12.8, 12.10, 12.13, and 12.14). Also, former customers must be contacted in efforts to bring them back (12.12), and it is always important to follow a salesman's call to a prospective customer with a letter (12.7).

INTRODUCING PRODUCTS AND SERVICES

Before you can introduce a product or service you must be thoroughly familiar with it and with the person or company you are contacting. This is imperative because sales promotion letters must be very skillfully composed or they will be ineffective. Even in large mail campaigns where you cannot possibly know a specific individual, an effort must be made to select a generally representative audience. The other preliminary information you must have is the nature of the entire sales program. If a series of letters are planned, for example, each one you write must fit properly into this total scheme.

1. Plan your remarks to arouse interest and stimulate action.
2. Describe the product or service being offered and its value to the customer.
3. Explain any special offers or incentives that are available.
4. Leave the door open for further contact.

Models 12.1 to 12.6 illustrate the major types of sales letters that introduce a product, service, salesman, or some related aspect such as a payment plan.

INTRODUCING A SERVICE

12.1 To Prospective Customer

Dear Mr. Wolf:

May we introduce to you our new office design and consulting service? We're happy to let you know that Macomb Office Interiors has expanded its line of modern office furniture and accessories and, along with it, has added this new service for customers.

With an experienced staff of office decorators and designers, we can now give you expert advice on all those things that together can make your office a more pleasant, efficient, and productive unit. Best of all, we can provide this important advice to our customers free of charge. That's right—on any purchase of $100 or more, we will be happy to visit your offices at no additional cost and give you our recommendations for a more efficient layout, better color coordination, improved lighting, and so on.

I'm enclosing a bulletin that describes our expansion, including our new design and consulting service as well as the many new office furnishings we have on the floor. If you would like more information, just call me at 923-7700 or, better yet, stop by our store at 11 Maple Avenue and see our many new selections.

Cordially,

There could be variations of model 12.1. For example, the letter might suggest the writer will soon phone for an appointment to have a representative call. Or the letter might ask the prospect if he would like a free catalog. Or the letter might invite the prospect to a special showing or open house. Circumstances will dictate specific details of the letter, but all introductions of this type must explain the service and why it should be of interest to the prospect.

INTRODUCING A PRODUCT—NO SAMPLE

12.2 To Prospective Customer

Dear Mr. Talbert:

Would you like to cut your heat and electric bills drastically this winter? Of course, who wouldn't? That's why more and more people are turning every day to a beautiful cast-iron stove for heating and cooking.

We just acquired a large supply of these magnificent heaters and are introducing them to residents of Morrison County during the month of August with a prewinter sale. Each cast-iron stove—and we have three models to fit any room size—will be available during August at 40 percent off regular retail prices ranging from $129.95 to $169.96. This amazing value includes delivery and installation.

These magnificent stoves include a grate basket that holds coal, wood, or charcoal. Doors can be closed when not in use. The cast-iron construction provides more heat than a regular fireplace because of radiation from all sides. Not only are these heaters practical, they are an attractive addition to any home and fit perfectly in both modern and traditional decors.

Come in today and see for yourself what a truly remarkable value you will find in these beautiful stoves. You'll be glad you did, especially when winter arrives with its inevitable high-cost heating and electric bills. In the meantime, if you have any questions, just call 632-8000 and speak with one of our sales personnel at Otega's Home Furnishings Center.

Sincerely,

When a sample product cannot be sent, and when sales literature is not available, the sales letter must provide enough details to satisfy and interest the prospective customer. Appeal is important in introduction letters. Model 12.2 appeals to the prospect's pocketbook by reminding him of expensive heating and electric bills with conventional heating and cooking methods. The letter closes by explaining how the prospect can learn more about the stoves. Notice the underlining in the body of the letter. Sales writers sometimes call attention to special inducements by underscoring them or using all capitals.

INTRODUCING A PRODUCT—SAMPLE ENCLOSED

12.3. To Prospective Customer

Dear Mrs. Anderson:

Please accept this free sample of the finest 35 mm slide-protector pages available today. For many years this distortion-free, clear, vinyl page has been a favorite means of protecting valuable slides and prints for professional photographers; now we are pleased that we can offer this same quality protector page to <u>all</u> camera enthusiasts. What's more, until April 30 we are offering a special introductory discount of <u>10 percent off on any purchase of fifty pages or more.</u>

Your sample of Modern Plastic Corporation's top-loading slide page is designed to hold twenty slides and will fit any standard three-ring binder or album. As the enclosed literature explains, we manufacture pages for all standard-size slides, transparancies, and prints. Although similar pages found in camera stores retail for as much as 50 cents each, our high-quality, durable plastic pages are available by mail for <u>as little as 20 cents each</u> on orders of fifty pages or more. Think of the savings when you also consider the 10 percent discount being offered until April 30.

Our pages are sent on a satisfaction-guaranteed basis. If you are not completely happy with your purchase, simply return it within thirty days for a full refund. Use the enclosed postage-paid envelope and send us your order today! We'll promptly mail your vinyl protector pages to you postpaid.

                                        Cordially,

If you can afford them, sample products, postage-paid return envelopes, and descriptive literature are frequently effective in increasing response. Coupons, premiums, and gifts are other types of gimmicks and enclosures employed to stimulate sales. But even when you use enclosures, your letter should sufficiently describe the product and its value to the customer. Model 12.3 also uses a special introductory discount to further encourage sales.

TRANSMITTAL LETTER TO PROSPECT

12.4. Literature Enclosed

Dear Ms. Daniels:

We're happy to send you the new Pomeroy Catalog of Imports you requested. This recent issue offers a choice of <u>more than 200 unusual buying opportunities</u> at overseas close-out prices.

Without ever leaving your home you can select quality merchandise from countries all over the world at <u>savings of up to 50 percent</u> off usual retail prices. All items are insured and the prices listed in the enclosed catalog represent your total cost—no hidden import fees, no extra insurance fees, just <u>one low price</u> that includes everything.

We hope you'll enjoy the excitement of shopping overseas the easy, inexpensive way. For your convenience, an order form is enclosed in the catalog, and we'll look forward to receiving your first order soon. In the meantime, if you have any other questions, just let me know. We sincerely appreciate your interest in Pomeroy's House of Imports.

Cordially,

Many transmittal letters are little more than brief indications of what is enclosed. Model 12.4 illustrates how a transmittal letter can also be used as a sales promotion letter. Like many other sales letters, this one could be prepared individually or as a form letter that might use a "Dear Customer" salutation.

INTRODUCING A PAYMENT PLAN

12.5. To Regular Customer

Dear Mrs. Adams:

Now that the Christmas shopping season is almost here we want to let you know about a new delayed-payment plan at Davidson's. We hope this new <u>shop-now</u> and <u>pay-later plan</u> for our charge customers will make it easier for you to prepare for the holidays without straining your budget during this heavy shopping period.

Here's the way it works: You can stop by our Credit Office the next time you shop at Davidson's and pick up delayed-payment coupons amounting to <u>$300 worth of instant purchases</u> that are not payable until next February. Just present the appropriate number of coupons with each purchase, along with your charge card, and the sales clerk will mark your sales slip for February billing. Your February statement, then, will show all coupon purchases, which will be payable in the usual manner—within thirty days or in monthly installments according to your choice. Of course, during this period you may also use your charge card alone without the coupons for additional purchases.

As always, we look forward to seeing you soon and hope this year you'll especially enjoy your holiday shopping at Davidson's.

Cordially,

Companies and stores offer a variety of payment plans. Since these plans are designed to increase sales, the letter explaining them should also promote sales. Model 12.5 introduces a special plan for the holidays, and the writer obviously tries to arouse interest in it to encourage the customer to do her holiday shopping at his store.

PAVING THE WAY FOR A
SALESMAN'S CALL

12.6. To Prospective Customer

Dear Mr. Feldman:

We have just added an amazing new set of aluminumware to our cookware line. Since the price of this new set is comparable to the other sets of cookware you carry, your customers should find this a very exciting discovery.

This remarkable new aluminumware has the most durable, nonstick cooking surface I've ever seen. Best of all, unlike other finishes, the interior can't be damaged by metal utensils; yet, it cleans just as easily as more sensitive nonstick surfaces. The finish is beautiful—heavy gauge aluminum exteriors with rich, pewter-look interiors—and each of the eleven pieces in a set has heat-resistant black plastic handles and knobs. I'm enclosing some manufacturing specs that describe each peice in the set and offer other market data. In all, the eleven-piece set retails for about $49.95 ($79.95 separately). Of course, sets are available to you at our usual 40 to 60 percent factory markdown, depending on quantities ordered.

Bob Willis, one of our salesmen, will be in your area the week of October 10 and will contact you before then to see when it would be convenient to stop by to show you a complete set. I just know you're going to be as impressed as I am with this magnificient cookware. In the meantime, do call if you have any questions.

Best regards,

Different approaches can be used to pave the way for a salesman. For instance, if the customer does not know the salesman, the letter might focus on introducing the person, rather than the product (see model 6.7). In model 12.6 the writer prefers to introduce the new product, and thus the letter is a typical introduction to a product, except that it closes by identifying the representative who will be calling on the customer.

FOLLOW-UP SALES LETTERS

Seldom do first letters or calls by salesmen produce enough sales to justify no further effort. Thus, the follow-up letter is essential in a sales program. Some companies plan a series of letters, assuming it may take as many as four to six contacts before adequate sales result. The follow-up letter should contain the same vital information covered in the initial letter of introduction.

1. Describe again the product or service being offered and again stress its value to the customer.
2. Repeat any special offers or incentives that are available.
3. Provide any additional or new information that may arouse the customer's interest and stimulate action.
4. Leave the door open for still further contact.

Models 12.7 to 12.14 illustrate the variety of sales promotion situations requiring a follow-up letter.

FOLLOWING A SALESMAN'S CALL

12.7. To a Prospective Customer

Dear Mr. Samuels:

Our representative Joe Devonshire sends his thanks along with mine for the time you spent with him last Tuesday. The information you gave him about your operations has been a tremendous help to us in determining how we might be of assistance to your company.

It's true that your bookkeeping and associated record-keeping system is unnecessarily complicated and cumbersome. Naturally, this creates added costs for you in staff time and year-end auditing expenses. If we were to devise a more appropriate system for your particular operation, the savings to you each year could amount to as much as $1,300 in in-house staff time as well as a reduction in auditing costs of at least $300—that's a potential of $1,650 in total annual savings. I'm enclosing a detailed report that explains this possibility more fully.

The most efficient procedure would be for us to implement a new program for you at the time we do your annual audit. The cost of devising and implementing the program at that time would be $950. With the new system your savings in year one alone would cover this cost and perhaps leave as much as $700 to spare.

I'll phone you in a couple weeks, Mr. Samuels, to see if I can add anything to the enclosed proposal. In the meantime, you can reach me at 493-0120 if you have any questions.

                                          Best regards,

Model 12.7 is a follow-up of a representative's call that gets right to the point: it suggests what service the customer needs and the cost of that service. Specific information is presented in an enclosed proposal. However, even this to-the-point type of follow-up leaves the door open for another contact in case the customer still does not agree to the proposal.

AFTER REJECTION OF MERCHANDISE

12.8. Article Returned

Dear Ms. Parsons:

I'm sorry to learn you want to return the TLT auto electric typewriter you were using on a trial basis. Our salesman has said you thought the quality of the type was insufficient for your needs.

Two possibilities occur to me: (1) if you were using a nylon rather than carbon ribbon, the type image would not have been as sharp and clear; and (2) if you require exceptional quality, you would probably be happier with our new TLT-10 model. This machine has all the features of the TLT and more. It is larger, heavier, and is designed for ultra-precision, high-quality type production.

I'm enclosing some literature on the new TLT-10, and I've asked Bob Wilson, our salesman, to phone you next week. I know he will be happy to discuss the advantages of the TLT-10 for your situation and will be glad to leave a machine with you to try for a week.

We sincerely appreciate your interest in our typewriters, Ms. Parsons. Now that we have a better idea of your expectations, I know we can show you exactly the right machine for your needs.

Cordially,

Model 12.8 illustrates a follow-up (after a rejection of merchandise) that does not give up. When a customer rejects a product, companies and their salesmen must quickly look for alternative products or some adjustment that will satisfy the customer. Thus, these follow-ups must present an appealing option immediately, before the customer goes elsewhere and purchases a competitor's product.

AFTER REQUEST FOR MORE INFORMATION

12.9. Interested Customer

Dear Ms. Eisenstadt:

I was very happy to learn that several persons in your department are considering attending our Advanced Photography Workshop in Buffalo on May 19. The 3:45 p.m. session on advanced darkroom technqiues will, indeed, cover the area in which your staff is most interested: creative techniques. These are but a few of the topics that will be discussed:

—Previsualization
—Designing a multiple print
—Exposure and development for each element
—Procedures for printing in new elements
—Posterization, Kodalith masking, and bas relief
—How to add new dimensions to your pictures

The workshop will provide an excellent opportunity for professionals to meet with other professionals. Generally, it will be a day of ultra-intensive training in the most advanced commercial techniques—something too good to miss!

I'm enclosing a dozen copies of our final program, with registration and hotel accommodation forms, for you to distribute among your staff. Since registration is limited to the first 100 enrollments, I would urge you to submit the forms as soon as possible.

Let me know if I can offer any further information, Ms. Eisenstadt. Otherwise, I'll look forward to meeting you and your staff on May 18 in Buffalo.

Cordially,

When a prospect requests information, he or she is obviously interested in the product or service being offered. The response, then, should be prompt, courteous, informative, and appealing.

INVITATION TO USE OTHER PRODUCTS

12.10. Following a Purchase

Dear Mr. Carlton:

Thank you very much for your order for twenty steel shelving units. We sincerely appreciate this opportunity to be of service to you.

The units you selected are our most popular space organizers. I know you'll be pleased with this exceptionally practical and durable shelving. High quality and low cost are features typical of our full line of space-saving storage units. A copy of our latest catalog is enclosed to show you some other products that could help you achieve maximum efficiency in storage the economical way. Notice in particular our pull-drawer storage files, literature trays, high-stack files, and flip-top storage files. These items are all designed to complement the steel shelving units you have chosen.

Please let me know if there is any way I can help you plan a more efficient, convenient, and economical filing and storage system for your business. It would be a pleasure to work with you, Mr. Carlton, and I'm delighted to welcome you as a customer of Modern Business Products, Inc.

Cordially,

Most companies take advantage of one sale to encourage more sales. A customer who has purchased one product is a good candidate for more purchases. Model 12.10 (1) thanks the customer, (2) introduces similar products that might interest the customer, (3) offers to be of help in planning and selecting other products, and (4) welcomes the new customer.

OFFERING ADDITIONAL INFORMATION

12.11. To a Customer

Dear Mrs. Hartley:

Early this month we let you know that LaRue's House of Art had acquired an original collection of hand-crafted colonial figures. Since then we have had numerous inquiries about the figures, especially in regard to the colors represented in the collection. As a discerning collector, I'm certain this aspect is of particular interest to you.

The thirteen sculptures are all hand-painted in full color, just like the native-lands collection you saw on display last month in our showroom. I'm enclosing a color print of the new colonial collection to show you how vivid and realistic the colors are on these superbly crafted figures. As you can see, the combination of nine colors, hand-painted with the finest detail, gives exceptional authenticity to each lifelike colonial sculpture. The collection is truly a remarkable and beautiful treasure.

Since we have only this one original colonial collection, do let me know right away if you would like to have me hold it for you, Mrs. Hartley. In the meantime, if I can offer any additional information, you can reach me at 852-7300, Monday through Saturday.

Cordially,

Follow-ups are often designed to provide additional information with each succeeding contact. Model 12.11, which takes this approach, provides new facts about the product being offered, even though the customer did not ask for the information. Naturally, the additional information must in some way make the product more desirable and thus arouse the customer's interest.

CONTACTING FORMER CUSTOMERS

12.12. To Renew Service

Dear Mr. Atkins:

We haven't heard from you for nearly six months and have missed working with you on your mail campaigns. It was always a pleasure to handle your addressing and mailing needs, and we very much appreciated your business.

I hope nothing serious has happened to discourage you from continuing to use our service. If something has escaped my attention, please do let me know. It has always been our policy to offer the best service possible, and I'm always prepared to take whatever steps are necessary to insure that our customers are fully satisfied. If there's anything we can do to satisfy your needs or help you in any way, Mr. Atkins, I would welcome an opportunity to talk to you about it.

Please do drop me a note or call me at 632-4000 sometime soon. I'd enjoy hearing from you again.

Cordially,

Letters soliciting business from former customers must be written with care. If you are unaware of any previous problem, it obviously would be a mistake to give the impression you gave poor service in the past. That could suggest that poor service is so typical of your company you automatically assume it is the cause of a customer's withdrawal. If you have nothing for which to apologize that you know of, avoid an apologetic tone. Stress your desire to satisfy the customer and try to find out why the customer left, but keep the tone of your letter positive.

REQUESTING REFERRALS

12.13. Regular Customer

Dear Mr. Jenkins:

In this fast-paced world of overcrowded cities and roads we all yearn for a taste of the "good life"—getting away from it all and enjoying the wonders of nature. Some of us—like you—have found a way to enjoy nature year-round without even leaving home. Of course, I'm referring to your recent purchase of our vinyl-paneled greenhouse. Since you're one of our regular customers I know how much you appreciate and enjoy the wonder of beautiful growing and thriving plants, right in your own backyard.

Mason's Greenery has been a leader in the field of indoor-outdoor plant and gardening supplies for more than a decade. We believe our greenhouses are the best available at prices that make them realistic for almost any size income. Moreover, as you know, all our gardening products are backed by guarantees. We also stock a full line of accessories—pots, benches, shelves, plants—for all our greenhouses.

We would like to tell others about the pleasure of year-round gardening in a Mason's greenhouse. If you have friends or relatives who share your enthusiasm for this wonderful hobby, we would like to let them know about our products and service. If you have no objection, just write the names and addresses that come to mind on the enclosed postage-paid card and mail it today. There's a space to indicate whether or not you want to have your name mentioned.

Many thanks for your help and cooperation, Mr. Jenkins. We'll be looking forward to seeing you soon again at Mason's Greenery.

Cordially,

Companies often ask for referrals from customers since this is an excellent means of locating prospects. The letter may or may not offer something in return. Model 12.13 makes no offer, unlike model 12.14, which includes a special incentive if the customer will actually contact friends and relatives.

ASKING CUSTOMER TO JOIN SALES FORCE

12.14 With Special Incentive

Dear Mrs. Lane:

How would you like to earn valuable gifts from McDaniel's Stemware Shop? Since you have been one of our regular customers for more than five years, I know how much you appreciate our lovely glassware. You are certainly well qualified to comment on the quality and beauty of McDaniel's stemware and glass serving sets.

Knowing your familiarity with our products, we were wondering if you would like to become a neighborhood representative of McDaniel's—showing friends, neighbors, and relatives the pieces you already have and others we would provide to you for showings. Sales resulting from these contacts would entitle you to free selections from our stemware and glassware serving sets.

In hopes you will like the idea of earning free gifts in such an easy and enjoyable way—right from your own home—I'm enclosing a booklet describing the procedure for becoming a McDaniel's neighborhood representative. After reading the booklet, all you need to do is sign and mail the enclosed postage-paid card. Your first shipment of items to show will soon be delivered and you can begin earning your free selections of stemware and serving sets right away.

It's been a pleasure to have you as one of our regular customers during the past years, Mrs. Lane, and I hope now we can also count you among our regular neighborhood representatives.

Cordially,

Model 12.14 illustrates a common sales technique: asking customers to show merchandise to friends and relatives in exchange for free gifts. Sometimes the free gifts are offered just in exchange for the names and addresses of friends and relatives.

Part II

MEMOS

13

MEMOS THAT GIVE INFORMATION

Memos traditionally have been regarded as a form of *internal* business communication. In that respect they have been less of a public relations tool than the external letter and more of a management and administrative tool. But the old, familiar patterns of business communication have been changing, and the memo has become prominent in external correspondence as well.

Memos, speed messages, note paper, preprinted forms, and other informal types of communication are familiar sights in the modern business office. To help cope with a massive flood of information, companies are seeking such time-saving devices at every turn. With the trend towards a more casual, friendlier tone in correspondence combined with the need to save time and costs, it is not surprising that the memo is becoming increasingly popular, both in internal and external communication. Not only does the memo usually take less time to set up and type than the formal letter, it also can be prepared on less expensive (sometimes smaller or different-sized) paper than formal letterhead stationery. (See 15.20–15.21 and 19.18–19.20.)

Of course, businesses must still use care in determining when a memo can or should be used in place of a letter. In part the choice is one of intent and format: what impression do you want to make; can the correspondence be informal or must it appear more formal, for example, with an inside address; must it be objective or subjective; and so on? Beyond that, the memo is the preferred in-house vehicle for conveying objective, factual information. Many offices also use this simpler format for certain outside contacts: (1) for routine transactions, for example, processing orders, transmitting material, confirming arrangements and receipts, and making inquiries; and (2) for easy, rapid communication with business friends, long-time customers, and other persons with whom you have developed a casual, friendly working relationship and with whom you must exchange objective, factual information.

Because most memos are objective, the tone is usually more straightforward than that of the letter. But even though facts and information are conveyed in a clear, logical, and concise style in the memo, it should never be used as an excuse to be inconsiderate. It is still a person-to-person contact—an exchange among people—and it can irritate and provoke the recipient just as much as a letter can. Cooperation and good human relations are obviously necessary among co-workers, business friends, and long-time customers as much as anyone else. However, the straightforward style definitely is basic to the memo, and a secretary should find it easy to use the models shown here as guides. Many of these memos will go out under the secretary's signature (e.g., Shipments Overdue). Others may be written by the secretary for the manager (e.g., 13.17, Shipment Delayed). A few will probably be written by the manager, although the secretary may be expected to refine and polish them (e.g., 13.11, Dismissals).

This chapter concentrates on memos that primarily *give* information (chapter 14 deals with those that primarily make a request).

1. Present your facts clearly and objectively, in a logical sequence.
2. Be concise but offer all essential information.
3. Indicate if any response is expected from the recipient.

Ten categories of memos that give information are discussed here, including analytical memos (13.1–13.3), follow-ups and reminders (13.4–13.6), announcements (13.7–13.12), explanations (13.13–13.17), recommendations (13.18–13.20), orders (13.21–13.22), instructions (13.23–13.25), reports (13.26–13.29), confirmations (13.30–13.33), and transmittal memos (13.34–13.37). Notice that although the basic purpose of these memos is to *give* information, many of them also include a *request* for something.

ANALYTICAL MEMOS

The analytical memo evaluates something—a person, product, service, or situation. It reports on the subject objectively, clearly, and concisely. The memo itself may contain all essential facts, or certain data (if lengthy or if in the form of tables, charts, and so on) may be provided in an attachment. (Notice the use of subheads in some instances to increase organizational clarity.) Models 13.1 to 13.3 are examples of typical in-house analytical memos.

EMPLOYEES

13.1. Performance

TO: Melvin Anderson
SUBJECT: Anita Reese—Performance Analysis

Here's the performance evaluation of Anita Reese you requested. Also attached are detailed rating charts concerning her (1) educational background, (2) job skills, and (3) personal characteristics.

EDUCATIONAL BACKGROUND: Ms. Reese is a high school graduate and a graduate of Wilton Secretarial School. She also has completed miscellaneous night courses in bookkeeping, data processing, and business communication.

JOB SKILLS: Ms. Reese has excellent abilities in typing, filing, taking and transcribing dictation, use of office machines, and simple bookkeeping. She has moderate to poor abilities in telephone communication and receptionist duties.

PERSONAL CHARACTERISTICS: Ms. Reese is neat and businesslike in appearance. She is a quiet, industrious, and careful worker, with above-average concern for detail and accuracy. She prefers to work alone and avoid contact with others and is generally ineffective in situations requiring telephone or other personal exchange.

SUMMARY: Ms. Reese is highly proficient in all office skills and duties with the exception of telephone and other personal communication. Therefore, I recommend that she be retained and advanced at appropriate intervals in positions where minimal personal contact is required.

Let me know if you need further information, Mel.

MACHINES

13.2. Performance

TO: Joe Carter
SUBJECT: Mimeograph Machine

The Martell mimeograph machine in Mr. Brownley's office is still functioning erratically. We've had servicemen look at it and adjust it on several occasions without success. As yet no one—here or from Martell—has discovered how to control the inking, with the result that copies have been either too faint or too dark.

Since the guarantee is still in effect I suggest we have the Martell representative pick up the machine immediately and replace it with one that is operating properly. If you agree, please ask the representative to provide another machine for our temporary use if there will be a delay in receiving the replacement.

Thanks very much, Joe.

TESTS—INTERVIEWS

13.3. Results

TO: Kevin Bradley
SUBJECT: Gerald McKinney—Application for Employment

Attached are test scores and the results of my interview with Gerald McKinney who is applying for the position of data-processing training instructor in our department.

BACKGROUND: Age 27, married—two children, B.A. in economics, four years' experience teaching data processing at Seaton Technical Institute.

INTERVIEW: Mr. McKinney was well prepared, organized, and supported his written application with a strong, personal desire to join our organization and progress within it. He demonstrated a good understanding of a company instructor's duties and a thorough knowledge of data processing. His oral presentation was pleasing and effective.

TESTS: Mr. McKinney scored very high on each of our departmental knowledge and skills tests in data processing and instruction.

RECOMMENDATION: Mr. McKinney is a highly qualified candidate for the training-instructor position and should be given serious consideration along with other exceptionally well-qualified applicants. He would be an asset to our organization and every effort should be made to place him in this or another suitable position.

If I can add anything, Kevin, just let me know.

FOLLOW-UPS AND REMINDERS

Many follow-ups and reminders are no more than brief, factual messages. Often in such cases it would be a waste of secretarial time and expensive stationery to type a formal letter. The memo is ideal for these situations, as you can see in models 13.4 to 13.6. (See chapter 4 for models of reminder and follow-up letters.) In certain instances this format can be used for external as well as internal follow-ups (e.g., models 13.5–13.6).

DEADLINE APPROACHING

13.4 For Report

TO: Maxine Arnold
SUBJECT: Customer Survey

Just a reminder that the customer survey report you're preparing is due March 11. I'd appreciate it if you would drop me a note indicating the present status of the project. Thanks, Max.

AWAITING INFORMATION

13.5. Agenda

TO: Donald Fox
SUBJECT: Agenda—Executive Committee Meeting

The executive committee meeting agenda is complete except for your item regarding the research proposal. Any luck yet in getting the information we need? Since the deadline for mailing the agenda is November 5, I'll need the proposal details from you by noon on the 4th—at the latest.

Thanks, Don.

SHIPMENTS OVERDUE

13.6. Office Supplies

TO: Kraus Business Forms, Inc.
SUBJECT: Order for Supplies (P.O. 060112)

On April 9 we ordered from you 5,000 #MACS Management Action Control Sheets (see enclosed copy of our purchase order no. 060112) to be delivered by May 15.

We are in urgent need of the control sheets but the shipment has not yet arrived. Would you please let me know right away whether the shipment has gone out and when you expect it will arrive. If the order has not yet been sent, please handle it on a "rush" basis and let me know the expected delivery date.

Thank you.

ANNOUNCEMENTS

Announcements are prepared in a variety of formats: letters, memos, news releases, bulletins, cards, and brochures. Content and audience will dictate which format to use. For example, an announcement of an open house might be prepared in the format of a formal invitation (see model 15.13); a timely announcement, such as the development of a revolutionary new product, might be sent as a press release (see model 15.27). But many announcements are primarily factual messages for in-house personnel, and the memo format is more appropriate in these instances.

MEETING NOTICES

13.7. Sales Meeting

TO: All Salesmen
SUBJECT: July Meeting

The next sales meeting will be held on Monday, July 12, from 10:00 a.m. until 3:00 p.m., at the Country Motor Lodge, Route 5, in Kingston. Lunch will be provided.

An agenda will be mailed on June 30. If you have any items to be included, they should be forwarded to my secretary by June 29.

I'd appreciate hearing from you right away if you're unable to attend. Thanks very much.

NEW POLICIES-PROCEDURES

13.8 Of Company

TO: Department Managers
SUBJECT: Cafeteria Shifts

Since our work force has been growing, so have the lines in the cafeteria! To solve this annoying problem we have arranged to serve lunch in three specific shifts: 11:30 a.m., 12:00 noon, and 12:30 p.m.

Please arrange within your own department which employees will be assigned to each luncheon shift, giving them a choice to the extent possible. However, to avoid an overload in one of the shifts, please try to assign about the same number of people to each period.

I sincerely appreciate your cooperation in implementing this new procedure. Let's hope we've seen the last of those long and tedious cafeteria lines.

COMPANY EVENTS

13.9. Party

TO: All Employees
SUBJECT: Summer Picnic—August 4

The directors of J. T. Anderson and Company are pleased to announce that our annual summer picnic will be held on Friday, August 4, from 11:00 a.m. until 4:00 p.m., at Maxwell Park.

A picnic lunch will be provided for each employee and his or her guest. After lunch there will be a choice of good conversation or outdoor recreational activities—tennis, softball, swimming, and so on—for everyone, concluding at 4:00 p.m. with a special drawing for a new color TV!

So we can make appropriate luncheon arrangements, please let Ms. Hollis in the Public Relations Department know whether you plan to attend and if you will bring a guest.

We're looking forward to seeing everyone on August 4.

APPOINTMENTS—PROMOTION

13.10. Of Employee

TO: Members of the Art Department
SUBJECT: Assistant Art Director Appointment

It's a pleasure to announce the appointment of Robert Carstairs, Jr., as assistant art director at the Lewis Press. He will fill the position left open by Jerry Kincaid, who recently moved to the East Coast.

Bob, who just completed his seventh year at Lewis Press, is very familiar with all aspects of production in our department, having handled each function—pasteup, stripping, camera, and so on—at some time. His solid background and full understanding of our varied needs and problems make him exceptionally well qualified to handle the challenges that face the assistant director every day.

I know he will welcome your full cooperation and consideration as he assumes his new duties. We all wish him much success.

DISMISSALS

13.11. Of Employee

TO: Members of the Service Department
SUBJECT: Customer Representative Positions

This is to let you know the employment of David Thurston as customer representative at Wright Motors was terminated effective October 1. We hope to announce his replacement by the end of this month.

Our service manager, Bill Grady, may be calling on some of you to serve temporarily as customer representative until we have a replacement. We hope you will give Bill your complete cooperation during this time so our customers will continue to receive full and thoughtful attention without interruption.

Thanks for your help and understanding.

PRICE-RATES

13.12. Increase

TO: Carla Brownell
SUBJECT: Rate Change

As we discussed by phone this morning, please take the necessary steps to show the following new advertising rates for the Daily Marketer:

Ad Size	New Rate (B&W)
One page	$600
Two-thirds page	475
One-half page horiz.	400
One-half page vert.	420
One-third page horiz.	320
One-third page vert.	320
One-sixth page	150
(Color addit.)	(No charge)

As soon as you've had an opportunity to draft a letter of notification to our advertisers and prospects, I'd like to see a copy of it. Also, could you let me know when the new rate cards will be ready?

Thanks very much, Carla

MAKING EXPLANATIONS

Explanations are part of the daily fare in any business office. The letter format is more appropriate in many instances, particularly in external contacts that also involve an apology or that in some way involve sensitive customer relations. But the memo is suitable when the explanation is basically routine and/or factual, as it is in models 13.13 to 13.17. Model 13.17 illustrates use of the memo format in external communication for a routine notice addressed only to "Purchasing Agent."

FOR ACTION

13.13. Of Company

TO: All Supervisors
SUBJECT: TV Monitoring System

We will soon be installing a visual monitoring system in all cautionary work areas at the mill. A pamphlet is enclosed that explains the operation of this new system.

Basically, the system provides twenty-four-hours-a-day visual contact with all work areas where full safety measures are needed. The contact is channelled to each supervisor's work station and to the office of the floor manager. This visual monitoring device will alert us to dangers and potential accidents—before they occur—that we might otherwise miss. So there will be no misunderstanding, I suggest you inform your crew right away that the TV monitoring system is a safety measure intended strictly to provide greater protection for employees in cautionary work areas.

If you have any questions, just let me know. I appreciate your help in letting our employees know about this new safety device.

REASON FOR NEW POLICY-PROCEDURE

13.14. In Office

TO: Administrative and Secretarial Staff
SUBJECT: Time-Work Studies

In the past month we have discovered some instances when a duplication of effort has occurred in this office and other instances when certain duties seemed unnecessarily time consuming and cumbersome. Apparently it is time to review our respective functions to see how our tasks and procedures can be improved.

Attached is a one-week supply of daily time-work analysis forms. For one week I would like to have each of you record on these forms the work you do and the time you spend doing it. Please include everything, from sharpening pencils to typing a report. At the end of the week, if you will return the completed forms to me, I will prepare individual activity summaries. Once we have this type of information we can easily spot the areas where we need to streamline our procedures and eliminate overlap and duplication of effort. To insure that we don't slip back into our old habits and old problems, I would like to repeat this type of analysis periodically, perhaps once every six months or once a year.

I sincerely appreciate your cooperation and am certain that with your help we can soon have our office running smoothly and efficiently.

CAUSE OF A PROBLEM

13. 15. In Scheduling

TO: Dan Polaski
SUBJECT: Gift House Catalog Schedule

The dummy for The Gift House catalog just arrived and your job ticket (no. 6177) says the customer wants to see a proof in two weeks. This presents a problem: we just started a large town report for Pine Hills—also due in two weeks. (Help!)

Ordinarily we could handle both with some overtime, but Roy Parker is on vacation this week and Joyce Kummel is still in the hospital. Since we're short-handed, there's no way we can finish the catalog in two weeks. Unless you can quickly find us some temporary help, we'll have to let The Gift House know it will be at least three weeks before their proof is ready.

Please let me know what you think, Dan. Thanks very much.

NEED FOR COOPERATION

13. 16. Of Employees

TO: All Employees
SUBJECT: Parking Lot Construction

I'm certain you've all noticed the poor condition of our parking lot. As a result of an unusually severe winter the surface is a mass of cracks and holes. Since this is a heavy vacation month and there are fewer cars around, it seems like the ideal time to resurface the entire lot.

We have arranged for repair and resurfacing work to begin on Wednesday, July 6, and conclude on Saturday, July 9. Unfortunately, from Wednesday through Friday it will be necessary to keep all cars out of the lot. Therefore, we will have to park our cars along the street during those three days. Some of you may even want to form car pools to cut down the number of vehicles needing parking spaces along the street.

As much as we all regret the temporary inconvenience, it will be a pleasure to have a much-improved parking lot after the resurfacing is completed. Your cooperation in making this possible will be greatly appreciated.

SHIPMENT DELAYED

13.17. To Customer

TO: Purchasing Agent
SUBJECT: Your Order No. 913—Portable Welders

We are sorry to let you know that the six portable welders you ordered on August 11 are temporarily out of stock. However, they have been back ordered and will be shipped promptly on September 1.

We regret any inconvenience this delay may cause. If there is any way we can be of help in the meantime, please let us know.

RECOMMENDATIONS

Certain recommendations are essentially in-house minireports or miniproposals. These recommendations, when they are primarily factual and objective, are particularly well suited for the memo format. Models 13.18 to 13.20 are examples of such communication.

PROPOSALS

13.18. For New Department

TO: John Norris
SUBJECT: Proposed Public Relations Department

Here are the preliminary recommendations I promised concerning the proposed Public Relations Department.

OBJECTIVE: To handle our public relations activities more effectively by collecting them in one office and having the same person be responsible for them at all times. At present, PR duties are scattered from office to office. There is too much overlap and inefficiency in collecting and generating information. Moreover, the PR function suffers since now it is always an extracurricular activity for everyone and thus is frequently neglected. The time each of us would save by moving these functions out of our own offices would more than pay for the services of one productive PR person.

ACTIVITIES: The major functions that should be transferred to this new office are:

1. Media contact (press releases, ads, press conferences)
2. Newsletter production (quarterly company bulletin)
3. Customer relations (complaints, special programs)
4. Survey supervision (assisting marketing and sales)
5. Research (miscellaneous fact finding)
6. Audiovisual supervision (assisting other departments)

There might be other activities we would want to add to this list later, but the above six points could be considered the basis for a job definition.

PERSONNEL: The reports I've received show that one person could handle the PR work, using our typing pool for support. This person could be selected from within our company (preferable in terms of knowing our operations) or brought in from the outside (might find someone with a better PR background). We should discuss this aspect with the personnel director.

CONCLUSION: We could greatly improve our public relations if we established a separate Public Relations Department. Functions now handled haphazardly in various offices would be centralized in the new PR office, thereby insuring greater efficiency and effectiveness.

Let me know if you would like to pursue this idea, John. I'll be glad to provide further details and discuss it all at your convenience.

RECOMMENDATIONS FOR CHANGE

13.19. In Methods

TO: Lois Van Dyke
SUBJECT: Supplies Control

I would like to suggest another method for maintaining and replenishing supplies in the storage closet. At present there are three of us on this floor who remove supplies at random, which often results in unexpected depletion of some supplies and the constant need to replenish them on a rush basis.

To introduce some sort of warning system, I recommend that supplies be stacked from front to back on shelves so the total number of any item on hand can be written boldly on the front package. Each person who removes any of them should cross out that number and write the current remaining number on the front package.

To further help us, we should establish for each item the point at which it is time to reorder and leave a typed list showing this in the storage closet. Each person who removes anything should check the remaining number of the item on hand with the reorder number on the list. For instance, perhaps after someone removes 1,000 letterhead there are 5,000 left and the typed list shows we should reorder when the supply is down to 5,000. That person then should immediately notify you that it is time to reorder stationery.

The control I'm suggesting should eliminate at least a large part of our problem of unexpected depletions. If you would like to try this method, I'll be glad to set it up and get us started. Just let me know.

TO SOLVE A PROBLEM

13.20. In Office

TO: Jack Webster
SUBJECT: Improving the Reception Area

Janice and I have been discussing a persistent problem in the reception area. Although the function of greeting visitors has been assigned to Janice, the reception room doesn't have a wall space near the door where her desk can be placed. Thus both Janice and I have our desks close together towards the back of the room. The result is that visitors sometimes walk directly to my desk, before Janice can get their attention. This means I have many unnecessary interruptions each day, which sometimes makes it difficult to accomplish anything.

Since the reception room isn't suitable for repositioning our desks, we want to recommend another solution: have a sign made for Janice's desk (or near it) that says "Receptionist" or "Information." It should be large enough for a visitor to spot instantly upon entering the room but not so large or awkward that it takes up important work space.

Please let us know if we may follow through with this idea. Thanks.

PROCESSING ORDERS

Orders are processed in many ways, often, when substantial numbers are involved, with special forms: requisitions, purchase orders, confirmation forms, and so on (See 15.24–15.25.) When very few orders are processed in an office, and special forms are not used, the letter (see chapter 2) or memo format is typical. Many routine orders can be processed easily and rapidly by using the memo format, as shown in models 13.21 and 13.22.

PLACING ORDERS

13.21. For Supplies

TO: Office Accessories, Inc.
SUBJECT: Order for Name Plates

Please send us the following name plates, to be billed to Dempsy Products, 113 Church Street, Marlborough, Massachusetts 01752:

One (1) #JAR-MT, 2″ × 8″ clear acrylic name plate, $8.50, for BEN RANDALL

One (1) #XTP-JV, 2″ × 8″ self-adhesive walnut acrylic door plate, $6.95, for BEN RANDALL.

One (1) #ROC-LN, 1″ × 3″ black acrylic name tag with white lettering, $2.50, for BEN RANDALL, BUSINESS MANAGER

These items should be sent to the attention of Susan Wyatt, Room 410, at Dempsy Products. Thank you.

CHANGING ORDERS

13.22. For Service

TO: Venus Office Machines
SUBJECT: Maintenance Contract 0710943-66

We would like to change the maintenance arrangement for our model 8 Venus copier from a one-year to a three-year contract. We understand there is no reduction in the annual charge with a longer term contract but that we are protected against servicing price increases during this time.

Please send an invoice for the additional two-year period to Mason Travel Service, 911 24th Street, Chicago, Illinois 60609. Thank you.

PROVIDING INSTRUCTIONS

Instructions represent another category of communication appropriate for the memo format. Many instructions, particuarly if they are in-house communications, are primarily brief, factual messages that do not require a formal letter. Models 13.23 to 13.25 are examples of memos that provide instructions (13.24 and 13.25 are external communications).

INSTRUCTING EMPLOYEES

13.23. About New Procedure

TO: Shipping Clerks
SUBJECT: Gift Enclosures

From November 1 through January 31 the following free gifts are to be enclosed with each customer's purchase:

Orders up to $10—Small memo calendar
Orders $10–$25—Large wall calendar
Orders over $25—Pocket calendar in vinyl wallet

Calendars, which are already wrapped, should be packaged carefully with the customers' orders so they will not be bent, crushed, or otherwise damaged during shipment. Our shipping supervisor, Joe Nichols, recommends placing the calendars at the bottom of each box with protective cardboard positioned on top of the calendar before other items are enclosed.

If you have any questions or problems with the gift calendars, please contact Joe Nichols in the Shipping Department right away. Thank you.

OPERATING INSTRUCTIONS

13.24. For Copier

TO: Balsam Insurance Agency
SUBJECT: Model 750 Spectrum Copier Operating Instructions

The model 750 Spectrum copier is particularly easy to operate. If you follow the simple instructions for operation and maintenance provided in the enclosed booklet you will enjoy many years of trouble-free copying. There are no messy chemicals to worry about—a simple dusting every so often is all that is required. Briefly, these are the steps to follow in making quality copies:

1. Turn the ON-OFF switch to ON and let the machine warm up.

2. Place a sheet of transparent copy paper, glossy side up, on top of the original to be copied.
3. Lay the two pieces on the exposure plate, with the transparent sheet next to the plate. Close the lid.
4. Set the exposure knob at number 6 (you may want to try several settings to find the one you prefer) and press the knob.
5. After the light goes off place the transparent sheet, glossy side up, on the clear side of the white copy paper.
6. Insert the two sheets into the feeder slot and wait for your copy to come out. Discard the transparent sheet upon removal.
7. Turn the ON-OFF switch to OFF.

That's all there is to it—a fast and easy process that produces copies of amazing clarity. Should you have any questions, however, please do let us know. We appreciate having you as a customer and want to be certain you are receiving the best results possible with your new Spectrum copier.

FOR MEETING LOCATION

13.25. Out of Town

TO: Members of the Conference Planning Committee
SUBJECT: February 12 Meeting Location

The 10:00 a.m. February 12 meeting of the Conference Planning Committee will be held in suite 101 at the Willowbrook Inn on Route 17. An agenda with full meeting details is enclosed.

The Willowbrook is a new facility about two miles west of town. If you are not familiar with its location, I suggest you follow these directions from the downtown area.

1. Pick up interstate 76 south off Branson parkway or off north 83rd Street.
2. Follow 76 south to the Route 11 exit about 3 miles from center city.
3. Take Route 11 west one-half mile and turn right onto Route 17 north. The Willowbrook is a quarter mile down the road on the left.

If you have any questions, please call my secretary at 202-1117 (I'll be away until February 9).

REPORTS

To many persons reports and memos are synonymous. They are not always the same thing, of course, although many reports—both internal and external—are presented in the memo format. Models 13.26 to 13.29 are examples of the short, informal memo report.

THE SHORT, INFORMAL REPORT

13.26. Status Report

TO: Wendall Morris
SUBJECT: Davis Reclamation Project Status Report

We have nearly reached the midway point in our reclamation project at Wintergreen Acres. The following steps have been completed:

Step 1: Surveying
Step 2: Removal of dead trees and underbrush
Step 3: Drainage of pond and associated swampland
Step 4: Burning off of remaining dead growth (anything presenting a fire hazard)

The following steps have been approved and funded and will be undertaken during August and September:

Step 5: Clearing four-acre site for the Wintergreen cottages
Step 6: Resoding public lawn area (2.5 acres)
Step 7: Planting fringe and park trees and shrubs

Our estimated completion date is September 25. No cost variations from our original estimate are evident at this time.

The next status report will be sent to you on August 15. In the meantime, if you have any questions just let me know.

TRANSMITTAL MEMO WITH FORMAL REPORT

13.27. To All Departments

TO: Department Managers
SUBJECT: Quarterly Report

A copy of our report on sales activity during the first quarter of this year is enclosed for your review. I would like to call your attention to two items that will be discussed at the next meeting of all departmental heads:

1. Although the figure for quantities of machines shipped shows an increase during this period over the previous quarter, there was actually a substantial decline in shipments compared with this same period last year (see page 7 of the report).
2. The closing of our Houston operation has created a serious bottleneck at our Kansas City plant (see page 11 of the report).

You will have an opportunity to comment on these problems and other matters in the report at the next meeting. Until then, I'll be glad to hear from you if you have any questions.

CREDIT REPORTS

13.28. On Customers

TO: Credit Department
SUBJECT: Credit Report—Pellitier Studios

Our records show that Pellitier Studios has an excellent credit standing with our company. They have maintained an account with us since 1975, with purchases averaging $350 monthly.

Our experience suggests you would be justified in extending a reasonable amount of credit to Pellitier Studios.

If I can offer any further information, do let me know.

INFORMAL MEETING NOTES

13.29. On Committee Meeting

TO: Warren Ricotti
SUBJECT: Publicity Committee—December Meeting

While waiting for the official minutes of the December 5 Publicity Committee meeting, you may want to review the key points we covered.

1. Miles Bradstreet will resign as chairman, effective February 1. We should elect a new chairman at the January 14 meeting.
2. Publicity for the Lawrenceville Arts and Crafts Festival on March 19 is underway. First press release was mailed December 7.
3. A copy of next year's budget will be mailed with the December meeting minutes. Discussion and approval to be on the January meeting agenda.

4. Tom Wilson proposed that we hold open house in July this year instead of June to take advantage of the heavier tourist traffic. Discussion slated for the January meeting.

After we receive the official minutes I'll contact you to discuss some of these matters before the January meeting. If you have any questions before then, Warren, just give me a call.

SENDING CONFIRMATIONS

Confirmations of routine matters—scheduled meetings, receipts, and so on—can frequently be prepared in memo format. If numerous notices with the same general information must be sent (e.g., confirming meeting registrations), the confirmations may even be prepared as preprinted forms, with only the pertinent facts filled in individually for each recipient. In any case, the confirmation must provide all necessary data, clearly and accurately, and it must be sent in time for the recipient to act or respond as required.

MEETING DETAILS

13.30. Staff Meeting

TO: All Staff Members
SUBJECT: April 4 Staff Meeting

This will confirm that the next staff meeting will be held on Thursday, April 4, at 9:30 a.m., in Mr. Cramer's office. Please let me know right away if you will be unable to attend.

Thanks very much.

CONFERENCE REGISTRATIONS

13.31. Annual Conference

TO: Marlene Singleton
SUBJECT: Conservationist Society Annual Conference

We are happy to confirm your preliminary registration for the Fourth Annual Conference of the Conservationist Society, May 14–15, at the Civic Center in Provo, Utah.

To complete your registration, a conference fee of $65 is payable by May 1. (Please make your check payable to the Conservationist Society and mail it to the society's offices at 114 Pine Grove, Logan, Utah 84322.)

Thank you.

INFORMATION—PAYMENTS RECEIVED

13.32. For Conference Proceedings

TO: Paul Fryatt
SUBJECT: Second Proceedings

We have received your check for $17.95 for one copy of our Second Annual Conference Proceedings: THE NEW MEDICAL FRONTIERS. Thank you very much.

As you requested, rather than mail the book to you, Mr. Adams will personally take it along to your meeting with him on Saturday evening, August 17.

ORDERS RECEIVED

13.33. For Survey Details

TO: Betty McKinsey
SUBJECT: Membership Survey

Thank you for your order for a copy of our recent membership survey report. There has been a slight delay in production, but the reports will be ready in two weeks and your copy will be sent promptly at that time.

TRANSMITTAL MEMOS

Transmittal correspondence is often a very simple type of communication: brief, factual, and straightforward. Thus the memo format is ideal for many transmittal communications and models 13.34 to 13.37 are examples of the type of transmittal correspondence suitable for the memo format.

COMPANY LITERATURE

13.34. To Prospective Customers

TO: Monte Evans
SUBJECT: Sartwell's Custom Lab Service

Here is the literature you requested on the Sartwell Company and our Custom Lab Service. The enclosed brochure explains in detail our various techniques and procedures for placing orders.

We very much appreciate your interest and hope you will let us know if we can be of service.

COMPANY PRODUCTS

13.35. To Customer

TO: David Lewis
SUBJECT: Century 2000 Gas Welder

Here, hot off the press, are the new specs on our Century 2000 Gas Welder. I'll have more details on the welder when I see you next week, Dave.

FOR MATERIAL-INFORMATION REQUESTED

13.36. Company Department

TO: Diane Warnecki
SUBJECT: Masking Film

Enclosed are four rolls of .003″ Rubylith film you ordered for your Art Department.

We also have the .003″ Amberlith film you asked about in pads of ten sheets each: 8½ × 11 ($10/pad) and 11 × 14 ($16.50/pad).

If we can be of further help, please do let us know. We appreciate your interest in our products.

REMITTANCES

13.37. For Book Sales

TO: Creighton's Book Store
SUBJECT: Book Order

Enclosed is our check for $34.90 along with a completed book sale order form. Please note that if any of the books are not available, we would appreciate receiving an immediate refund rather than credit on future purchases.

Thank you.

14

MEMOS THAT MAKE A REQUEST

Like the memo that *gives* information (see chapter 13), the memo that *requests* something has traditionally been used primarily in internal business communication. But now it is being used more and more for external contacts as well. In both internal and external correspondence the memo format is often ideal for rapid communication that is basically factual and objective. In many offices the memo is also used as an economy measure since it usually takes less time to set up and type than a formal letter and can be prepared on less expensive paper than formal letterhead stationery (see 15.20 and 19.18–19.20).

Memos that request something, like those that give information, follow a specific pattern. They are usually factual and concise, written with a straightforward, objective style and tone. This pattern will make it easy for you to follow the examples given in this chapter. Many of the memos shown here can be written and sent under the secretary's name (e.g., 14.4, Planning a Company Event). Others may be sent by the manager but the secretary will likely write them (e.g., 14.7, To Determine Interest). Occasionally the manager may prefer to draft the memo (e.g., 14.29, Budget Approval) but will expect his or her secretary to polish and refine it. (See chapter 1 for requests handled by letter and consult the Selector Guide for models of other requests throughout the book.)

Memos often differ from letters in their tendency to be more objective than subjective. Nevertheless, all requests, whether made by memo or letter, should be specific and clear.

1. Tell what you want (possibly why you want it).
2. Explain what action you want the reader to take.
3. Specify all pertinent facts, such as time, place, price, delivery.
4. Express appreciation if a favor or special effort is required.

Thirty-three models are illustrated in the following nine categories of memos that make a request: asking for help (14.1–14.5); conducting surveys (14.6–14.8); follow-up inquiries (14.9–14.12); information for reports (14.13–14.16); personal information (14.17–14.20); product-service information (14.21–14.28); requesting action (14.29–14.30); and soliciting contributions (14.31–14.33). Although the basic purpose of these memos is to *ask* for something, they may, in the process, also *give* information.

ASKING FOR HELP

Examples of assistance needed in a business office are endless, but all situations share common features. The right person must be contacted, the need for help must be explained, and pertinent details—when, where, and so on—must be given. Many requests of this type are essentially factual, straightforward messages, which means they can be conveyed by memo. Models 14.1 to 14.5 illustrate the types of requests for help that are suitable for the memo format.

TEMPORARY OFFICE ASSISTANCE

14.1. For Secretary

TO: Joan Flowers
SUBJECT: Temporary Clerical Help

I'm in need of temporary clerical assistance for my secretary, Margie Woodward. Since we're in the midst of our annual sales campaign, Margie's work load has increased substantially, and her usual duties are suffering as a result.

I'd like to have someone from the typing pool or from the mail department assist us during the next two weeks—through Friday, May 5. Our principal needs are (1) typing envelopes and (2) folding inserts and stuffing and sealing envelopes.

Anything you can do to help will be much appreciated, Joan. Thanks very much.

SPECIAL WORK PROJECTS

14.2. For Department

TO: Scott Aldrich
SUBJECT: List Conversion

Would it be possible for your assistant, Bob Watts, to spend a couple of days next week helping us check over the Public Relations Department's mailing list?

We're converting the list from metal plates to computer and want to go through the Southwest section, which hasn't been checked for at least five years. Since Bob is more familiar with the names in this section than anyone in our department, it would be helpful if he could assist us in selecting rejects.

Please give me a call if you can spare him on Monday and Tuesday next week. I'd really appreciate it, Scott. Thanks very much.

PERMANENT COMMITTEES

14.3. For Club

TO: Rita Farnsworth
SUBJECT: Business Women's Club Entertainment Committee

Our Entertainment Committee co-chairman recently informed me that her committee lost two members and is in need of assistance to complete the entertainment plans for our August and October dinner meetings and for our December Christmas party. Since all of the regular programs seem to be fairly well established and some of your Program Committee members will be without assignments most of the year, I was wondering if anyone on your committee could transfer to the Entertainment Committee on a permanent basis.

If this sounds feasible to you, I'd appreciate it if you would let me know right away. Thanks very much, Rita.

PLANNING A COMPANY EVENT

14.4. Picnic

TO: Ben Byse
SUBJECT: August 11 Company Picnic—Transportation

Our office is in charge of plahning for the company picnic on August 11, so I'm contacting a number of persons who might be able to help us with arrangements. Since you're in charge of the motor pool, I was wondering if you could make arrangements for transportation from the company to Carnegie Lake and back again on the day of the picnic.

Basically, what we will need are enough cars and drivers for about fifty employees and guests. The cars should leave from the motor pool entrance at noon and return from the Carnegie Lodge entrance at four o'clock.

I'd very much appreciate your help in making these arrangements. Please let me know right away if we can count on you for our transportation needs on August 11. Thanks, Ben.

TO SOLVE A PROBLEM

14.5. In Meeting a Deadline

TO: Nancy Almond
SUBJECT: Management Newsletter

Would you be able to submit your marketing report for our April issue of MANAGEMENT NEWS one week early this month—by Friday, March 23? Since I'll be away during the regularly scheduled week of production, I'll have to give all copy to the printer in advance to meet our deadline.

Let me know if you can manage an early report. Your help will be greatly appreciated. Thanks very much, Nancy.

CONDUCTING SURVEYS

The memo format is often ideal for conducting surveys. Sometimes the questions to be asked can be incorporated into the body of the memo; at other times it is more practical to use the memo for transmittal information and enclose a separate questionnaire. Models 14.6 to 14.8 show different ways the memo can be used in surveys.

TO ESTIMATE ATTENDANCE

14.6. At Meeting

TO: Members of the Community Service Association
SUBJECT: Annual Meeting

The Program Committee is making arrangements for the October 15 annual meeting of the Community Service Association at the Lakeville Civic Center. (A program was sent to you earlier this month.) To help us make adequate room and luncheon reservations, we would appreciate knowing whether you plan to attend this meeting.

For your convenience, space is provided below for you to indicate your intention. Please return this memo in the enclosed postage-paid envelope by September 5. Thank you.

( ) Yes, I will attend.   ( ) No, I will be unable to attend.

_____
Signature

TO DETERMINE INTEREST

14.7. In Seminar

TO: Joan Ricardo
SUBJECT: Recruitment Seminar

A bulletin is enclosed describing a one-day recruitment seminar for admissions personnel. The program is scheduled for April 9 at the Holiday Inn in Dumont.

I'd appreciate knowing whether you believe any of the Admissions Office personnel should attend this seminar. If you think it would be worthwhile, Joan, let me know and we can discuss arrangements for registrations and transportation.

TO UPDATE RECORDS

14.8. Personnel Data

TO: Department Heads
SUBJECT: Personnel Records

Periodically we need to review and update our personnel records at the Oxford Company so they are as current and accurate as possible. Nonconfidential information (e.g., marriages, prizes, and so on) is used by our publicity department in preparing news releases and by our executive board in selecting recipients for special recognition and commendation.

I'm enclosing a supply of one-page questionnaries to be completed by all employees in your department. (If you need more forms, let me know.) I'd appreciate it if you would distribute and collect these forms and return them to me by January 1.

Thanks very much for your help and cooperation.

FOLLOW-UP INQUIRIES

Although the letter format is often used for follow-ups (see chapter 4), there are many occasions when follow-up inquiries can be made by memo. Some of these inquiries are routine follow-ups concerning factual data about shipments, appointments, and so on. Models 14.9 to 14.12 are examples of follow-up inquiries prepared in the memo format.

FOR MEETING DETAILS

14.9. About the Agenda

TO: Dave Montgomery
SUBJECT: Executive Committee Meeting Agenda

The agenda for our June 4 executive committee meeting is almost ready. All I need are final details from you on the construction plans. Have you had an opportunity to confirm the Fraser Construction bid we discussed last week?

I'd appreciate it if you would let me know by Friday whether the bid is firm. Thanks, Dave.

DATE OF SHIPMENT

14.10. Of Order

TO: All-Season Greenery
SUBJECT: Order 06102

On March 11 we placed an order for eleven large floor plants to be shipped from your greenhouse to Martek Engineering at 421 North Fordham Street in Brockton. A copy of our order number 06102 is enclosed.

Would you please let us know the date of shipment and anticipated delivery date to our offices? We are expecting out-of-town clients to arrive on April 17 and want to be certain the plants will be here before that date.

Thank you.

ABOUT APPOINTMENT

14.11. Tentative Date

TO: Harold Crosby
SUBJECT: Building Inspection

I was wondering if you're in a position yet to confirm our tentative date to inspect the vacant building at 11 Waterfront Avenue next week. There's a note on my calendar to meet you on-site at 3 o'clock on October 5.

I'd appreciate a call as soon as you know if you can make it. Thanks very much, Hal.

FOR FURTHER INFORMATION

14.12. On Product

TO: Art Supplies, Inc.
SUBJECT: Drafting Tables

Thank you for sending a copy of your general catalog. The equipment section shows four light tables, each available in three sizes. We are particularly interested in one of the large floor models, number 1250, and would like to receive more information about this table.

Please send full specifications and an order form to Jarred Phillips, Manager, Burr and Hodges, Communications Consultants, Highway 51, Columbia, Missouri 65201. Thank you.

INFORMATION FOR REPORTS

Reports are based on information that often must be collected from various sources. The written request for this information can be handled in a number of ways: letter, form, or memo. Routine communications soliciting information are frequently well suited for the memo format, as models 14.13 to 14.16 illustrate.

GENERAL GUIDANCE-INFORMATION

14.13. From Research Department

TO: Margaret Eddington
SUBJECT: Report—Use of Plastics in Appliance Manufacture

Mr. Steinberg is preparing a report on the use of plastics in the manufacture of household appliances. He was wondering if your department has compiled any information in this area that might be helpful.

Specifically, Mr. Steinberg is concerned with the effect of plastics on life expectancy of appliances. For instance, many vacuum cleaner manufacturers are now using more plastic and less metal in their products—how has this reduced life expectancy or otherwise contributed to replacement and repair needs?

I know Mr. Steinberg would greatly appreciate any information you have on the use of plastics in appliance manufacture. Thank you very much for your help.

STATISTICAL INFORMATION

14.14. From Accounting Department

TO: Shaun Fenton
SUBJECT: Payroll Data for Report

Ms. Damione is preparing a five-year review of staff salaries for the general manager and would like to know if you have payroll data that would be pertinent to her study. She will be looking for general patterns in salary changes and specific patterns related to job level.

Would you please let Ms. Damione know sometime next week whether you have payroll data she might find helpful. Thank you very much.

PERMISSION TO QUOTE—EXTRACT

14.15. From Publisher

TO: Permissions Editor
SUBJECT: Permission to Use Material from Computer Studies

We are preparing an article for the August issue of our association newsletter Computer Briefs. May we have your permission to include the description of "debugging" on page 411 of Computer Studies, by Mark Cromwell (1978)? A photocopy of the section we would like to use is enclosed.

For your convenience a form is provided below to grant your permission and to indicate your preferred credit line.

Your consent will be greatly appreciated. Thank you very much.

CREDIT LINE: _____

_____

I (we) grant permission for the use requested above.

_____   _____
Signature   Date

CREDIT INFORMATION

14.16. On Distributor

TO: Credit Department
SUBJECT: References for Smith and Harris, Inc.

Smith and Harris, Inc., a local distributor of automotive parts and accessories, has filed a request with us to purchase goods on account at our usual terms. According to their application you have extended credit to them on previous occasions.

We would appreciate knowing something about your experience with Smith and Harris. Your comments, of course, will be held in the strictest confidence.

Thank you very much.

PERSONAL INFORMATION

Businesses frequently use personal as well as professional information about employees in preparing publicity releases, in evaluating candidates for awards and promotions, and in making suitable work assignments. Such information could be collected by letter, form, or memo. Since this type of request is essentially factual and objective, the memo is often appropriate. Sometimes it serves primarily as a transmittal communication, with the information request prepared as an attachment such as a questionnaire form. Models 14.17 to 14.20 show how personal information is requested in the memo format.

FOR A NEWS RELEASE

14.17. About Branch Manager

TO: Stephen Libby
SUBJECT: Data for News Release

We're preparing a release on your upcoming transfer to our Denver office. To be certain we have our facts correct, I'd appreciate it if you would complete the attached personal data sheet and return it to me by November 1.

Thanks very much, Steve.

FOR COMPANY RECORDS

14.18. For Public Relations Office

TO: Charles Wright
SUBJECT: Executive Data File

We're updating our executive data files and would appreciate your help in bringing our records up to date. These files are used by our writers in preparing press releases and newsletter announcements that concern company executives.

To simplify matters, I'm enclosing your complete file for you to review, along with a new data sheet for you to complete. If you spot anything in the file that's out of date, please replace it and destroy the dated item. For instance, should the photographs of you be replaced with something more current?

I'd like to have the updated file back by December 1. In the meantime, if you have any questions just let me know. Thanks very much for your help and cooperation, Mr. Wright.

TO MAKE WORK-COMMITTEE ASSIGNMENTS

14.19. To Staff

TO: Donna Margolis
SUBJECT: Committee Staff Assignments

I'm enclosing a list of newly elected chairmen for our budget, social relations, and training resources committees. These chairmen will soon be calling on us to provide staff assistance during the coming year.

Last year we provided assistance on a random basis—whoever was free at the time a task was presented. This year I would like to try a more organized approach. Let's select six persons from our staff in advance, two for each committee. The same individuals, then will assist the same committee throughout the year. This consistency and their growing familiarity with the work and the committee's needs should make everyone's job easier.

To help me make appropriate assignments, I'd appreciate it if you would have each person in our office complete the enclosed biographical fact sheets. Any recommendations you have will also be welcome. As soon as I have the assignments ready, I'll forward the information to you.

If you have any questions, Donna, let me know. Many thanks for your help.

FOR EMPLOYEE RECOGNITION

14.20. Awards Night

TO: Sam Sorensen
SUBJECT: Personal Data for Awards Introduction

Mr. Barkley is preparing his presentation speech for the award you are to receive on June 11 and would like to have some more background information about you. Would you please complete the enclosed biographical data sheet and return it to Mr. Barkley by June 5.

Thank you very much.

PRODUCT-SERVICE INFORMATION

Most requests for information about products and services are factual, objective communications—hence ideal for the memo format. Such requests may involve external as well as internal communication as shown in models 14.21 to 14.24. Frequently these requests are just directed to the company rather than to a specific individual, or they may be addressed to a department such as the Service Department or Sales Department.

INQUIRIES ABOUT SERVICE

14.21. For Pickup and Delivery

TO: Rossetti's Uniform Pressing and Cleaning Service
SUBJECT: Schedule and Rates

A recent newspaper advertisement indicates you are now providing pickup and delivery service in East Lansing. Please send us a schedule of rates with hours and days when you would be able to pick up and deliver fifty uniforms at Jones Tool and Die Works, 1450 Juniper Lane, in East Lansing.

Thank you.

INQUIRIES ABOUT EQUIPMENT

14.22. For Maintenance

TO: Bromley's Office Equipment Center
SUBJECT: Maintenance Contract for Dictating Equipment

Several months ago we purchased three Starlite model 50 dictation and transcription units from you. Now that the warrenties have expired we would like to have the units covered by a maintenance service agreement. Please have one of your representatives call on us within the next couple weeks or send us full details on your contracts by mail.

Thank you.

PRICE AND DELIVERY DETAILS

14.23. On Office Equipment

TO: Major Office Suppliers, Inc.
SUBJECT: Paper Shredders

Please send us information, including price, warranty, and delivery details, on your paper shredders. We are primarily interested in models that will adjust to fit any standard wastebasket with automatic start and stop features.

Thank you.

FOR FURTHER INFORMATION

14.24. On New Equipment

TO: The Complete Entertainment Center
SUBJECT: Computerized TV Converter

Thank you for sending a brochure describing your new minicomputer TV converter with snap-in cartridges. Since we would be interested in a number of these units, we were wondering if multiple TV adaptors are available for plug-in operation on several sets.

Any further information you can provide on multiple use will be very much appreciated. Thank you.

REQUEST FOR LITERATURE

Businesses and other organizations must constantly request literature of all sorts—product and service brochures, reports, travel information, educational literature, and so on. Such material is frequently requested by letter, but the routine literature request is also suitable for the memo format. Models 14.25 to 14.28 illustrate several types of brief, straightforward requests for literature that can be made by memo.

PRODUCT BROCHURES

14.25. For Manager

TO: The Pro Camera Shop
SUBJECT: Sound-Zoom Movie Outfit

Please send a brochure on your new AL 160 zoom movie camera, mike, and projector outift to David Collins, Manager, Hartz Custom Studios, P.O. Box 100, Dallas, Texas 75221. Thank you.

REPORTS AND STUDIES

14.26. For the Library

TO: The Wheeler Technical Institute
SUBJECT: Index to Reports and Studies

Please send an index to your reports and studies, along with a current price list and order form, to the attention of Ms. Marlene Baker, Librarian.

Thank you.

MEETING NOTES

14.27. For Files

TO: Joe Cossetti
SUBJECT: March 9 Executive Committee Meeting Notes

Since the minutes of our March 9 meeting won't be available for several weeks, I'd appreciate having a copy of your meeting notes for our files. Thanks, Joe.

TRAVEL LITERATURE

14.28. For Upcoming Trip

TO: Sue Johnston
SUBJECT: Information for Trip to England

Mrs. Hoffman would like to arrange a trip to England—leaving New York September 1 and returning September 22—and would like to see some literature on two- and three-day excursions from her base in London. She will attend meetings in London on September 5, 12, and 16 but would like to travel and sightsee the rest of the time.

Any descriptive literature you have on sightseeing opportunities suitable for her schedule will be very much appreciated.

Thanks very much, Sue.

REQUESTING ACTION

Communications that ask someone to take action are often sent by letter (see chapter 1) but in certain instances are also suitable for the memo format. If the request is basically objective and factual and does not involve subjective discussion or persuasion, the memo is often preferable. Models 14.29 to 14.30 depict this type of action request.

BUDGET APPROVAL

14.29. For Department

TO: Jim Stockton
SUBJECT: Approval of Advertising Department Budget

I'm enclosing a copy of our proposed departmental budget for the coming fiscal year. The figures are essentially those you gave me with only three minor refinements, which I've marked in red. If you'll OK the budget, I'll submit it to the Finance Committee right away.

Thanks very much, Mr. Stockton.

CHANGE IN PROCEDURE

14.30. For Staff

TO: Training Department Staff
SUBJECT: Supplies

To help the Supply Office streamline its operations, the training director has asked us to employ better control measures in ordering supplies for our department. The procedure has been for each person to go to the Supply Office independently and select whatever he or she needs at the time. The new procedure, effective immediately, will be for each person to fill out a requisition form in my office, which the director will initial, and then take this form to the Supply Office.

I know the director will appreciate your help and cooperation in improving our procedure in this area. Thanks very much.

SOLICITING CONTRIBUTIONS

Many organizations have a standard procedure for collecting contributions to charities or for special events. Depending on the size of the organization and the number of people to reach, the procedure may involve personal contact or some type of mailing. Sometimes envelopes are circulated with printed instructions, and sometimes letters or memos accompany the envelopes. Models 14.31 to 14.33 are examples of several types of solicitations that could be handled by memo.

COMPANY PICNIC DONATIONS

14.31. From All Employees

TO: All Employees
SUBJECT: Company Picnic Contributions for Orphans

This year Harris Manufacturing Company will entertain children from the Pine Grove Orphanage at its August 14 company picnic in Kennedy Park. The company will provide transportation and lunch for all children plus admission to the entertainment facilities at the park.

Many of us at Harris want to do one other thing—have a grabbag of gifts so each child will receive one small present. The Personnel Office has volunteered to select the gifts and make arrangements for the grabbag distribution. It is up to us now to contribute generously to a fund to support this effort.

Please place your donation in the enclosed envelope and return it to the Personnel Office by August 1. Thank you very much for helping to make this worthwhile effort possible.

EMPLOYEE RECOGNITION FUND

14.32. From Department Staff

TO: Staff Members
SUBJECT: Employee Recognition Fund

Two years ago by unanimous agreement we established an Employee Recognition Fund to finance an annual award to the employee who made the greatest contribution to successful departmental operations during the year. Once again it is time to honor one of our staff at the annual departmental banquet on December 13.

The fund, as you know, is supported by our own donations. Therefore I'm enclosing an envelope for you to use this year in making the contribution of your choice. Please return the envelope to me by November 15.

Thanks very much for your continuing support and generosity.

FOR CHARITABLE ORGANIZATIONS

14.33. From Business Associate

TO: Bill Jamison
SUBJECT: Annual Charity Drive

I've been asked by the United Community Drive to encourage the support of executives in our company this year for this worthwhile cause.

Funds collected by the United Community Drive go to all needy organizations in our community. Donations, of course, may be earmarked for a particular need such as the Lowrey Home for Underprivileged Children or the new Cancer Treatment Center at the hospital. Without a successful drive, many of these vital organizations would have to reduce their services and some that are struggling just to exist might even have to close their doors.

I'm convinced the need is real and important, and I plan to make a generous contribution this year. I sincerely hope you can do the same. Just make your check payable to the United Community Drive and mail it to P.O. Box 40 here in Evanston.

Thanks for your help, Bill.

Part III

FORMS

15

FORMS FOR EFFECTIVE COMMUNICATION

If there were no forms in an office to facilitate the communications function, the staff might have to be doubled. The time spent in recording and transmitting messages and notices would be overwhelming and the work load facing the secretary each day would be formidable. However, numerous forms designed for rapid,

Date _____
From _____
To _____
( ) Please telephone _____.
( ) Please reply to the attached.
( ) Please prepare a reply for _____'s signature.
( ) Please furnish information re attached.
( ) Please reply to appropriate person to handle.
( ) Please discuss attached with _____
( ) Please advise if we can handle.
( ) Please note and return.
( ) _____ _____

15.1. Action-Requested Slip. A form for requesting action will save countless hours of memo- and letter-writing time. Depending on the type of activity in your office, you can add to or revise the items shown here as needed.

effective communications are available. Many can be ordered through office supply catalogs or found in stationery and office supply stores; some can easily be prepared by the secretary on a stencil or master and a supply run off by copier or duplicator. Since successful business operations are dependent on effective communications, the time spent in running off a supply of forms or the money spent in purchasing a supply of them is well worthwhile.

Many secretaries maintain a forms file (or notebook) with a sample of every form used in the office and full details regarding reordering and stenciling procedures. Some sort of inventory control is also helpful so the secretary knows when the supply of a particular form is running low and needs replenishing before it is exhausted.

Models 15.1 to 15.32 are examples of the most common forms used in the modern business office to facilitate the communications function. (For record-keeping and travel and meeting forms, see chapters 16 and 17.) If any one of the forms is not precisely appropriate for your office, simply modify it as you wish to fit your own needs.

ANNOUNCEMENT

Date: _____

From: _____

To: _____

This is to inform you that the following activity is planned. Please make appropriate arrangements to attend.

Event: _____

Date: _____

Time: _____ _____

Place: _____

For further information, contact: _____

_____

15.2. Announcements: Event. This form has a multitude of uses, from notifying employees of a training session to announcing a plant tour. You can easily modify the form to be more appropriate for the types of announcements common in your own office.

_____ Company

is pleased to announce that

_____

will be offered to members

of _____

effective _____.

This _____ is brought

to you as part of our continuing

effort to improve the quality of service

to all our members.

15.3. Announcements: New Product-Service. This is just one of numerous formats that can be used to introduce new products or services to a community or organization when something less detailed than a form letter or bulletin is desired. Stationery stores and printers usually have samples of such announcements for a variety of purposes. The objective is to avoid writing individual letters and, as briefly and clearly as possible, to make people aware of the new product or service.

Gerald F. Griffin

General Manager
Watson & Beale, Inc.

P.O. Box 700
Lewisburg PA 17837
717-521-2600

15.4. Business Card: Men. Styles of business cards vary greatly, although 3½″ × 2″ is the usual size. Some cards employ color; others use only black ink. High-level executives may have their cards engraved, although raised offset printing is widely used among executives and company representatives at all levels. High-level executives sometimes have their name centered on the card; company representatives almost always center the company's name.

COLBY INTERIORS
complete home decorating service

600 Oak Drive
Fairfax VA 22030
703-621-0101

Elaine Nelson
Interior Decorator

15.5 Business Card: Women. Women's cards are similar to men's except the titles *Miss*, *Mrs.*, or *Ms.* may (but need not) precede the name. However, a married woman should not use the title *Mrs.* with her first name; rather, if she wants to use her first name, she should (1) also use her maiden name and the title *Miss* or *Ms.* or (2) use her first name and married name without any title.

CHANGE OF ADDRESS

Please complete (print or type) and forward to

_____

NAME

_____

Last, first, middle initial

OLD ADDRESS

_____

No. & Street, Apt., Suite, POB, or RD No.

_____

City, State, Zip Code

NEW ADDRESS

_____

No. & Street, Apt., Suite, POB, or RD No.

_____

City, State, Zip Code

15.6. Change of Address Form. Most businesses use a notice of some sort to encourage their customers to notify them when they move. Model 15.6 is one of many possibilities (standard forms are available from the U.S. Postal Service).

Name: Account No.:
Address: Ref. No.:

Type of Account:
Amount Due:
Terms:
Due Date(s):
Past-Due Amount/Date:

Collection Action:

                                   Date:

15.7. Collection Notices: Card Follow-up Record. A card follow-up record or tickler system is filed by date on which the next collection step should be taken. Information on each card will vary according to the type of account.

LETTERHEAD

Dear Customer:

Just a friendly reminder that your payment of $_____ has not yet reached us and your account is now past due.

If your check is in the mail, please disregard this notice and accept our sincere thanks. If it is not, we would very much appreciate it if you would give this your usual prompt attention.

                              Cordially,

                              Credit Department

15.8. Collection Notices: Form Letters. In the early stages of collection efforts, forms and form letters are frequently used. Usually these are brief, friendly reminder letters, sometimes with basic data such as the amount due typed in each form letter individually. (See also chapter 11.)

FORGET SOMETHING?????

Yes, your payment is past due . . . won't you take a moment to mail us your check now?
Many thanks for your cooperation.

Invoice _____ Date Due _____ $_____

TO

Company Name
Address

15.9. Collection Notices: Reminder. The reminder is just a variation of the form letter sent in the early stages of collection efforts. Sometimes these reminders are designed for use in a window envelope. (See also chapter 11.)

Addressee: Date of
                                              Letter:

                        HOLD

Re:

15.10. Executive Reminder: Note. When carbon copies of correspondence are returned to the manager for further attention before filing, attach a reminder note summarizing the action still to be taken. Make a copy of the note for yourself to remind you that your carbon copy of the original letter is still in the manager's office.

```
┌─────────────────────────────────────────────────────────┐
│                      DEPARTMENT                          │
│                                                          │
│  Due date:                                               │
│  Re:                                                     │
│                                                          │
│  Submit to:                                              │
│  Requested by:                          Date:            │
│  Action taken:                                           │
│                                                          │
│                                                          │
│                              Date:       By:             │
└─────────────────────────────────────────────────────────┘
```

15.11. Follow-ups: Note. In addition to the regular follow-up (tickler) files, forms are often used as a secretary's personal reminder of pending communications. These follow-up notes, which could be prepared either on paper or card stock, are used to summarize action to be taken. (For an example of a similar reminder form that can be attached to follow-up file folders and used as a record of follow-up data, see model 16.31.)

Mr. and Mrs. Jason Spencer
accept with pleasure
the kind invitation of
Mr. and Mrs. Roberts
to be present at dinner
on Wednesday, the fourteenth of June
at half-past seven o'clock
at Nineteen Wilshire Boulevard

15.12. Invitations: Acknowledgments-Thank Yous. When a reply card is not enclosed, the acceptance of a formal invitation should be handwritten, in the third person, on folded note paper. Envelopes should be handwritten, too, and carry a postage stamp. (A refusal may but need not give a reason, e.g., ". . . regret that a previous engagement prevents their accepting . . .")

> The Directors and Officers
> of
> Lamp-Lite Incorporated
> cordially invite you to attend
> a cocktail party and reception
> at their new offices
> 1211 Orange Grove Avenue
> Los Angeles
> on Monday, August ninth
> from three until six o'clock
>
>
> R.S.V.P.

15.13. Invitations: Formal. A formal invitation may be handwritten or engraved. Businesses sometimes send typed or printed invitations. Envelopes should be handwritten and carry a postage stamp. Consult printers and stationery stores for samples.

> *Dinner*
> *Friday, January 5, 8 o'clock*
> *Mr. and Mrs. Samuel Kingston*
> *18 Fenway Place*
>
> *R.S.V.P.*   *Black Tie*

15.14. Invitations: Informal. The informal invitation can be issued by typed or handwritten letter or handwritten on folded note paper or calling cards. Model 15.14 could be sent on folded note paper or, if the address is omitted, on the host's calling card. The envelope should also be handwritten with a postage stamp applied.

```
Please respond on or before
        August 2, 19—


M _____

      will _____ attend.
```

15.15. Invitations: Reply Cards. Reply cards vary, of course, as do the invitations themselves. Often they contain as little as this model. Matching envelopes are included and they should be addressed in handwriting with a postage stamp applied. Consult printers and stationery stores for samples.

```
                    LONG-DISTANCE CALLS

Telephone number: _____
To: _____
    _____
Re: _____
    _____
Placed by: _____  Date: _____
Time: _____  Charges: _____
```

15.16. Long-Distance Calls: Record. Calls can be recorded in loose-leaf notebooks or on forms such as this. The amount of information that must be recorded depends on company practice.

CORRESPONDENCE DIGEST				
(Date)				
Date of Corresp.	From	Summary of Message	Action Required	Action Taken

15.17. Mail: Correspondence Digest. When the manager is away or so busy that he or she cannot read the mail immediately, a digest of incoming correspondence is helpful.

FOR YOUR INFORMATION

Date: _____

From: _____

Please review and forward.

NAMES	INITIALS	DATE
1. _____	_____	_____
2. _____	_____	_____
3. _____	_____	_____
4. _____	_____	_____
5. _____	_____	_____
6. _____	_____	_____

15.18. Mail: Routing (Circulation) Slip. When something must be sent to more than one person, a mimeographed routing slip with the name of each person typed on it can be used in place of individually prepared letters or memos.

MAIL SUMMARY SHEET

Date Received	From	Subject	To Whom Sent	Action Required	Follow-up Date

15.19. Mail: Summary Sheet (Record). A loose-leaf record of all mail going out of the office will serve as a reminder of action to be taken and as a check on the receipt and disposition of mail that gets misplaced.

```
┌─────────────────────────────────────────────────────────┐
│                    COMPANY NAME                          │
│                    Address/Phone                         │
├─────────────────────────────────────────────────────────┤
│                                                          │
│   From:                        Date:                     │
│      To:                                                 │
│  Subject:                                                │
│                                                          │
└─────────────────────────────────────────────────────────┘
```

15.20. Memorandum: Interoffice-Communication Form. The memo is a fast, economical method for one-way correspondence. Although, traditionally, the memo is often referred to as an interoffice form, it can be used for external correspondence as well (see chapters 13 and 14). Notice that memos generally have no salutation, no complimentary close, and no written signature (see 19.18–19.20). Designs vary greatly. Some forms are available in convenient multiple-carbon sets; others (see model 15.21) have a reply section. Printers and suppliers of business forms have samples available.

```
┌─────────────────────────────────────────────────────────┐
│                    COMPANY NAME                          │
│                    Address/Phone                         │
├───────────────────────────┬─────────────────────────────┤
│         MESSAGE           │           REPLY             │
├───────────────────────────┼─────────────────────────────┤
│       To:                 │   Date:                     │
│   Subject:                │                             │
│      Date:                │                             │
│                           │                             │
│                           │                             │
│  Signed _____        │  Signed _____          │
└───────────────────────────┴─────────────────────────────┘
```

15.21. Memorandum: Speed Letter (Message) Form. Like the interoffice-communication form, the speed message is a fast and economical method of correspondence. Unlike the interoffice form, however, it is designed for two-way correspondence through the use of a carbon interleaf or carbonless set. Printer and suppliers of business forms have samples available.

TELEPHONE MESSAGE

To: _____   Date: _____

Taken by: _____   Time: _____

Caller: _____

Company: _____

_____

Phone: _____

    ( ) telephoned   ( ) please phone

    ( ) returned your call   ( ) will call again

Message: _____

_____

_____

_____

15.22 Message Form: Telephone. To save time in recording messages, colored forms for taking phone messages are available in office supply stores and from suppliers of business forms. Or you can design and mimeograph your own form.

VISITOR MESSAGE

To: _____   Date: _____

Taken by: _____   Time: _____

Visitor: _____

Company: _____

_____

Phone: _____

Message _____

_____

_____

_____

    ( ) please call   ( ) please write

15.23. Message Form: Visitor. Forms to record messages from visitors provide an excellent record of the call and a reminder to acknowledge the visitor's message or request.

COMPANY NAME
Address

Yes, please continue my enrollment in _____
_____, with all rights and privileges to which I am thereby entitled.
My check for $_____ is enclosed.

( ) 1 year $12   ( ) 2 years $20   ( ) 3 years $28

Name: _____

Company: _____

Address: _____

City, State, Zip: _____

15.24. Orders: Order-Renewal Form. Renewal forms are used for many purposes—subscriptions, memberships, and other orders. If your needs are specialized, you can design a form as brief or as detailed as you like and mimeograph it or have supplies of it printed on paper or card stock.

REQUISITION

( ) Supplies/Stock   ( ) Forms   Date _____
( ) _____   No. _____

To _____   Deliver to _____
_____   _____
_____   _____

Qty	Cat. No.	Description	Unit Price	Total Price
			Total	

Charge to Dept. _____Account No. _____
Requisitioned by _____Date Required _____
Remarks _____
Authorized by _____

15.25. Orders: Requistion Form. Interoffice supply requests can be handled quickly and efficiently by preprinted or mimeographed forms. Copies also serve as a record for inventory control.

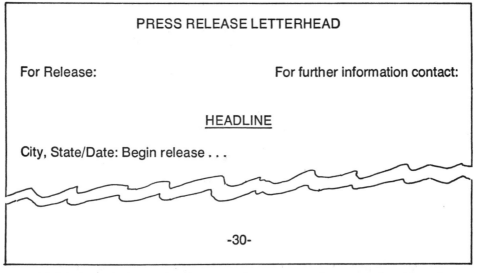

PETITION
(date)

WHEREAS _____

_____

WHEREAS _____

_____

WHEREAS _____

_____

WE, the undersigned _____ of _____
do hereby petition _____ to _____

_____

_____

_____

(signatures)   (signatures)

15.26. Petitions: Form. The form of a petition depends on what you want to say, but this model can be modified to fit many situations.

PRESS RELEASE LETTERHEAD

For Release: For further information contact:

HEADLINE

City, State/Date: Begin release . . .

-30-

15.27. Press Release: Form. News releases are usually compiled and issued rapidly by some economical means such as mimeographing or offset printing. Often special letterhead is designed and printed for this purpose. The symbol -30- signifies the end of the release. When the release runs to another page, the word "more" is typed at the bottom. The body of the release should be typed in factual, straightforward language, void of flowery prose, and double spaced with paragraph indent.

BIBLIOGRAPHY

Jared, Frank R., and Dixon, Robert P. A Manual of Group Relations. Chicago: The Harrison Press, 1965.

Miller, Allan J., et al. "The Urban Conflict." Journal of Urban Economics 60 (1971): 149–51.

Paulette, Harold. "The Fall of Rome." In Roman History, edited by T. R. Davis. New York: Maxwell Publishers, Inc., 1977.

15.28. Reports: Bibliography. An alphabetical list of reading material pertaining to the subject of a report is often included at the end of the report, just before the index (if there is one). The preferred style for bibliographies varies from company to company. This model shows a style popular in many organizations. Regardless of the order of facts presented, however, entries should always include all pertinent data: author's name, title of work, place (city) of publication, name of publisher, and date published. The examples here are for a book, an article, and a paper in a multiauthor book.

REPORT TITLE

I.   Section Head
     A.   First-Level Subhead
          1.   Second-Level Subhead
               a.   Third-Level Subhead
               b.   Third-Level Subhead
          2.   Second-Level Subhead
               a.   Third-Level Subhead
               b.   Third-Level Subhead
     B.
          1.
               a.
               b.
II.
     A.
          1.
               a.

15.29. Reports: Outline. Outlining is an effective way to organize report material. Frequently Roman numerals are used for section heads (e.g., Background); capital letters are used for first-level subheads (e.g., Early History); and Arabic numerals and small letters are used for further subdivisions (e.g., Revolutionary Period).

Title

Author
Author's Department

Company Name
City, State

Date

15.30. Reports, Title Page. Content of a title page will vary from report to report, but this model is appropriate in many instances. Separate each item on the title page by at least four lines but use only two line spaces between the lines of a particular item (e.g., author and author's department).

CONTENTS

Preface		0
Introduction		0
I.	Main Section Head	0
	Subsection Head I.1	0
	Subsection Head I.2	0
II.	Main Section Head	00
	Subsection Head II.1	00
	Subsection Head II.2	00
III.	Main Section Head	00
	Subsection Head III.1	00
	Subsection Head III.2	00
Appendix		000
Bibliography		000

15.31. **Reports: Table of Contents.** A table of contents is useful if it contains an accurate listing of sections and, if desired, subsections. The table should also include other features of the report such as a preface, introduction, appendix, and bibliography.

CHRONOLOGICAL RESUME	QUALIFICATION RESUME
Title of position desired	Title of position desired
Name, address, phone, age	Name, address, phone, age
Objective:	Objective:
Employment:	Employment Highlights:
19— to 19—	1.
19— to 19—	2. .
Education:	Job Record:
19— to 19—	19— to 19—
19— to 19—	19— to 19—
Licenses Earned:	Education:
Military Record:	19— to 19—
Other Qualifications:	19— to 19—
Personal Data:	Licenses Earned:
References:	Military Record:
Salary Desired:	Other Accomplishments:
Availability:	Personal Data:
	References:
	Salary Received:
	Availability:

15.32. **Resumes: Format.** The chronological resume, the most popular style in use today, emphasizes for prospective employers a summary of the applicant's job experience. The qualifications resume, preferred by many executives with particular skills, stresses special accomplishments.

16

RECORD-KEEPING FORMS

Efficiency is a principal objective in the modern business office. Secretaries must constantly seek simpler and better ways to organize and control the daily flow

	Time Spent per Activity								
ACTIVITY RECORD: YOUR NAME (Period Covered)									
Date	(A)	(B)	(C)	(D)	(E)	(F)	(G)	(H)	Total Hrs. per Day
Mon, _____									
Tues., _____									
Wed., _____									
Thrs, _____									
Fri, _____									
Total Hrs. per Activity									

16.1. Activity Records: Chart. In some offices it is standard practice to record time expenditures. Even when this is not a requirement, it is a useful exercise and will help you understand the allocation of time in your work day. After daily time-work studies (see 16.36, Time-Work Analysis) have been made for a week or two, the figures can be totaled and charted as shown here. (The letters A, B, and so on represent the type of activity such as typing or filing.) It will soon be clear where you are spending most of your time, which may point to an area of activity needing some streamlining.

of information in and out of the office. An indispensable tool in the proper handling of information is the record-keeping form, which may be anything from a
cross-reference sheet to a petty cash voucher.

Some record-keeping forms, like the communications forms described in chapter 15, can be purchased from suppliers such as stationery and office supply stores.
Many, however, can be either (1) designed and reproduced especially for you by
printers or forms manufacturers or (2) designed and typed personally in your own
office and run off on your office mimeograph machine or copier. You will often find
the forms you design yourself are more suitable for your needs and easier to work
with.

This chapter illustrates thirty-six useful record-keeping forms. The purpose of
each is to provide a fast and easy way to record and maintain information. Most of
the models are intended as suggestions only and you can change them as necessary
to suit your own work requirements. (See chapters 15 and 17 for communications
and travel and meetings forms.)

APPOINTMENT SCHEDULE		
(Date)		
Time	With Whom	Nature of Appointment

16.2. Appointments: Daily Schedule. Depending upon the number of appointments you usually have to record, your daily schedule can be typed on
small note or memorandum sheets (6 by 9 inches or less). Paper is preferable to
index cards so you can make a carbon copy for yourself.

SEPTEMBER 19__				
MEMOS	Sun, 4th	Sun, 11th	Sun, 18th	Sun, 25th
	Mon, 5th	Mon, 12th	Mon, 19th	Mon, 26th
	Tues, 6th	Tues, 13th	Tues. 20th	Tues, 27th
	Wed, 7th	Wed, 14th	Wed, 21st	Wed, 28th
Thrs, 1st	Thrs, 8th	Thrs, 15th	Thrs, 22nd	Thrs, 29th
Fri, 2nd	Fri, 9th	Fri, 16th	Fri, 23rd	Fri, 30th
Sat, 3rd	Sat, 10th	Sat, 17th	Sat, 24th	MEMOS

16.3. Appointments: Monthly Schedule. The only practical way to show appointments for an entire month at a glance is by calendar. Consult stationery and office supply stores for special calendars with days of the week arranged in rows, as shown in this model. You can also make up your own calendar each month in whatever size you need for your office.

APPOINTMENT SCHEDULE (week of _____ to _____)			
Date	Time(s)	With Whom	Nature of Appointment(s)
Mon, _____			
Tues, _____			
Wed, _____			
Thrs, _____			
Fri, _____			

16.4. **Appointments: Weekly Schedule.** Lists can be typed for one or more weeks in form similar to the daily schedule shown in model 16.2. If you design your own form, keep in mind the number of appointments you usually record in a week when selecting paper size. If there are a substantial number, you may prefer a size of 8½ × 11 inches over the smaller note or memorandum paper that is often used for a daily schedule.

ABC CORPORATION
Balance Sheet
December 31, 19___

Assets		
Current Assets		
Cash		$ 9,000
Accounts Receivable	$ 5,500	
Less: Allowance for Doubtful Accounts	500	5,000
Notes Receivable		11,000
Merchandise Inventory		30,000
Total Current Assets		55,000
Fixed Assets		
Furniture & Fixtures	28,000	
Less: Accumulated Depreciation	5,000	23,000
Land		40,000
Buildings	170,000	
Less: Accumulated Depreciation	40,000	130,000
Total Fixed Assets		193,000
Total Assets		$248,000

Liabilities		
Current Liabilities		
Accounts Payable		$ 15,000
Notes Payable		10,000
Accrued Taxes Payable		7,000
Total Current Liabilities		32,000
Long-Term Debt		
Mortgage Payable		60,000
Bonds Payable, 5% due 19___		100,000
Total Long-Term Debt		160,000
Capital and Surplus		
Common Stock $50 par 1,000 shares authorized, issued, and outstanding		50,000
Retained Earnings		6,000
Total Capital and Retained Earnings		56,000
Total Liabilities and Capital		$248,000

16.5. Balance Sheet: Sample. If you are involved in keeping records for your company, you should be familiar with the balance sheet: a financial statement showing at a specified time and in a systematic manner the balance in the accounts representing the assets, liabilities, and capital of an organization. Model 16.5 shows the common account form balance sheet.

Reconciliation, January 31, 19___

Bank statement balance	$2,114.30
Add late deposit	400.00
Subtotal	$2,514.30

Subtract checks outstanding: #614	300.00	
#620	14.75	314.75
Balance		$2,199.55

16.6. Bank Reconciliation Statement: Sample. If your bank statement does not provide a place to reconcile its balance with the checkbook balance, you can work out your own reconciliation as shown in this model. The balance shown on the reconciliaton statement should agree with the balance in your checkbook after deducting service or other fees.

COMPANY NAME

Address
Telephone

1.

2.

3.

16.7. Card Index: Form. Cards of varying sizes (e.g., 3 by 5, 4 by 6, and 5 by 8 inch) can be used to record a variety of reference data: address lists, bibliographies, library titles, and so on. The reason for using card stock instead of sheets of paper is that these records are handled regularly and only card stock would hold up under such conditions. This model illustrates the form for a card index prepared for a company reference file. The form you adopt depends strictly on the information you want to record. (Notes on the company are itemized beneath the address.) However, be certain the information you want to see first (probably the name or an identification number) when you scan through your card file appears at the top of each card.

CHARGE-OUT SLIP
(Department)

Date Removed _____   Return Date _____

Subject _____

Description of Material _____

_____

_____

Name _____   Phone _____

Department _____

16.8. Charge-Out Slip (Sign-Out Sheet): Form. To avoid having material disappear without knowing who has it, you can use a special form to maintain control of material removed from your office. Charge-out slips may be filed in the OUT folders, which are substituted in the file cabinet for regular folders that have been removed, or they can be kept together in a separate charge-out file.

CONTRIBUTIONS, 19____

(Name)

Date	Organization	Amount

16.9. Contributions Record: Form. This model, which could be set up on loose-leaf accounting sheets, shows the simplest form for recording contributions. It assumes that donations are made in one lump sum to each organization. But if contributions to the same group are made monthly or several times a year, it would be better to expand the form to show a column for each month in which the amounts contributed could be recorded and then totaled in the final column at the end of the year.

| CREDIT CARDS/ACCOUNT NUMBERS |||||
| (Name) |||||
Date Card Issued or Account Opened	Expiration Date	Issuing Company	Card or Account No.

16.10. **Credit Card Record (Account Number Register): Form.** It is advisable to keep a record of all credit cards and/or accounts. The form shown in this model can be used for either purpose and can be set up on a loose-leaf accounting sheet.

CROSS-REFERENCE SHEET

Subject/Name _____

Description _____

_____

_____

See _____

_____

_____

_____

16.11. **Cross-References: Sheet.** If a record might logically appear in more than one place, cross referencing is the only way to insure quick retrieval. A cross-reference sheet can have as much information as you like on it, but usually the basic facts—subject or name, brief description of the material, and location of the material—are adequate.

DIVIDEND RECORDS, 19___															
Stock (Bond)	Shares	J	F	M	A	M	J	J	A	S	O	N	D	Annual Total
Monthly Total															

16.12. **Dividends (Income) Received: Record.** If you keep personal tax records for the manager you will need to record dividends received. Such income often comes in throughout the year and your form should thus include a column for each month as shown in this model. Loose-leaf accounting sheets can be used for your record.

GIFTS, 19____ (Name)					
To Whom Given	Gift Given	Occasion	Cost	Other Suggestions	Suggested Price

16.13. Gifts: Record. In most offices the manager gives a number of presents each year, especially during the holiday seasons such as Christmas. Records from previous years are most helpful in avoiding duplications and in making new decisions. Your record each year might include space such as that shown in the last two columns of this model for you to write in suggestions for the future and for the manager to indicate his or her preferred price range.

```
┌─────────────────────────────────────────────────────────────┐
│                      XYZ COMPANY                             │
│                 Profit and Loss Statement                   │
│               Year Ended December 31, 19____                │
│                                                             │
│  Income:                                                    │
│                                                             │
│      Net Sales                              $250,000        │
│      Dividend Income                           2,500        │
│         Total Income                        $252,500        │
│                                                             │
│  Expenses:                                                  │
│                                                             │
│      Cost of Goods Sold        $160,000                     │
│      Selling Expenses            20,000                     │
│      Administrative Expenses     11,000                     │
│      Interest Expense               900                     │
│      Federal Income Tax          17,000                     │
│         Total Expenses                       208,900        │
│                                                             │
│  Net Income                                 $ 43,600        │
│                                                             │
└─────────────────────────────────────────────────────────────┘
```

16.14. Income (Profit and Loss) Statement: Sample. This is one of the financial statements you will likely handle if you are involved in keeping company books and records. A profit and loss statement summarizes the income and expenses of a business in classified form and shows the net income or loss for a specified period.

LIFE INSURANCE
(Name of Insured)

| Type of Policy | Company | Date of Issue | Bene-ficiary | Amt. | Annual Prem-ium | Disability | | Dble. Indem-nity | Prem. Due Dates |
						Prem. Waiver	Monthly Income		

16.15. Insurance Records: Life. Forms for keeping life insurance records are sometimes more detailed than those for other types of insurance. You might, for instance, need to have medical or other details about the insured on the record. However, if you do not need extensive personal information, the form shown in this model is useful in most instances.

INSURANCE POLICIES

(Name of Insured)

Type of Ins.	Company	Policy No.	Agent	Premium	Period Covered	Due Dates	Dates Paid	Ck. No.

16.16. **Insurance Records: Policies.** Although you will probably maintain separate records for each type of insurance, it is helpful to have information on *all* types of policies recorded on a single sheet such as that illustrated in this model. This allows you to see the total insurance picture at a glance. Your record can have as many columns as you need, depending on how much information you want to show. In most cases the information shown here will be adequate.

PROPERTY INSURANCE

(Name of Insured)

Type of Policy	Company	Policy No.	Agent	Kind of Prop.	Loca-tion	Prem-ium	Period Covered	Dates Due	Dates Paid	Ck. No.

16.17. **Insurance Records: Property.** Your property insurance record might be similar to the general record of all policies (model 16.16), except there should be columns to show the kind of property and its location.

Company _____   Policy No. _____

Type of Policy _____   Coverage _____

Insured _____

Agent _____

Premium _____   Expiration Date _____

Due Dates _____

Pay to _____
_____

16.18. Insurance Records: Tickler File—Premiums. Tickler cards (e.g., 3 by 5 inch) are commonly used for reminders of premium due dates. The card can contain as little or as much information as you wish but should at least include policy number and issuing company, premium due dates and amount, type of policy and what is covered, the name of your agent, and the name of the insured person or company.

INTEREST INCOME (Owner's Name) (Period)					
Taxable Income			Tax-Exempt Income		
Description	Date Received	Amount Received	Description	Date Received	Amount Received
Total $			Total $		

16.19. Interest Income: Record. Information on interest income must be kept for income tax purposes. Your record should show taxable interest income (e.g., corporate bonds, mortgage bonds, notes, and bank deposits) and tax-exempt interest income (e.g., state and municipal bonds and securities).

| CURRENT INVESTMENTS | | | | | |
| (Name of Investor) | | | | | |
Type of Security	Name of Security	No. of Shares & Face Val.	Cost of Security	Current Market Price	Date of Maturity
Stocks					
Bonds					
Mutual Funds					
Investment Totals	—	—	$	$	—

16.20. **Investments (Securities—Bonds—Mutual Funds): Current List.** A list of all investments allows the investor to view his or her complete market position quickly. To keep the list current, additions and deletions should be made periodically (weekly, monthly, or as often as activity warrants).

INVESTMENT TRANSACTIONS		
(Name of Investor)		
Transaction Information	Purchases	Sales
Registered Name		
Certificate No.		
Date of Purchase/Sale		
No. of Shares		
Kind of Security		
Price per Share		
Total Sales/Purchase Price		
Commission		
Misc. Charges (e.g., Taxes)	N/A	
Short-Term Capital Gain (Loss)	N/A	
Long-Term Capital Gain (Loss)	N/A	

16.21. Investments (Securities—Bonds—Mutual Funds): Record Sheet
(Card) of Purchases-Sales. A record should be kept of purchases and sales for
each security. Either loose-leaf sheets or cards can be used. Notice that some
information in model 16.21 is not applicable to purchases.

LONG-RANGE SCHEDULE			
Project _____ Completion Date _____ Director _____ Phone _____			
Type of Activity	Summary of Activity	Dates and Times	Deadlines
Transportation			
Meetings			
Special Assignments			
Miscellaneous			

16.22. Long-Range Schedule: Form. Long-range schedules are a must for important projects that have numerous steps and deadlines. Each schedule will have to be tailored to the particular project: for example, one project might involve extensive travel and another, none. Model 16.22 can serve as a general format guide in creating your own type of schedule.

			Amount Paid	
			Medicine	Other
Date	Description of Expenses	To Whom Paid	& Drugs	Expenses

MEDICAL EXPENSES, 19_____
(Name)

16.23. **Medical Expenses: Record.** A record of medical expenses must be kept throughout the year for income tax purposes to determine if a deduction is allowable at the end of the year. Receipts should be kept for each item recorded on the expense form.

MERIT RATING CHART
(date/employee)

Performance Factor	Above Average	Average	Below Average
Personality Cooperation Disposition Neatness Leadership Ability Initiative Industriousness Judgment Accuracy Quality of Work Quantity of Work			

16.24. **Merit Rating: Chart.** A merit rating form is used to evaluate the employee (as opposed to the job). Characteristics, which are listed and scored, should be selected according to the particular work situation of an employee and/or the position for which he or she is being considered. This model shows many of the traits commonly included on most rating charts. The evaluator checks off each trait as above average, average, or below average. (Instead of those three degrees you could also devise a rank of 1 to 10 or something else to indicate a wider range of capability.)

Date	Voucher Number	Explanation	Receipts	Payments

PETTY CASH RECORD
(Department)

16.25. Petty Cash: Record. A record of petty cash expenditures is sometimes kept in a standard cash book when a number of columns are needed to show the distribution of payments according to specific categories (e.g., postage). Such a record would vary from office to office. This model shows the basic data that would be recorded in any office, whether or not additional columns were used to show specific categories of expenses.

PETTY CASH VOUCHER
(Department)

Date _____   No. _____

Chg. to Acct. _____   Amount _____

Paid to _____

For _____

Approved by _____

Received _____

16.26. Petty Cash: Voucher. When authorization is needed to make a petty cash expenditure, a voucher with a signature line should be used. Preprinted forms are available in office supply stores, but you can also prepare and mimeograph your own form.

REAL ESTATE

LOCATION

DESCRIPTION

PURCHASED FROM	DATE PURCHASED	PURCHASE PRICE	AGENT EMPLOYED	ASSESSED VALUE
RECORDED IN	COUNTRY OF	STATE OF	DEED BOOK NO.	PAGE NO.	WHERE DEED KEPT

MORTGAGE DATA

REMARKS

SOLD TO	DATE SOLD	SALE PRICE	AMOUNT CASH RECEIVED	NOW BALANCE PAYABLE
AGENT EMPLOYED		AGENT'S FEE		PROFIT OR LOSS

MORTGAGE DATA

REMARKS

DATE	DESCRIPTION	EXPENSE	DEPRECIATION AND REPAIRS	✓ 10	FIXED IMPROVEMENTS	NET INVESTMENT	RETURNS RECEIVED ✓ 4	5
	TOTALS BROUGHT FORWARD							
	MAKE AS FIRST ENTRY UNDER "NET INVESTMENT." ORIGINAL PURCHASE PRICE							
	TOTALS CARRIED FORWARD							

16.27. **Real Estate: Record.** Records of real estate showing depreciation, expenditures for repairs, and so on are necessary to determine deductible items for income tax purposes. The form shown here would be adequate for the majority of situations.

From the book, COMPLETE SECRETARY'S HANDBOOK, 4th Edition by Mary A. DeVries, Reviser. ©1977 by Prentice-Hall, Inc. Published by Prentice-Hall, Inc. Englewood Cliffs, New Jersey.

DOCUMENTS RECEIPT
(Department)

Date Removed _____   Due Date _____

Released to _____

_____ Phone _____

For _____

Description of Document _____

_____

Approved _____

16.28. Receipts: Documents. A record must be kept of any document that goes out of your office. These forms can best be prepared on paper (not cards) so you can make a carbon copy (one for the follow-up files and one to go with the rest of the papers pertaining to the document).

No. _____

COMPANY NAME

Address

Date _____

Received from _____

The Sum of _____   Dollars $ _____

For _____ ( ) cash ( ) check ( ) M. O.

Amount of Account $_____

Amount Paid $_____   THANK YOU!

Balance Due $_____   By _____

16.29. Receipts: General. Pads or booklets of receipt forms are available in most office supply stores. If you want to prepare your own personalized forms, this model can be used as a guide.

RECORDS-RENTENTION CONTROL FORM (Department)		
Description of Record	Period to be Retained	Special Requirements
1.		
2.		
3.		
4.		
5.		
6.		

16.30. Records-Retention Control: Form. A system should be devised to govern the control and retention of records. Usually this is handled by a records manager or other executive who decides what should (or must) be kept. This model includes a third column, which is optional, where special requirements can be noted. Some records, for instance, must be kept to comply with state and federal laws or to meet some other rules and regulations.

REMINDER FORM

Date Requested _____   Date Due _____

Requested by _____

Subject _____

Action Requested _____

_____

Action Taken _____

_____   By_____

16.31. Reminder Form (Card): File-Folder Attachment. To provide a record of follow-up information at a glance, reminder sheets or cards can be clipped to the outside of a file folder, which is then filed in the follow-up section of the file cabinet. Later, the form can be placed in the folder with the other material when it is time to return it all to the regular files. (For an example of a general follow-up note, see model 5.11.)

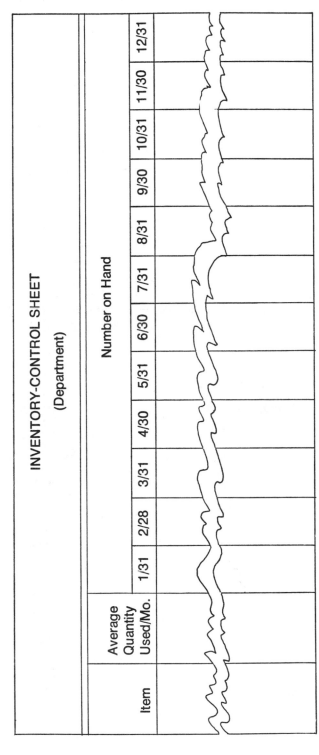

16.32. Supplies-Inventory File: Inventory-Control Sheet. Supplies (stationery, forms, and miscellaneous materials such as paperclips) are usually kept in a closet or storeroom, and the secretary is expected to keep an adequate amount of everything on hand. To avoid running out of some item, a record should be kept periodically (weekly or monthly) to show how many of each item are currently on hand. When the record shows that only enough for a month or a few weeks remain, it is probably time to reorder. Rather than count everything each week or month, mark the number on the front of the nearest package. Then, each time you remove something, cross out the old figure and jot the current balance on the front of the package.

INVENTORY-CONTROL SHEET

(Department)

Item	Average Quantity Used/Mo.	Number on Hand											
		1/31	2/28	3/31	4/30	5/31	6/30	7/31	8/31	9/30	10/31	11/30	12/31

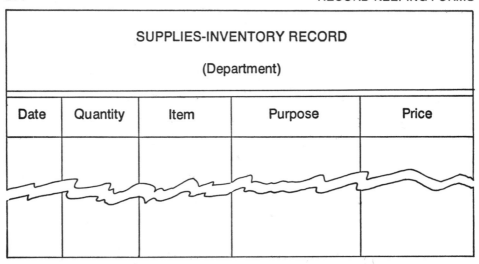

16.33. Supplies-Inventory File: Record Form. The only way to know what is in the supply cabinet, when it was ordered, and what it cost is to keep a record of every item purchased. Without such a record you would have to page back through the accounting records or paid-bills file to search out items and amounts. This type of record is especially useful for reviewing data on special-order items such as holiday stationery.

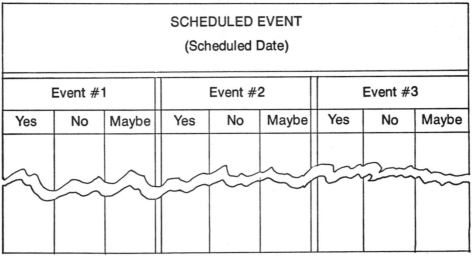

16.34. Tabulated Sheet: Scheduled Events Form. When replies are received for a special event such as attendance at a meeting they must be tabulated. If the number of replies are recorded daily, and you pencil in up-to-the-minute totals for each column, a running total will be constantly available. If the event includes replies concerning a number of things (such as attendance at a workshop, attendance at a cocktail party afterwards, followed by attendance at dinner), you can use as many columns as necessary.

				Item			
Date	Paid to	For	Amount	Taxes	Interest	Losses & Bad Debts	Other

TAX DEDUCTIONS, 19____

(Name)

16.35. Tax-Deductions: Record. Among the personal records you keep for the manager should be a record of income tax deductions. It can have as many columns as necessary to show all types of deductions of concern to the manager.

TIME-WORK ANALYSIS

(date)

Job	Morning		Afternoon		Total Minutes
	Start	Finish	Start	Finish	
(A)					
(B)					
(C)					
(D)					
(E)					

16.36. Time-Work Analysis: Form. Daily time-work studies are needed to help you evaluate how you generally spend your time. Once these daily figures have been compiled over a period of a week or two, they can be totaled and charted on an activity record such as that shown in model 16.1.

17

FORMS AND TRAVEL RECORDS
FOR MEETINGS AND CONFERENCES

Much of an executive's time is spent either at a meeting or on the way to one. Much of the secretary's time, therefore, is spent making travel arrangements, assisting in preparations for meetings and conferences, and maintaining accurate records of all such activity. Without adequate forms to use for these tasks, a secretary

---

AGENDA
(Meeting Title, Time, Place, Date)

  1. Call to order
  2. Roll call or verification of members present
  3. Determination of quorum
  4. Reading and correction of minutes of previous meeting
  5. Approval of minutes
  6. Reading of correspondence
  7. Reports of officers
  8. Reports of standing committees
  9. Reports of special committees
10. Unfinished business
11. New business
12. Appointments of committees   _____
13. Nominations and elections
14. Announcements
15. Adjournment

17.1 **Agenda: Form.** Meeting agenda items should be typed in the order shown here. For further guidelines on the amount of detail to include under the various items, study the agendas and minutes of previous meetings and follow the manager's instructions.

would find it difficult to get everything organized quickly and accurately, especially for unexpected trips and meetings.

Fortunately, there are communications and record-keeping forms especially intended to handle travel and meeting plans. Just like the forms described in chapters 15 and 16, these can be specially designed for your particular requirements and some can be purchased in stationery and office supply stores. For instance, you might find one of the preprinted standard travel expense forms adequate for your purposes but prefer to devise (and mimeograph or photocopy) your own facilities checklist for a meeting.

Models 17.1 to 17.18 are examples of basic travel and meetings forms that will save you time and make your work a lot easier and more enjoyable. Many of these forms are suitable for use with all kinds of travel and meeting arrangements. However, if you prefer to create your own forms, there is no reason why you cannot tailor each one specifically to your own situation.

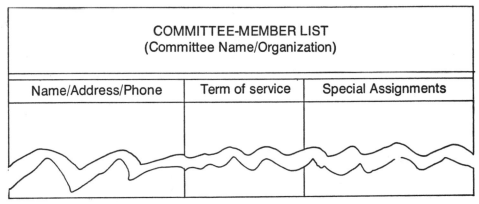

17.2 Committee-Member List: Form. If you are responsible for sending meeting notices and other announcements to committe members, a convenient list of names, mailing addresses, and phone numbers will be useful. When members have special assignments (e.g., preparing a report), keep a list of such duties so you will know where to send information that could be helpful to the members. Also include the term of service so you will know (1) when a replacement member may be expected and (2) when you should check to see if special mailings to the retiring member should be terminated.

FACILITIES CHECKLIST (Meeting Title, Time, Place, Date)					
Item	Room	Equipment Needed	Special Requirements (or problems)	Deadline for Arrangements	Date Completed
1.					
2.					
3.					
4.					
5.					
6.					
7.					
8.					
9.					
10.					
11.					
12.					

17.3. Conferences: Facilities Checklist. The extent of your duties in arranging for facilities will depend on available outside assistance (e.g., special committees) and the service provided by the hotel. Examples of items included in facilities arrangements are special lighting equipment, tables, floor plans, lecterns, chairs, air conditioning, acoustics, audiovisual aids, union requirements, and security.

CONFERENCE PLANNING FORM (Meeting Title, Date)			
Duties	Contact (Person, Organization)	Deadline for Arrangements	Date Completed
1. 2. 3. 4. 5. 6. 7. 8. 9. 10. 11. 12.			

17.4. Conferences: Planning Form. Your duties will vary, depending on the type of meeting, available outside assistance (e.g., special committees), and so on. Often the secretary must notify participants; help with arrangements for rooms, special equipment, meals, and coffee breaks; prepare and distribute attendance lists; order and organize registration and general meeting materials; prepare an agenda; process registrations; send speaker and guest invitations; and help prepare the program and press releases.

REGISTRATION-CONFIRMATION FORM
(Meeting Title, Place, Date)

M_____

_____

Your registration is confirmed for the following events:

Conference/Workshop Sessions: ( ) Tuesday   ( ) Wednesday
Lunch: ( ) Tuesday ( ) Wednesday   Dinner: ( ) Tuesday

Received $_____   Due on or before (date) $_____

NAME OF SPONSORING ORGANIZATION/ADDRESS/PHONE

17.5. Conferences: Registration-Confirmation Form. It is common practice to confirm preregistrations for conferences, seminars, and similar meetings. This can be done by form letter, printed slips, or a tearoff section of the
registration form itself. Naturally, the information on the form will vary, depending on what the meeting offers. (It will save typing time if the form is
designed to fit into a window envelope.)

MEETING DATES RECORD
(Period Covered)

Type of Meeting	Scheduled Dates											
	Jan	Feb	Mar	Apr	May	Jun	Jul	Aug	Sept	Oct	Nov	Dec

17.6. Meeting Dates: Record. You can design a variety of forms to record
prescheduled meeting dates. This form covers a calendar year. Dates are recorded as they are established. At a glance, then, you can tell what days the
manager will be busy and if there are any conflicting dates.

```
+--------------------------------------------------+
|                 MEETING NOTICE                   |
|               BOARD OF DIRECTORS                 |
+--------------------------------------------------+
|                                                  |
| To: _____|
|                                                  |
| Meeting Date: _____ Time: _____ |
| Place: _____|
|       _____|
|                                                  |
| Deadline for Submission of Agenda Items: _____|
|                                                  |
|            ORGANIZATION/ADDRESS/PHONE            |
+--------------------------------------------------+
```

17.7. Meeting Notice: Directors: The form and content of notices of a regular or special directors meeting are determined by the bylaws. If the notice can be sent on printed cards or paper slips with only blanks to fill in, it will save time and make the task much easier. Model 17.7 is an example of an informal notice of a regular meeting.

```
+--------------------------------------------------+
|                 MEMO LETTERHEAD                  |
|                                                  |
| Date:                                            |
| To:                                              |
| From:                                            |
|                                                  |
| The next regular monthly staff meeting will be   |
| held on _____ at _____ in room _____.    |
| Please notify this office (ext. 210) if you      |
| are unable to attend.                            |
|                                                  |
| Thank you.                                       |
+--------------------------------------------------+
```

17.8. Meeting Notice: Employees. A variety of forms could be used to notify employees of a meeting: memos, cards, slips, and so on. This form illustrates a simple notification by memo. Each memo could be typed individually if there are only a few involved; otherwise, a supply could be printed with blanks to fill in later.

COMPANY LETTERHEAD

NOTICE OF SPECIAL MEETING OF STOCKHOLDERS
TO BE HELD ON _____

A special meeting of the stockholders of _____, a corporation in the state of _____, has been called and will be
held on _____ at _____ at the registered
office of the company, _____.
The meeting will be held for the following purposes.

1.
2.
3.

If you do not expect to attend, please fill in, date, sign, and promptly return the enclosed postage-paid proxy.

By order of the Board of Directors.

_____
Secretary

(Place)
(Date)

17.9. Meeting Notice: Stockholders. As with the directors meeting described in model 17.7, the form and content of a stockholders meeting are
determined by the bylaws. This model is an example of a notice sent on company letterhead for a special meeting. A postage-paid proxy form should be
enclosed (see model 17.14).

```
                              RESOLUTION
                          Adopted _____

        WHEREAS _____
        _____
        WHEREAS _____
        _____
        WHEREAS _____
        _____
        RESOLVED, That _____
        _____
        _____
        FURTHER RESOLVED, That _____
        _____
        _____

        _____        _____
        Secretary                    Chairman
```

17.10. Minutes: Form of Resolutions. To simplify the recording task, a special form can be prepared to guide you in filling in details in the proper sequence and format. Notice the use of all capitals for WHEREAS and RESOLVED, and the use of a capital initial letter for That.

```
                          TOPIC
        Date _____ Page _____
        Date _____ Page _____
        Date _____ Page _____
        Date _____ Page _____
        Date _____ Page _____
        Date _____ Page _____
```

17.11. Minutes: Indexed Reference Card. When meeting activity is extensive, an index to the minutes is essential for finding things quickly and easily. Usually one topic (e.g., computer survey) is assigned to a 3- by 5-inch card with all references to it listed below by date of minutes involved and the appropriate page number.

```
┌──────────────────────────────────────────────────────────────────┐
│                           MINUTES                                  │
│                           (Date)                                   │
│                                                                    │
│  Meeting Date _____    Place _____           │
│                                                                    │
│  Present:                                                          │
│                                                                    │
│  _____    _____              │
│                                                                    │
│  _____    _____              │
│                                                                    │
│  _____    _____              │
│                                                                    │
│  Call to Order:                                                    │
│                                                                    │
│  Reading, Correction, and Approval of                              │
│  Minutes of Previous Meeting:                                      │
│                                                                    │
│  Correspondence:                                                   │
│                                                                    │
│  Reports of Officers:                                              │
│                                                                    │
│  Reports of Standing Committees:                                   │
│                                                                    │
│  Reports of Special Committees:                                    │
│                                                                    │
│  Unfinished Business:                                              │
│                                                                    │
│  New Business:                                                     │
│                                                                    │
│  Appointment of Committees:                                        │
│                                                                    │
│  Nominations and Elections:                                        │
│                                                                    │
│  Announcements:                                                    │
│                                                                    │
│  Adjournment:                                                      │
│                                                                    │
│                                          _____           │
│                                             Secretary              │
└──────────────────────────────────────────────────────────────────┘
```

17.12. Minutes: Recording Guide Form. A form similar to the resolutions form shown in model 17.10 may help you take minutes easily and accurately. Items on the form could follow the same order as those on the final agenda. If you study previous minutes you should be able to determine logical headings and judge how much space to leave by each item for taking notes. (The form may well run into several pages.)

PROXY

I hereby constitute _____, _____, and
_____(who are officers or directors of the company), or a
majority of such of them as actually are present, to act for me in my stead
and as my proxy at the _____ meeting of the stockholders of
_____, to be held in _____, on
_____, at _____, and at any adjournment or adjourn-
ments thereof, with full power and authority to act for me in my behalf, with
all powers that I, the undersigned, would possess if I were personally present.

Effective Date _____

Signed _____   _____
       Stockholder   City   State

17.13. Proxy: Form. Proxies are usually enclosed with the meeting notice. Often they are printed on self-addressed, postage-paid business-reply post-cards, although they may be prepared on sheets of paper as well. In that case a separate stamped envelope should be enclosed with the mailing.

TRAVEL AUTHORIZATION

Name _____

Department _____

Date _____

Travel Order No. _____

From/To	Dates	Purpose	Type of Transp.	Transp. Cost	Living Expense	Enter- tainment	Misc.	Total Cost

Total Travel Advance $ _____ cash $ _____ check

Date _____

Approved _____

17.14. Travel: Authorization Form. Some companies require that a summary of the proposed trip, with cost estimates, be submitted before a travel advance can be issued. Model 17.14 is a basic authorization form. Depending on company policy, either more or less detail might be suitable for your needs.

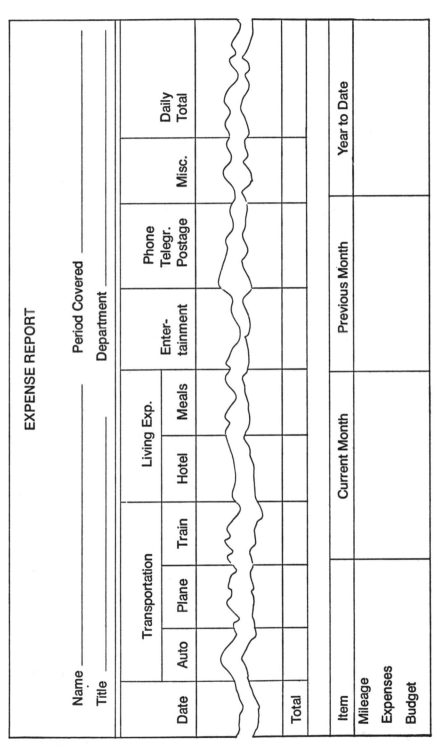

EXPENSE REPORT

Name _____ Period Covered _____
Title _____ Department _____

| Date | Transportation | | Living Exp. | | Enter-tainment | Phone Telegr. Postage | Misc. | Daily Total |
	Auto	Plane	Train	Hotel	Meals				
Total									

Item	Current Month	Previous Month	Year to Date
Mileage			
Expenses			
Budget			

17.15. Travel: Entertainment-Expense Record. Since certain business expenses are tax deductible, everyone who travels must keep a careful record of expenditures. Stationery and office supply stores have standard forms available for this purpose. Or you can make up your own form as shown here to summarize individual expenditures.

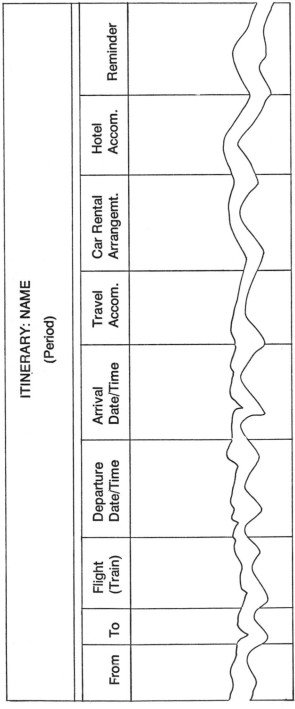

From	To	Flight (Train)	Departure Date/Time	Arrival Date/Time	Travel Accom.	Car Rental Arrangemt.	Hotel Accom.	Reminder

ITINERARY: NAME

(Period)

17.16. **Travel: Itinerary Form.** A travel itinerary should show points of departure and arrival, mode of transportation, dates and times of departure and arrival, travel accommodations, car rental arrangements, and the hotel accommodations. (The itinerary should also specify time differentials.)

ITINERARY WORKSHEET

Name _____   Period Covered _____

DATE

Lv: _____ Time _____ Plane/Train _____ Accom. _____
Ar.: _____ Time _____ Airport/Sta _____ Car Rental _____
Hotel _____ Address _____

Appointments:

Reminders:

17.17. Travel: Itinerary Worksheet. This model is an example of a work-sheet you could use in the preliminary planning stages of a trip. The form shown here would then be repeated for each day of the trip. Details would be summarized on the final itinerary illustrated in model 17.16.

TRAVEL SUPPLIES CHECKLIST

( ) travel tickets   ( ) misc. stationery, envelopes, etc.
( ) itinerary   ( ) calendar
( ) credit cards   ( ) address book
( ) travel funds, checkbook, etc.   ( ) dictating equipment
( ) reservation confirmations   ( ) pens, pencils, erasers
( ) expense forms   ( ) scissors, bottle opener
( ) business files   ( ) clips, rubber bands, tape, etc.
( ) business cards   ( ) first-aid
( ) passport   ( ) postage
( ) maps and timetables   ( ) stamp pad/rubber stamps
( ) appointment schedule

17.18. Travel: List of Supplies. If you do not have a checklist of supplies to pack for the manager before a trip you may forget something. You can add or subtract from this list as appropriate for your situation.

Part IV

LETTER-WRITING AIDS

18

BASIC LETTER STYLES AND
FORMS OF ADDRESS

The first impression of a letter comes from the way it looks—its general appearance, including neatness, accuracy, and style. Most readers then glance at the inside address and salutation, often to see if their names are spelled correctly. Since first impressions are so important, it is clear that an acceptable letter style and a correct form of address are essential to the effectiveness of the letter. In fact, all the technical aspects of a letter are important in creating the desired impression (see chapter 19 for instructions concerning proper use of the principal elements of letters and memos).

LETTER STYLES

The four most common letter setups are the full-block, block, semiblock, and official styles. Most companies use some variation of the block-style letter. Models 18.1 to 18.4 illustrate the distinguishing characteristics of these standard letter styles. (See models 15.20 and 15.21 for examples of memo and speed message forms.)

18.1. Full-Block Style

January 4, 19—

Ms. Janet Grove
1121 Baker Lane
Princeton NJ 08540

Dear Ms. Grove:

This is an example of the full-block letter style. The full-block format is popular in organizations seeking the most efficient letter form.

No indentations are used in this style. Everything is set flush left, which saves time and energy in typing. Open punctuation is used in both the inside address and signature.

Because the dictator's name is typed in the signature, his or her initials are not included in the identification line.

Sincerely yours,

Annette Carson
Correspondence Secretary

18.2. Block Style

January 4, 19—
Your reference 20:631

Ms. Janet Grove
1121 Baker Lane
Princeton NJ 08540

Dear Ms. Grove:

Most businesses use some variation of the block style. Like the full-block style, the block letter also saves time and energy.

The inside address and paragraphs are typed flush left. However, the dateline and reference line are typed flush right. The dateline is positioned two spaces below the letterhead and the reference line two spaces below the dateline. The complimentary close is typed slightly to the right of the center of the page, with the signature aligned beneath it. Open punctuation is used in the inside address.

Since the dictator's name is typed in the signature, there is no need to include his or her initials in the identification line.

> Sincerely yours,
>
> Annette Carson
> Correspondence Secretary

18.3. Semiblock Style

> January 4, 19—

Ms. Janet Grove
1121 Baker Lane
Princeton NJ 08540

Dear Ms. Grove:

The semiblock style is preferred in many companies because of its pleasing appearance. It does not, however, have all of the time-saving features of the full-block and block styles.

Unlike the block style, the paragraphs are indented five to ten spaces in the semiblock letter. In all other respects it resembles the block form. For example, the dateline and reference line are flush right; the complimentary close begins slightly to the right of the page center; the signature aligns beneath the complimentary close; and open punctuation is used in the inside address.

Because the dictator's name is typed in the signature, his or her initials may be omitted from the identification line.

> Sincerely yours,
>
> Annette Carson
> Correspondence Secretary

rl

18.4. Official Style

January 4, 19—

Dear Ms. Grove:

The official style is often used in personal correspondence on executive-size (or monarch) stationery. The principal difference in this style from the others is the placement of the inside address.

The salutation in the official style is typed about five or six spaces below the dateline. Paragraphs are indented, and the body of the letter, the complimentary close, and the signature are positioned the same as they are in the semiblock style. The inside address, however, is placed two spaces below the last signature line, flush left.

An identification line is usually not typed on the original but the typist's initials may appear on the carbon copy.

Sincerely yours,

Annette Carson
Correspondence Secretary

Ms. Janet Grove
1121 Baker Lane
Princeton NJ 08540

FORMS OF ADDRESS

Some people are easily offended or at least annoyed when they are addressed incorrectly. The careful secretary will make certain she is using the latest forms of address for men and women and the correct forms for people in official or honorary positions. Sections 18.5 and 18.6 discuss the most recent changes in forms of address for men and women. Sections 18.7 to 18.15 list the proper forms of address, salutation, and complimentary close to use on letters written to persons holding official or honorary titles. Women in such positions are formally addressed as *Madam*. Informally they are addressed as *Mrs.*, *Miss*, or *Ms.* The proper form of address for ths wife of an official is *Mrs.* (Governor and Mrs. Hendricks). The husband of an official is addressed as *Mr.* (Governor Ellen and Mr. Kent Barrington).

18.5. Men

Precede a man's name by a title such as *Mr.* or *Dr.* (Mr. Douglas Clark) unless *Esquire* or initials for a degree follow the name (Douglas Clark, LL.D.). If the person has two high-level degrees, use the one pertaining to his profession first (Douglas Clark, LL.D., Ph.D., for a lawyer). The abbreviations *Sr.*, *Jr.*, *2nd*, and *III* and business titles such as *Manager* do not take the place of the title *Mr.* (thus, Mr. Douglas Clark, Jr., Manager). Address a firm of men as *Messrs.* (Messrs. Davis, Wright, and Carter) but not a company (*not* Messrs. Clark Manufacturing Company).

18.6. Women

Socially and in business, use *Miss* or *Ms.* for an unmarried woman (*Ms.* if her marital status is unknown). Socially, address a married woman or a widow by her husband's full name (Mrs. Keith Bernard). A divorcee may keep her former husband's surname and be addressed as *Mrs.* (Mrs. Joy Campbell), or use her maiden name combined with his surname and *Mrs.* (Mrs. Joy Foster Campbell), or use her maiden name only with *Mrs.*, *Miss*, or *Ms.* (Ms. Joy Foster). In business, some married women use their given and married names with *Mrs.* (Mrs. Helen Bernard); others prefer *Ms.* with their given and married names (Ms. Helen Bernard) and sometimes with their maiden names (Ms. Helen Baxter). In all cases, follow the form the woman prefers. Address a firm of women as *Mesdames* or *Mmes.* Women are never addressed by their husband's titles and men are never addressed by their wive's titles (thus, Dr. and Mrs. John Dixon; Dr. Mary and Mr. John Dixon; or if both are titled, Drs. John and Mary Dixon).

18.7. United States Government Officials

Charts from the book COMPLETE SECRETARY'S HANDBOOK, 4th Edition by Mary A. DeVries, Reviser. ©1977 by Prentice-Hall, Inc. Published by Prentice-Hall, Inc. Englewood Cliffs, New Jersey.

Personage	Envelope and Inside Address (Add City, State, Zip)	Formal Salutation	Informal Salutation	Formal Close	Informal Close
The President	The President The White House	Mr. President	Dear Mr. President:	Respectfully yours,	Very respectfully yours, Very truly yours, or Sincerely yours,
Former President of the United States[1]	The Honorable William R. Blank (local address)	Sir:	Dear Mr. Blank:	Respectfully yours,	Sincerely yours,
The Vice-President of the United States	The Vice-President of the United States United States Senate	Mr. Vice-President:	Dear Mr. Vice-President	Very truly yours,	Sincerely yours,
The Chief Justice of the United States Supreme Court	The Chief Justice of the United States The Supreme Court of the United States	Sir:	Dear Mr. Chief Justice:	Very truly yours,	Sincerely yours,
Associate Justice of the United States Supreme Court	Mr. Justice Blank The Supreme Court of the United States	Sir:	Dear Mr. Justice:	Very truly yours,	Sincerely yours,

[1] If a former president has a title, such as *General of the Army*, address him by it.

Retired Justice of the United States Supreme Court	The Honorable William R. Blank (local address)	Sir:	Dear Justice Blank:	Very truly yours,	Sincerely yours,
The Speaker of the House of Representatives	The Honorable William R. Blank Speaker of the House of Representatives	Sir:	Dear Mr. Speaker: *or* Dear Mr. Blank:	Very truly yours,	Sincerely yours,
Former Speaker of the House of Representatives	The Honorable William R. Blank (local address)	Sir:	Dear Mr. Blank:	Very truly yours,	Sincerely yours,
Cabinet Officers addressed as "Secretary"[2]	The Honorable William R. Blank Secretary of State The Honorable William R. Blank Secretary of State of the United States of America (if written from abroad)	Sir:	Dear Mr. Secretary:	Very truly yours,	Sincerely yours,
Former Cabinet Officer	The Honorable William R. Blank (local address)	Dear Sir:	Dear Mr. Blank:	Very truly yours,	Sincerely yours,

[2] Titles for cabinet secretaries are Secretary of State; Secretary of Defense; Secretary of the Treasury; Secretary of the Interior; Secretary of Agriculture; Secretary of Commerce; Secretary of Labor; Secretary of Health, Education, and Welfare; Secretary of Housing and Urban Development; Secretary of Transportation.

United States Government Officials continued

Personage	Envelope and Inside Address (Add City, State, Zip)	Formal Salutation	Informal Salutation	Formal Close	Informal Close
Postmaster General	The Honorable William R. Blank The Postmaster General	Sir:	Dear Mr. Postmaster General:	Very truly yours,	Sincerely yours,
The Attorney General	The Honorable William R. Blank The Attorney General	Sir:	Dear Mr. Attorney General:	Very truly yours,	Sincerely yours,
Under Secretary of a Department	The Honorable William R. Blank Under Secretary of Labor	Dear Mr. Blank:	Dear Mr. Blank:	Very truly yours,	Sincerely yours,
United States Senator	The Honorable William R. Blank United States Senate	Sir:	Dear Senator Blank:	Very truly yours,	Sincerely yours,
Former Senator	The Honorable William R. Blank (local address)	Dear Sir:	Dear Senator Blank:	Very truly yours,	Sincerely yours,

Senator-elect	Honorable William R. Blank Senator-elect United States Senate	Dear Sir:	Dear Mr. Blank:	Very truly yours,	Sincerely yours,
Committee Chairman— United States Senate	The Honorable William R. Blank, Chairman Committee on Foreign Affairs United States Senate	Dear Mr. Chairman:	Dear Mr. Chairman: *or* Dear Senator Blank:	Very truly yours,	Sincerely yours,
Subcommittee Chairman— United States Senate	The Honorable William R. Blank, Chairman, Subcommittee on Foreign Affairs United States Senate	Dear Senator Blank:	Dear Senator Blank:	Very truly yours,	Sincerely yours,
United States Representative or Congressman[3]	The Honorable William R. Blank House of Representatives The Honorable William R. Blank Representative in Congress (local address) (when away from Washington, DC)	Sir:	Dear Mr. Blank:	Very truly yours,	Sincerely yours,
Former Representative	The Honorable William R. Blank (local address)	Dear Sir: *or* Dear Mr. Blank:	Dear Mr. Blank:	Very truly yours,	Sincerely yours,

[3]The official title of a "congressman" is *Representative*. Strictly speaking, senators are also congressmen.

United States Government Officials continued

Personage	Envelope and Inside Address (Add City, State, Zip)	Formal Salutation	Informal Salutation	Formal Close	Informal Close
Territorial Delegate	The Honorable William R. Blank Delegate of Puerto Rico House of Representatives	Dear Sir: *or* **Dear Mr. Blank:**	Dear Mr. Blank:	Very truly yours,	Sincerely yours,
Resident Commissioner	The Honorable William R. Blank Resident Commissioner of (Territory) House of Representatives	Dear Sir: *or* **Dear Mr. Blank:**	Dear Mr. Blank:	Very truly yours,	Sincerely yours,
Directors or Heads of Independent Federal Offices, Agencies, Commissions, Organizations, etc.	The Honorable William R. Blank Director, Mutual Security Agency	Dear Mr. Director (Commissioner, etc.):	Dear Mr. Blank:	Very truly yours,	Sincerely yours,
Other High Officials of the United States, in general: Public Printer, Comptroller General	The Honorable William R. Blank Public Printer The Honorable William R. Blank Comptroller General of the United States	Dear Sir: *or* **Dear Mr. Blank:**	Dear Mr. Blank:	Very truly yours,	Sincerely yours,
Secretary to the President	The Honorable William R. Blank Secretary to the President The White House	Dear Sir: *or* **Dear Mr. Blank:**	Dear Mr. Blank:	Very truly yours,	Sincerely yours,

Assistant Secretary to the President	The Honorable William R. Blank Assistant Secretary to the President The White House	Dear Sir: *or* Dear Mr. Blank:	Very truly yours,	Sincerely yours,
Press Secretary to the President	Mr. William R. Blank Press Secretary to the President The White House	Dear Sir: *or* Dear Mr. Blank:	Very truly yours,	Sincerely yours,

18.8. State and Local Government Officials

Governor of a State or Territory[1]	The Honorable William R. Blank Governor of New York	Sir:	Dear Governor Blank:	Respectfully yours,	Very sincerely yours,
Acting Governor of a State or Territory	The Honorable William R. Blank Acting Governor of Connecticut	Sir:	Dear Mr. Blank:	Respectfully yours,	Very sincerely yours,
Lieutenant Governor	The Honorable William R. Blank Lieutenant Governor of Iowa	Sir:	Dear Mr. Blank:	Respectfully yours, *or* Very truly yours,	Sincerely yours,

[1] The form of addressing governors varies in the different states. The form given here is the one used in most states. In Massachusetts by law and in some other states by courtesy, the form is *His (Her) Excellency, the Governor of Massachusetts.*

State and Local Government Officials continued

Personage	Envelope and Inside Address (Add City, State, Zip)	Formal Salutation	Informal Salutation	Formal Close	Informal Close
Secretary of State	The Honorable William R. Blank Secretary of State of New York	Sir:	Dear Mr. Secretary:	Very truly yours,	Sincerely yours,
Attorney General	The Honorable William R. Blank Attorney General of Massachusetts	Sir:	Dear Mr. Attorney General:	Very truly yours,	Sincerely yours,
President of the Senate of a State	The Honorable William R. Blank President of the Senate of the State of Virginia	Sir:	Dear Mr. Blank:	Very truly yours,	Sincerely yours,
Speaker of the Assembly or The House of Representatives[2]	The Honorable William R. Blank Speaker of the Assembly of the State of New York	Sir:	Dear Mr. Blank:	Very truly yours,	Sincerely yours,
Treasurer, Auditor, or Comptroller of a State	The Honorable William R. Blank Treasurer of the State of Tennessee	Dear Sir:	Dear Mr. Blank:	Very truly yours,	Sincerely yours,

[2] In most states the lower branch of the legislature is the House of Representatives. The exceptions to this are: New York, California, Wisconsin, and Nevada, where it is known as the Assembly; Maryland, Virginia, and West Virginia—the House of Delegates; New Jersey—the House of General Assembly.

State Senator	The Honorable William R. Blank The State Senate	Dear Sir:	Dear Senator Blank:	Very truly yours,	Sincerely yours,
State Representative, Assemblyman, or Delegate	The Honorable William R. Blank House of Delegates	Dear Sir:	Dear Mr. Blank:	Very truly yours,	Sincerely yours,
District Attorney	The Honorable William R. Blank District Attorney, Albany County County Courthouse	Dear Sir:	Dear Mr. Blank:	Very truly yours,	Sincerely yours,
Mayor of a city	The Honorable William R. Blank Mayor of Detroit	Dear Sir:	Dear Mayor Blank:	Very truly yours,	Sincerely yours,
President of a Board of Commissioners	The Honorable William R. Blank, President Board of Commissioners of the City of Buffalo	Dear Sir:	Dear Mr. Blank:	Very truly yours,	Sincerely yours,
City Attorney, City Counsel, Corporation Counsel	The Honorable William R. Blank, City Attorney (City Counsel, Corporation Counsel)	Dear Sir:	Dear Mr. Blank:	Very truly yours,	Sincerely yours,
Alderman	Alderman William R. Blank City Hall	Dear Sir:	Dear Mr. Blank:	Very truly yours,	Sincerely yours,

265

18.9. Court Officials

Personage	Envelope and Inside Address (Add City, State, Zip, or City, Country)	Formal Salutation	Informal Salutation	Formal Close	Informal Close
Chief Justice[1] *of a State Supreme Court*	The Honorable William R. Blank Chief Justice of the Supreme Court of Minnesota[2]	Sir:	Dear Mr. Chief Justice:	Very truly yours,	Sincerely yours,
Associate Justice of a Supreme Court of a State	The Honorable William R. Blank Associate Justice of the Supreme Court of Minnesota	Sir:	Dear Justice Blank:	Very truly yours,	Sincerely yours,
Presiding Justice	The Honorable William R. Blank Presiding Justice, Appellate Division Supreme Court of New York	Sir:	Dear Justice Blank:	Very truly yours,	Sincerely yours,

[1] If his or her official title is *Chief Judge* substitute *Chief Judge* for *Chief Justice*, but never use *Mr., Mrs., Miss,* or *Ms.* with *Chief Judge* or *Judge*.
[2] Substitute here the appropriate name of the court. For example, the highest court in New York State is called the Court of Appeals.

Judge of a Court[3]	The Honorable William R. Blank Judge of the United States District Court for the Southern District of California	Sir:	Dear Judge Blank:	Very truly yours,	Sincerely yours,
Clerk of a Court	William R. Blank, Esquire Clerk of the Superior Court of Massachusetts	Dear Sir:	Dear Mr. Blank:	Very truly yours,	Sincerely yours,

[3]Not applicable to judges of the United States Supreme Court.

18.10. United States Diplomatic Representatives

American Ambassador	The Honorable William R. Blank American Ambassador[1]	Sir:	Dear Mr. Ambassador:	Very truly yours,	Sincerely yours,
American Minister	The Honorable William R. Blank American Minister to Rumania	Sir:	Dear Mr. Minister:	Very truly yours,	Sincerely yours,

[1]When an ambassador or minister is not at his or her post, the name of the country to which he or she is accredited must be added to the address. For example: *The American Ambassador to Great Britain.* If he or she holds military rank, the diplomatic complimentary title *The Honorable* should be omitted, thus *General William R. Blank, American Ambassador (or Minister).*

United States Representatives continued

Personage	Envelope and Inside Address (Add City, State, Zip, or City, Country)	Formal Salutation	Informal Salutation	Formal Close	Informal Close
American Chargé d'Affaires, Consul General, Consul, or Vice Consul	William R. Blank, Esquire [2] American Chargé d'Affaires ad interim (or other title)	Sir:	Dear Mr. Blank:	Very truly yours,	Sincerely yours,
High Commissioner	The Honorable William R. Blank United States High Commissioner to Argentina	Sir:	Dear Mr. Blank:	Very truly yours,	Sincerely yours,

[2] Do not use *Esquire* to refer to a woman in this position.

18.11. Foreign Officials and Representatives

Foreign Ambassador[1] in the United States	His Excellency,[2] Erik Rolf Blankson Ambassador of Norway	Excellency:	Dear Mr. Ambassador:	Very truly yours,	Sincerely yours,

[1] The correct title of all ambassadors and ministers of foreign countries is *Ambassador (Minister) of ———* (name of country), with the exception of Great Britain. The adjective form is used with reference to representatives from Great Britain—*British Ambassador, British Minister.*

[2] When the representative is British or a member of the British Commonwealth, it is customary to use *The Right Honorable* and *The Honorable* in addition to *His (Her) Excellency,* wherever appropriate.

Foreign Minister[3] in the United States	The Honorable George Macovescu Minister of Rumania	Sir:	Dear Mr. Minister:	Very truly yours,	Sincerely yours,
Foreign Diplomatic Representative with a Personal Title[4]	His Excellency,[5] Count Allesandro de Bianco Ambassador of Italy	Excellency:	Dear Mr. Ambassador:	Very truly yours,	Sincerely yours,
Prime Minister	His Excellency, Christian Jawaharal Blank Prime Minister of India	Excellency:	Dear Mr. Prime Minister:	Respectfully yours,	Sincerely yours,
British Prime Minister	The Right Honorable Godfrey Blank, K.G., M.C., M.P. Prime Minister	Sir:	Dear Mr. Prime Minister: _or_ Dear Mr. Blank:	Respectfully yours,	Sincerely yours,
Canadian Prime Minister	The Right Honorable Claude Louis St. Blanc, C.M.G. Prime Minister of Canada	Sir:	Dear Mr. Prime Minister: _or_ Dear Mr. Blanc:	Respectfully yours,	Sincerely yours,

[3]The correct title of all ambassadors and ministers of foreign countries is _Ambassador (Minister) of_ _____ (name of country), with the exception of Great Britain. The adjective form is used with reference to representatives from Great Britain–_British Ambassador, British Minister._

[4]If the personal title is a royal title, such as _His (Her) Highness, Prince,_ etc., the diplomatic title _His (Her) Excellency or The Honorable_ is omitted.

[5]_Dr., Señor Don,_ and other titles of special courtesy in Spanish-speaking countries may be used with the diplomatic title _His (Her) Excellency or The Honorable._

Foreign Officials and Representatives continued

Personage	Envelope and Inside Address (Add City, State, Zip, or City, Country)	Formal Salutation	Informal Salutation	Formal Close	Informal Close
President of a Republic	His Excellency, Juan Cuidad Blanco President of the Dominican Republic	Excellency:	Dear Mr. President:	I remain with respect, Very truly yours, *(formal general usage)* Sincerely yours, *(less formal)*	Sincerely yours,
Premier	His Excellency, Charles Yves de Blanc Premier of the French Republic	Excellency:	Dear Mr. Premier:	Respectfully yours,	Sincerely yours,
Foreign Chargé d'Affaires (de missi)[6] in the United States	Mr. Jan Gustaf Blanc Chargé d'Affaires of Sweden	Sir:	Dear Mr. Blanc:	Respectfully yours,	Sincerely yours,
Foreign Chargé d'Affaires ad interim in the United States	Mr. Edmund Blank Chargé d'Affaires ad interim[7] of Ireland	Sir:	Dear Mr. Blank:	Respectfully yours,	Sincerely yours,

[6] The full title is usually shortened to *Chargé d'Affaires.*

[7] The words "ad interim" should not be omitted in the address.

18.12. The Armed Forces

General of the Army	General of the Army William R. Blank, U.S.A. Department of the Army	Sir:		Dear General Blank:	Very truly yours,	Sincerely yours,
General, Lieutenant General, Major General, Brigadier General	General (Lieutenant General, Major General, or Brigadier General) William R. Blank, U.S.A. [1]	Sir:		Dear General Blank:	Very truly yours,	Sincerely yours,
Colonel, Lieutenant Colonel	Colonel (Lieutenant Colonel) William R. Blank, U.S.A.	Dear Colonel Blank:		Dear Colonel Blank:	Very truly yours,	Sincerely yours,
Major	Major William R. Blank, U.S.A.	Dear Major Blank:		Dear Major Blank:	Very truly yours,	Sincerely yours,
Captain	Captain William R. Blank, U.S.A.	Dear Captain Blank:		Dear Captain Blank:	Very truly yours,	Sincerely yours,
First Lieutenant, Second Lieutenant [2]	Lieutenant William R. Blank, U.S.A.	Dear Lieutenant Blank:		Dear Lieutenant Blank:	Very truly yours,	Sincerely yours,
Chief Warrant Officer, Warrant Officer	Mr. William R. Blank, U.S.A.	Dear Mr. Blank:		Dear Mr. Blank:	Very truly yours,	Sincerely yours,
Chaplain in the U.S. Army [3]	Chaplain William R. Blank, Captain, U.S.A.	Dear Chaplain Blank:		Dear Chaplain Blank:	Very truly yours,	Sincerely yours,

Note: Air Force titles are the same as those in the Army. *U.S.A.F.* is used instead of *U.S.A.* and *A.F.U.S.* is used to indicate the Reserve. Marine Corps titles are the same as those in the Army, except that the top rank is *Commandant of the Marine Corps*. *U.S.M.C.* indicates regular service; *U.S.M.R.* indicates the Reserve. Coast Guard titles are the same as those in the Navy, except that the top rank is *Admiral. U.S.C.G.* indicates regular service; *U.S.C.G.R.* indicates the Reserve.

[1] *U.S.A.* indicates regular service. *A.U.S.* (Army of the United States) signifies the Reserve.

[2] In all *official* correspondence, the full rank should be included in both the envelope address and the inside address, but not in the salutation.

[3] Roman Catholic chaplains and certain Anglican priests are introduced as *Chaplain Blank* but are spoken to and referred to as *Father Blank.*

271

The Armed Forces continued

Personage	Envelope and Inside Address (Add City, State, Zip, or City, Country)	Formal Salutation	Informal Salutation	Formal Close	Informal Close
Fleet Admiral	Fleet Admiral William R. Blank, U.S.N. Chief of Naval Operations, Department of the Navy	Sir:	Dear Admiral Blank:	Very truly yours,	Sincerely yours,
Admiral, Vice Admiral, Rear Admiral	Admiral (Vice Admiral or Rear Admiral) William R. Blank, U.S.N. United States Naval Academy[1]	Sir:	Dear Admiral Blank:	Very truly yours,	Sincerely yours,
Commodore, Captain, Commander, Lieutenant Commander	Commodore (Captain, Commander, Lieutenant Commander) William R. Blank, U.S.N. U.S.S. Mississippi	Dear Commodore (Captain, Commander) Blank:	Dear Commodore (Captain, Commander) Blank:	Very truly yours,	Sincerely yours,
Junior Officers: Lieutenant, Lieutenant Junior Grade, Ensign	(Lieutenant, etc.) William R. Blank, U.S.N. U.S.S. Wyoming	Dear Mr. Blank:	Dear Mr. Blank:	Very truly yours,	Sincerely yours,
Chief Warrant Officer, Warrant Officer	Mr. William R. Blank, U.S.N. U.S.S. Texas	Dear Mr. Blank:	Dear Mr. Blank:	Very truly yours,	Sincerely yours,
Chaplain	Chaplain William R. Blank Captain, U.S.N. Department of the Navy	Dear Chaplain Blank:	Dear Chaplain Blank:	Very truly yours,	Sincerely yours,

[1] *U.S.N.* signifies regular service; *U.S.N.R.* indicates the Reserve.

18.13 Church Dignitaries
(Catholic Faith)

			Always Formal	Respectfully,	Always Formal
The Pope	His Holiness, The Pope *or* His Holiness Pope _____ Vatican City	Your Holiness: Most Holy Father:			Respectfully,
Apostolic Delegate	His Excellency, The Most Reverend William R. Blank Archbishop of _____ The Apostolic Delegate	Your Excellency:	Dear Archbishop Blank:	Respectfully yours,	Respectfully,
Cardinal in the United States	His Eminence, William Cardinal Blank Archbishop of New York	Your Eminence:	Dear Cardinal Blank:	Respectfully yours,	Respectfully, *or* Sincerely yours,
Bishop and Archbishop in the United States	The Most Reverend William R. Blank, D.D. Bishop (Archbishop) of Baltimore	Your Excellency:	Dear Bishop (Archbishop) Blank:	Respectfully yours,	Respectfully, *or* Sincerely yours,
Bishop in England	The Right Reverend William R. Blank Bishop of Sussex (local address)	Right Reverend Sir:	Dear Bishop:	Respectfully yours,	Respectfully,
Abbot	The Right Reverend William R. Blank Abbot of Westmoreland Abbey	Dear Father Abbot:	Dear Father Blank:	Respectfully yours,	Sincerely yours,

Church Dignitaries
(Catholic Faith) continued

Personage	Envelope and Inside Address (Add City, State, Zip)	Formal Salutation	Informal Salutation	Formal Close	Informal Close
Canon	The Reverend William R. Blank, D.D. Canon of St. Patrick's Cathedral	Reverend Sir:	Dear Canon Blank:	Respectfully yours,	Sincerely yours,
Monsignor	The Right (or Very)[1] Reverend Msgr. William R. Blank	Right Reverend and Dear Monsignor Blank: *or* Very Reverend and Dear Monsignor Blank:	Dear Monsignor Blank:	Respectfully yours,	Sincerely yours,
Brother	Brother John Blank 932 Maple Avenue	Dear Brother:	Dear Brother Blank:	Respectfully yours,	Sincerely yours,
Superior of a Brotherhood and Priest[2]	The Very Reverend William R. Blank, M.M. Director	Dear Father Superior:	Dear Father Superior:	Respectfully yours,	Sincerely yours,
Priest	*With scholastic degree:* The Reverend William R. Blank, Ph.D. Georgetown University	Dear Dr. Blank:	Dear Dr. Blank:	Respectfully,	Sincerely yours,
	Without scholastic degree: The Reverend William R. Blank **St. Vincent's Church**	**Dear Father Blank:**	**Dear Father Blank:**	Respectfully,	Sincerely yours,

[1] Dependent upon rank. See the *Official* (Roman) *Catholic Directory.*
[2] The address for the superior of a Brotherhood depends upon whether or not he is a priest or has a title other than superior. Consult the *Official Catholic Directory.*

Sister Superior	The Reverend Sister Superior (order, if used)[3] Convent of the Sacred Heart	Dear Sister Superior:	Dear Sister Superior:	Respectfully,	Respectfully, *or* Sincerely yours,
Sister	Sister Mary Blank St. John's High School	Dear Sister:	Dear Sister Blank:	Respectfully,	Sincerely yours,
Mother Superior of a Sisterhood (Catholic or Protestant)	The Reverend Mother Superior, O.C.A. Convent of the Sacred Heart	Dear Reverend Mother: *or* Dear Mother Superior:	Dear Reverend Mother: *or* Dear Mother Superior:	Respectfully,	Sincerely yours,
Member of Community	Mother Mary Walker, R.S.M. Convent of Mercy	Dear Mother Walker:	Dear Mother Walker:	Respectfully,	Sincerely yours,

[3] The address of the superior of a Sisterhood depends upon the order to which she belongs. The abbreviation of the order is not always used. Consult the *Official Catholic Directory.*

Church Dignitaries
(Jewish Faith)

Rabbi	*With scholastic degree:* Rabbi William R. Blank, Ph.D.	Sir:	Dear Rabbi Blank: *or* Dear Dr. Blank:	Respectfully yours, *or* Very truly yours,	Sincerely yours,
	Without scholastic degree: Rabbi William R. Blank	Sir:	Dear Rabbi Blank:	Respectfully yours, *or* Very truly yours,	Sincerely yours,

Church Dignitaries
(Protestant Faith)

Personage	Envelope and Inside Address (Add City, State, Zip, or City, Country)	Formal Salutation	Informal Salutation	Formal Close	Informal Close
Archbishop (Anglican)	The Most Reverend Archbishop of Canterbury *or* The Most Reverend John Blank, Archbishop of Canterbury	Your Grace:	Dear Archbishop Blank:	Respectfully yours,	Sincerely yours,
Presiding Bishop of the Protestant Episcopal Church in America	The Most Reverend William R. Blank, D.D., LL.D. Presiding Bishop of the Protestant Episcopal Church in America Northwick House	Most Reverend Sir:	Dear Bishop Blank:	Respectfully yours,	Sincerely yours,
Anglican Bishop	The Right Reverend The Lord Bishop of London	Right Reverend Sir:	My dear Bishop:	Respectfully yours,	Sincerely yours,
Methodist Bishop	The Very Reverend William R. Blank Methodist Bishop	Reverend Sir:	My dear Bishop:	Respectfully yours,	Sincerely yours,
Protestant Episcopal Bishop	The Right Reverend William R. Blank, D.D., LL.D. Bishop of Denver	Right Reverend Sir:	Dear Bishop Blank:	Respectfully yours,	Sincerely yours,

	Address	Formal Salutation	Informal Salutation	Formal Closing	Informal Closing
Archdeacon	The Venerable William R. Blank Archdeacon of Baltimore	Venerable Sir:	My dear Archdeacon:	Respectfully yours,	Sincerely yours,
Dean[1]	The Very Reverend William R. Blank, D.D. Dean of St. John's Cathedral	Very Reverend Sir:	Dear Dean Blank:	Respectfully yours,	Sincerely yours,
Protestant Minister	*With scholastic degree:* The Reverend William R. Blank, D.D., Litt.D. *or* The Reverend Dr. William R. Blank	Dear Dr. Blank:	Dear Dr. Blank:	Very truly yours,	Sincerely yours,
	Without scholastic degree: The Reverend William R. Blank	Dear Mr. Blank:	Dear Mr. Blank:	Very truly yours,	Sincerely yours,
Episcopal Priest (High Church)	*With scholastic degree:* The Reverend William R. Blank, D.D., Litt.D. All Saint's Cathedral *or* The Reverend Dr. William R. Blank	Dear Dr. Blank:	Dear Dr. Blank:	Very truly yours,	Sincerely yours,
	Without scholastic degree: The Reverend William R. Blank St. Paul's Church	Dear Mr. Blank: *or* Dear Father Blank:	Dear Mr. Blank: *or* Dear Father Blank:	Very truly yours,	Sincerely yours,

[1] Applies only to the head of a Cathedral or of a Theological Seminary.

18.14. College and University Officials

Personage	Envelope and Inside Address (Add City, State, Zip)	Formal Salutation	Informal Salutation	Formal Close	Informal Close
President of a College or University	*With a doctor's degree:* Dr. William R. Blank *or* William R. Blank, LL.D., Ph.D. President, Amherst College	Sir:	Dear Dr. Blank:	Very truly yours,	Sincerely yours,
	Without a doctor's degree: Mr. William R. Blank President, Columbia University	Sir:	Dear President Blank:	Very truly yours,	Sincerely yours,
	Catholic priest: The Very Reverend William R. Blank, S.J., D.D., Ph.D. President, Fordham University	Sir:	Dear Father Blank:	Very truly yours,	Sincerely yours,
University Chancellor	Dr. William R. Blank Chancellor, University of Alabama	Sir:	Dear Dr. Blank:	Very truly yours,	Sincerely yours,
Dean or Assistant Dean of a College or Graduate School	Dean William R. Blank School of Law *or* (*If he holds a doctor's degree*) Dr. William R. Blank, Dean (Assistant Dean) School of Law University of Virginia	Dear Sir: *or* Dear Dean Blank:	Dear Dean Blank:	Very truly yours,	Sincerely yours,

Professor	Professor William R. Blank *or* *(If he holds a doctor's degree)* Dr. William R. Blank *or* William R. Blank, Ph.D. Yale University	Dear Sir: *or* Dear Professor (Dr.) Blank:	Dear Professor (Dr.) Blank:	Very truly yours,	Sincerely yours,
Chaplain of a College or University	The Reverend William R. Blank, D.D. Chaplain, Trinity College *or* Chaplain William R. Blank Trinity College	Dear Chaplain Blank: *or* *(If he holds a doctor's degree)* Dear Dr. Blank:	Dear Chaplain (Dr.) Blank:	Very truly yours,	Sincerely yours,
Associate or Assistant Professor	Mr. William R. Blank *or* *(If he holds a doctor's degree)* Dr. William R. Blank *or* William R. Blank, Ph.D. Associate (Assistant) Professor Department of Romance Languages Williams College	Dear Sir: *or* Dear Professor (Dr.) Blank:	Dear Professor (Dr.) Blank:	Very truly yours,	Sincerely yours,
Instructor	Mr. William R. Blank *or* *(If he holds a doctor's degree)* Dr. William R. Blank *or* William R. Blank, Ph.D. Department of Economics University of California	Dear Sir: *or* Dear Mr. (Dr.) Blank:	Dear Mr. (Dr.) Blank:	Very truly yours,	Sincerely yours,

18.15. United Nations Officials [1]

Personage	Envelope and Inside Address (Add City, State, Zip, or City, Country)	Formal Salutation	Informal Salutation	Formal Close	Informal Close
Secretary General	His Excellency, William R Blank Secretary General of the United Nations	Excellency: [2]	Dear Mr. Secretary General:	Very truly yours,	Sincerely yours,
Under Secretary	The Honorable William R. Blank Under Secretary of the United Nations The Secretariat United Nations	Sir:	Dear Mr. Blank:	Very truly yours,	Sincerely yours,
Foreign Representative (with ambassadorial rank)	His Excellency, William R. Blank Representative of Spain to the United Nations	Excellency:	Dear Mr. Ambassador:	Very truly yours,	Sincerely yours,
United States Representative (with ambassadorial rank)	The Honorable William R. Blank United States Representative to the United Nations	Sir: *or* Dear Mr. Ambassador:	Dear Mr. Ambassador:	Very truly yours,	Sincerely yours,

[1] The six principal branches through which the United Nations functions are The General Assembly, The Security Council, The Economic and Social Council, The Trusteeship Council, The International Court of Justice, and The Secretariat.

[2] An American citizen should never be addressed as "Excellency."

19

PRINCIPAL ELEMENTS
OF LETTERS AND MEMOS

The preparation of correspondence involves more than a mastery of effective letter-writing techniques—clarity, persuasiveness, good grammar, and so on. Appearance is extremely important, too. A sloppy setup or outmoded letter style can cause otherwise effective written communication to lose its impact and create an unfavorable impression. A writer must therefore pay special attention to the technical as well as the creative aspects of a business letter.

TECHNICAL ASPECTS OF THE BUSINESS LETTER

The business letter has a number of principal elements such as the reference line, the salutation, and the complimentary close. Chances are your office follows a certain practice in the use and placement of these technical aspects of correspondence. If not, you should study the letter styles shown in chapter 18, select the one most appropriate for your needs, and follow that style's requirements in typing and positioning the various elements of your letters. Models 19.1 to 19.17 discuss the proper placement and use of the principal elements of the business letter (see chapter 18 for correct forms of address).

19.1. Addressing the Envelope

The address on an envelope should be typed exactly as you type the inside address with one exception: type a foreign country in all capitals on the envelope but initial capitals only on the inside address. The U.S. Postal Service prefers that you use their two-letter state abbreviations followed by the zip code (Des Moines IA 50322). The notation PERSONAL is typed about two spaces above the address just to the left of it. The attention line (Attention John Jones) is typed in the lower left corner of the envelope. A special notation such as SPECIAL DELIVERY is typed below the stamp. Some companies single-space all addresses over two lines; others double-space two- and three-line addresses and single-space four lines and over.

19.2. Attention Line

Business letters addressed to a firm may be directed to the attention of an individual. In this case the letter will be opened whether or not the individual is there. The attention line (Attention Mr. Arthur Brown) is typed two spaces below the inside address. The salutation on the letter should then be general (Gentlemen).

19.3. Blind Carbon-Copy Notation

When you want a copy of a letter to go to someone without the addressee knowing about it, type a blind-copy notation (b.c. Jeanne Sims) in the upper left corner of the letter *only* on the carbon copies. For instructions regarding a regular carbon-copy notation, see 19.5, below.

19.4. Body of the Letter

Unless a letter is only two or three lines, it should be single spaced with a double space between paragraphs. Chapter 18 (18.1 to 18.4) discusses rules for paragraph indentation for each letter style. When you have lists within the body of the letter, center this copy by indenting five or more spaces from each margin. Begin each item with a number enclosed in parentheses or alone and followed by a period. Single-space within an item and double-space between items.

19.5. Carbon-Copy Notation

A regular carbon-copy notation is used when a carbon copy is to be sent to another person. (See 19.3 for use of the blind-copy notation.) Type the notation (c.c. John Williams or Copy to John Williams) flush left two spaces below the identification and enclosure lines.

19.6. Complimentary Close

Except in the full-block style letter, the complimentary close is typed slightly to the right of the center of the page two spaces below the body of the letter. Type it flush left in the full-block style (see 18.1). Keep at least two lines of the body of the letter on the final page with the complimentary close. The first word of the close is capitalized (Sincerely yours). Popular closings are *Sincerely*, *Sincerely yours*, *Cordially*, *Best regards*, and *Best wishes* (each is followed by a comma).

19.7. Enclosure Notation

When items are enclosed with the letter, type *Enclosure* or *Enc.* flush left two spaces below the identification line. Identify important enclosures (Enc. Cert. Ck. $500) and specify if there is more than one enclosure (Enc. 3). Also, indicate special instructions (enc. Lease, to be returned).

19.8. Identification Line

Businesses use an identification line to determine later who dictated and typed the letter. The typist's initials in lowercase letters are typed flush left two spaces below the last signature line (or across from it). On the official style letter (see 18.4) they are typed two spaces below the inside address. The initials can be omitted from the original unless company practice requires that they appear there as well as on the carbon copies. If required, also type the initials of the person signing the letter, followed by those of the transcriber (DR:ek). When the person signing the letter is not the same as the person who dictated it, place the initials of the person signing the letter first, followed by those of the dictator, and finally those of the transcriber (DR:FS:ek).

19.9 Inside Address

The inside address is typed flush left two to twelve spaces below the dateline on all letters except the official style. With the official form (see 18.4), place it flush left two spaces beneath the last signature line. When a long line in the address runs over to the next line, indent the runover line three spaces. (See also Addressing the Envelope, 19.1)

Use the full, official name of a company (Jones and Company, Inc., *not* Jones & Co.) and spell out street names of twelve or under (444 Fifth Avenue). Abbreviate only standard names (St. Louis) but not full names (*not* L.A. For Los Angeles). Use the two-letter state abbreviations, however, for states (Des Moines IA) followed by the zip code. Leave two spaces, but no comma, after the state abbreviations (New York NY 10017). Keep the city, state, and zip code on one line even when there is no street address. A post office box, instead of a street, should be used if there is one.

Do not abbreviate business titles such as *president*. *Mr.*, *Mrs.*, *Miss*, or *Ms.* precedes a name even when a business title follows it (Ms. Adele Simmons, Art Director). But omit the title when it causes the address to run over four lines. When it is used, however, and when it is not too long, the title may go on the same line as the name (Mr. Ralph Bell, Treasurer). A person's name goes on the first line, the company on the second line (assuming the title is omitted or stays on the first line after the name), the street or post office box on the third line, and the city, state, and zip code on the last line.

19.10. Mail Instruction Placement

Type instructions such as SPECIAL DELIVERY or REGISTERED only on the carbon copies above the address. Type the same notation on the envelopes under the stamps. (See 19.1.)

19.11. "Personal" Notation

Type notations such as PERSONAL or CONFIDENTIAL four spaces above the inside address. Type the same notation on the envelope about two spaces above the address just to the left of it (see 19.1).

19.12. Postscript

Type the postscript (P.S.)—a comment unrelated to the message in the body of the letter—two spaces beneath the identification line or the last notation on the letter. When the letter's paragraphs are indented, indent the postscript also. Type the dictator's initials immediately after the postscript. P.P.S. is used for a second postscript.

19.13. Reference Line

Some letterheads have a line printed in the upper right corner: *In reply please refer to*. A file reference, for example; 16:310 or File 617J, is typed immediately after that line. When there is no printed line, type the reference four spaces below the date. Always include someone else's reference line when you reply to his or her letter. When you, too, have a reference line, position yours directly under the other person's reference. Examples of reference lines are Your File 7020, Our Order 16-0100, Our File 162, and 13:220R.

19.14. Salutation

Except in the official-style letter, type the salutation flush left two spaces below the inside address. In the official style type the salutation five or six spaces below the dateline. Capitalize the first word, the title, and the name (Dear Mr. Green or My dear Ms. McKay). All major words are capitalized in titles such as *To Whom It May Concern* or *Ladies and Gentlemen*. A colon follows the salutation in business letters (a comma in social letters). The trend is toward informal salutations (Dear Ms. Crosby *not* My dear Ms. Crosby).

Do not use designations such as *C.P.S.* or a business title such as *secretary* in a salutation (Dear Ms. Lewis, *not* Dear Ms. Lewis, C.P.S., and *not* Dear Secretary Lewis). Do not use *Miss* alone (*not* Dear Miss). With a firm of several women the salutation is *Ladies* or *Mesdames*. When two women have the same name use Dear Mesdames Clark (married) or Dear Misses Clark (unmarried). For individual women use the form of address they prefer—*Mrs.*, *Miss*, or *Ms*. (see chapter 18 for instructions concerning the correct forms of address for men, women, and persons in official or honorary positions).

19.15. Second-Page Headings

If your company does not have specially printed stationery for continuation sheets, use plain paper of the same size and quality as the letterhead. Keep at least two lines of the body copy on the last page. There is no need to type "continued" at the bottom of any page. About three spaces from the top of the continuation page, type the name of the addressee flush left, the page number centered, and the date flush right (Dale Moss   -2-   January 5, 19—). Below this heading leave two or three spaces and continue with the body copy.

19.16. Signature

The signature is aligned beneath the complimentary close: (1) four spaces below the close to the writer's signature or (2) two spaces below to the firm name and then the writer's name four spaces below that. (See 18.1 to 18.4 for variations in position depending on letter style.) The writer's business title (Manager) appears directly beneath his or her name. When a firm name is included, the title may immediately follow the name on the same line, separated by a comma. A firm name is used mostly with formal or contractual letters. The writer's name may be omitted when his or her name appears on the letterhead.

When the firm name is used, however, type it in capitals. Type the writer's name exactly as he or she signs it. Only *Miss* or *Mrs.* (never *Ms.* or *Mr.*) precedes a name, with the title in parentheses. Degree initials such as *M.D.* follow the name (Jack Monroe, M.D.). An unmarried woman may omit the title *Miss* or place it in parentheses before her name. A married woman may use her given and married names preceded by *Mrs.* in parentheses—(Mrs.) Evelyn Stone—or place her full married name in parentheses—(Mrs. Arthur Stone). In either case she would sign the letter with her given and married names. A widow signs her name as she did before her husband's death. A divorcee may use her given name with her former husband's surname preceded by *Mrs.* in parentheses—(Mrs.) Diane Carter—or use *Mrs.* and combine her maiden name with her former husband's surname and place it all in parentheses—(Mrs. MacDonald Carter). In either case she would sign the letter with her given name and her former husband's surname (with or without the initial of her maiden name). She might also simply use her given and maiden names with no title.

When you must sign the manager's signature in his or her absence, write your initials directly below the written signature. When you sign a letter of your own, write your name above a typed line that includes your title and the manager's name. (Secretary to Ms. Cole). There is no need to include the manager's initials unless there are two persons in the firm with the same last name.

19.17. Subject Line

Except in the full-block style of letter, center the subject line two spaces beneath the salutation. In full-block letters, type it flush left. Introductory words such as *In re* or *Subject* are not necessary. *In re* is used primarily in legal correspondence. When the word *Subject* is used, place a colon after it. Capitalize all major words (Quarterly Budget Report and Analysis). Avoid underlining. Double-space after the subject line to the first line of the body of the letter.

TECHNICAL ASPECTS OF THE MEMO

The principal elements of a memo differ slightly from those of a letter. Most noticeably, there is no inside address, no salutation, and no complimentary close. Printed memo forms or memo letterhead may be used for this type of correspondence. Sizes and styles vary greatly. Often the memo stationery is smaller and less expensive than the regular letterhead. The form of a memo is designed for easy, rapid communication. Traditionally, the memo has been a means of interoffice communication, although it is being used more and more in external correspondence as well (see chapters 13 and 14).

19.18. Body

The memo message may be typed much the same as the body of a letter (see 19.4 and 18.1 to 18.4), with paragraphs indented five to ten spaces or typed flush left. The body copy should be single spaced with double spacing between paragraphs. Lists are usually treated as they are in the body of a letter (see 19.4).

19.19. Envelope

Although there is no inside address on the memo, the address on the envelope (when it is going out of the office) should be typed exactly as you would type the envelope for a letter. Follow the instructions given in section 19.1. Within the office, interoffice envelopes and/or routing slips may be used (see 15.18).

19.20. Heading

A number of styles are possible for a memo heading (see 15.20 and 15.21 for examples). Usually the memo has these headings printed at the top of the page: DATE, TO, FROM, and SUBJECT (or RE). The appropriate information is then typed after each printed line. Often initials are used in place of first names (TO: J.T. Van Dyke). The sender's name is typed after *FROM* but is usually not signed at the end of the memo. Sometimes, however, the sender writes his initials at the end of the message. All major words in the subject line are capitalized (SUBJECT: Information Storage and Retrieval).